Contents

Foreword   7
Archbishop Dermot Clifford

Introduction   11
Joseph Putti

The Changing Face of Ireland Today   15
Canon Conor Ryan

Proclaiming the Good News: 25
Changing Perspectives and Emerging Trends
Joseph Putti

Connecting the Good News with   50
Contemporary Living: Irish Perspectives
Donal Dorr

The Changing Shape of the Family   63
in Contemporary Ireland: Challenges to Faith
Cathy Molloy

Nurturing the Faith through Religious Education   82
Joe Collins

Proclaiming the Good News to the Young   98
Gerard Gallagher

The Parish as an Agent of Change   116
Clare Slattery RSM

Good Celebration of Liturgy: 133
A Primary Source of Evangelisation
Seamus Ryan

Bringing it all Back Home: The Retrieval of   170
Gregorian/Plainchant and the Forgotten Sense
Nóirín Ní Riain

New Paradigms for Proclaiming the Gospel: 186
Religious Orders in Search of Identity Today
Anne Codd PBVM

News and Good News: Christ in the Marketplace   195
Salvador Ryan

Nourishing the Faith through the Lens of   206
Patrick Kavanagh's Poetry
Una Agnew SSL

Connecting the Good News   224
with Contemporary Living: European
and Global Perspectives
Cardinal Keith O'Brien

Witnessing to Solidarity and Justice in the World: 242
Trócaire's Contribution to the Church's Mission Today
Lorna Gold

TIME [to] CHANGE

*Connecting the Good News
with Contemporary Living*

Edited by Joseph Putti

VERITAS

First published 2006 by
Veritas Publications
7/8 Lower Abbey Street
Dublin 1
Ireland
E-mail publications@veritas.ie
Website www.veritas.ie

ISBN 1 85390 927 0

Cover Design by Niamh McGarry
Printed in the Republic of Ireland
by Betaprint Dublin

Veritas books are printed on paper made from the wood pulp of managed
forests. For every tree felled, at least one tree is planted, thereby renewing
natural resources.

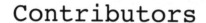

Contributors

Canon Conor Ryan is the Parish Priest of Hospital and Herbertstown, Co. Tipperary. He has lectured in sociology for over thirty years and has a lifelong interest in the role of religion in society.

Joseph Putti is currently the Director of Development at St Patrick's College, Thurles. He has lectured globally in theology, spirituality, world religions and related areas and has a number of publications to his credit.

Cathy Molloy is a theologian presently working as a researcher at the Jesuit Centre for Faith and Justice in Dublin.

Donal Dorr is widely published and internationally known for his work in the area of justice and spirituality.

Joseph Collins is the Registrar at St Patrick's College, Thurles and Director of Catechetics in the Archdiocese of Cashel and Emly.

Gerard Gallagher is Head of the World Youth Day Office in Catholic Youth Care, Dublin. He has worked with young people for many years and has written about the challenges and opportunities of youth ministry in the Church.

Clare Slattery has been the Director of Religious Education for the Diocese of Killaloe and is, at present, a member of the Parish Team at Nenagh, with special responsibility for Catechetics and Adult Education.

Seamus Ryan is the Parish Priest of St Matthew's, Ballyfermot. A former Professor of Theology at St Patrick's College, Thurles, and Chairman of the National Conference of Priests of Ireland, he is well known for his work in liturgical and pastoral renewal.

Nóirín Ní Riain is an internationally acclaimed singer of spiritual songs. She has recently been awarded a Ph.D. in Theology by the University of Limerick.

Anne Codd is a Presentation Sister who is currently resource person for the Irish Bishops' Commission on Pastoral Renewal and Adult Faith Development.

Salvador Ryan teaches history at National University of Ireland, Maynooth and St Patrick's College, Thurles. He has published widely on popular piety and ritual in late medieval and early modern Ireland and also on contemporary religious issues.

Una Agnew is the Head of the Department of Spirituality in Milltown Institute and among her published works is *The Mystical Imagination of Patrick Kavanagh*.

Antrim born **Cardinal Keith O'Brien** is the Roman Catholic Archbishop of Edinburgh.

Lorna Gold currently works as policy analyst in Trócaire. She has wide experience in global social issues.

Foreword

Archbishop Dermot Clifford

Shortly before his election to the Chair of Peter, Pope Benedict XVI was asked by a journalist to describe the essence of Christianity. His reply:

> A love story between God and humanity. If this could be understood in the language of our time, everything else would follow. There is a difficulty in accepting Christianity on the existential level. The current life styles are very different and so an intellectual response is not enough. We need to provide living spaces of community and ways of growth. Only through concrete experiences and lived witness is it possible to make the reality of the Christian message accessible to people now ... Faith becomes free and adult (born) from a 'yes' of the heart to Christ.

Cardinal Ratzinger got to the heart and core of the challenge which faces the Church in our time. How are we to recover the feeling of joy and liberation which the Good News brought when first preached? How can humanity be brought to welcome it as it did 'when all the world was young'? This is the challenge which Dr Joseph Putti and his Committee set out to address in the second Summer School at St. Patrick's College, Thurles in July last. Under the title: *Time to Change: Connecting the Good*

News with Contemporary Living, the fruits of those pleasant summer days now appear in this fine publication.

A team of fourteen well-known theologians, writers and Church people came to the subject from their different areas of expertise. All write from the authority of experience.

In a short period of ten years, or twenty at most, Ireland has found itself suddenly in what is called 'the post-modern age'. It took France two hundred years to make the same journey! Coincidentally, the scandals of other days came to haunt us during that same decade. But the writers do not dwell too long on how we got to this sad state. What matters is not what happened or why it happened but how we respond to the situation.

The task which faces us and the universal Church is called the 'new evangelisation'. The term was coined by Pope Paul VI and it became a priority for Pope John Paul II. The challenge is how to communicate the freshness and lightness of the Gospel in a way which will answer the hunger which money and pleasure and even the Celtic Tiger are unable to satisfy. Spiritual hunger is widespread today but it is not to the Church that many of the hungry are turning. The first summer school in 2004 AD on the theme of 'Spirituality' outlined some of the strange paths which people take to satisfy their spiritual hunger. The ever expanding shelves in our religious bookshops on New Age topics bear this out.

Although each of the contributors was assigned a specific topic in his/her area, a number of common threads appear throughout the book. The first is that faith, as presented up to now, relies too heavily on an appeal to reason. St Thomas Aquinas defined faith as follows: 'to believe is an act of mind assenting to divine truths by virtue of the command of the will as this is moved by God through grace ...' Pope Benedict XVI feels that 'an intellectual response is not enough in our times.'

Imagination also has a role to play in the presentation of the faith. Cardinal Newman once wrote that, 'It is at the level of the imagination that we find faith. The assent of the heart is essential.' 'Faith is knowledge born of love' as Bernard Lonergan put it. This is essentially what St Thomas Aquinas said but it says it in a new language. Imagination brings poetry to mind and Patrick Kavanagh receives honourable mention. 'The Spirit blows where He chooses' — not only through our rational faculties but perhaps even more in the 'deep unconscious room of our hearts', as Kavanagh says in one of his poems.

Undoubtedly, modern people are somewhat sceptical and they apply a credibility test to heralds of the message. Are the preachers' words matched by action? Is their faith a lived one or is it mere words? It is notable that old and young relate to Mother Theresa of Calcutta, Brother Roger of Taizé and Pope John Paul II, because their actions matched their words and they were not afraid to set out the challenge of the Gospel to young and old alike. The media, who are similarly suspicious, have been won over by such authentic witness. Genuine witness to the Gospel is the surest way of communication today.

Young people who have gone on pilgrimage over the years to World Youth Day, to Lourdes or to Taizé, have received a new understanding and appreciation of their faith. Young Irish boys and girls began to take pride in their faith as they shared with their fellow pilgrims from other countries in Rome 2000 AD and Cologne 2005 AD. Youth 2000 is the most promising youth organisation in the Church today. Pope John Paul II is rightly described as 'the greatest youth minister in the history of the Church!' as well as being 'the greatest evangeliser of our times'. He made the evangelisation of the young a priority and set an example for us all.

Another recurring theme is the importance of Liturgy in the life of the Church, the Community or the Parish. It has been a primary vehicle of evangelisation since the earliest times. Contributors urge the wider use of music, the restoration of plainchant in particular, and a greater participation in congregational singing. The careful preparation of the Sunday

Mass should be given quality time by the priest and the Parish Liturgical Committee every week. 'No Christian community can be built up unless it has its basis and centre in the celebration of the most Holy Eucharist', according to Vatican II.

This book is a significant contribution to making the Good News understood in the language of our time. In Pope Benedict's analogy, it adds further chapters to 'the love story between God and humanity'. I congratulate the editor, Dr Joseph Putti, on his second fine publication and I thank the contributors. This book is a credit to them.

It has been said that a foreword should be like a church porch – not so Spartan that the worshipper will turn back but not so well appointed and comfortable that he/she will go no further! I invite you then to come inside!

Most Rev. Dermot Clifford, DD,
Archbishop of Cashel & Emly.

Introduction

Joseph Putti

Change has been a much debated theme in Ireland, particularly in the recent decades. It invites a whole range of responses. Some glorify it. Others vehemently oppose it. Yet others sit on a fence and withhold judgement. But change itself is inevitable. It is one of the fundamental facts of life. Resisting it at all costs can cause irreparable harm at times. As Cardinal Newman said a long time ago, to be perfect means to have changed often. However, constant flux tends to destabilise society and individuals. Wisdom consists in recognising when change is appropriate and when it is not. As the Prayer of Serenity puts it: Dear Lord, give me the grace to change the things I can; to accept the things I can't; and the wisdom to know the difference!

It is fair to say that the Catholic Church has not always had the best record when it comes to dealing with change. Sometimes it tried to demonise it. At other times it tended to reject it altogether and gather the faithful into a fortress. And at yet other times it was forced to deal with it kicking and fuming. A sense of permanence traditionally pervaded the Catholic world-view. Stability was the sought after goal. Society as it existed represented the will of God. It should not be tampered with. Catholic philosophers have in the past tended to side with Parmenides rather than Heraclitus (both ancient Greek philosophers) in their interpretation of change. These reactions are understandable. And they may not always have been wrong and often quite natural. As sociologists point out, every institution tends to protect itself. And change can come across as threatening since it is not always easy to decode. It is often hard to discern what is permanent and what is fleeting in it.

Change poses risks, no doubt. But it also presents rare opportunities. If one is concerned too much with the former, then, one can miss out on the latter. As the vision of a new world was being hammered out in the universities and coffee houses of Europe, the Catholic Church, the most powerful institution of the time, chose to reject it altogether and gather the faithful into a ghetto. This choice, however understandable given the context of the time, has, nevertheless, proved to be, in the light of subsequent history, myopic. By refusing to dialogue with the new world that was emerging, the Church failed to retain a voice in shaping the direction of Europe to come. That must certainly be seen as an opportunity missed.

The theme that links this book is change. The reflections in this book are based on the conviction that change must not be demonised but must be accepted, analysed and responded to appropriately. This might sometimes mean going back and sometimes going forward. Ireland has changed drastically in the past few decades. Change has been fast and furious. The situation of the Church has been transformed dramatically. Therefore, our proclamation of the Good News cannot go on as usual. We must take the new realities into serious consideration and respond to them appropriately if we want to revitalise the life of faith among parishes and people. This remains the ultimate goal of this publication.

A word or two about our authors and their themes. Canon Conor Ryan analyses the changing face of Ireland today from the perspective of religion and concludes that the areas that register the most serious decline are attendance at religious services and confidence in the leadership and moral authority of the Church. Joseph Putti deals with evangelisation in general and new evangelisation in particular, and shows how, increasingly, the future of Christianity in Europe is becoming the focus of reflection and action. Donal Dorr asks why the rich vision made available by Vatican II has not really caught on here in Ireland. Cathy Molloy outlines some aspects of the changing shape of the family in contemporary Ireland, considers the challenges posed by this change and offers some suggestions for meeting these challenges. Joe Collins distinguishes between religious education and catechesis, and reflects on the many ways in which faith can be nurtured through religious education. Gerard Gallagher, basing himself on his experience of working with young people in Ireland, points out some of the ways in which the Gospel is proclaimed in a meaningful way to young people today. Clare Slattery shows how the various sectors of a parish can become powerful agents of change and revitalise the life of the parish and the local community.

Seamus Ryan shows how a meaningful celebration of the Sunday Eucharist can become a powerful source of evangelisation in and for the community. Nóirín Ní Riain makes a plea for the retrieval of plainchant in liturgical music and points out how the entire human sense of hearing has been neglected and ignored in Western theology. Anne Codd struggles with the question: Has the identity of the religious been too closely linked to what they do, and has not enough attention been give to religious life as a life form within the Church in its mission in the world? Salvador Ryan tries to come to terms with the relationship between the Church and the media in Ireland today. Una Agnew outlines how Patrick Kavanagh's poetry can open up new and meaningful avenues to encounter God afresh in our secular society. Cardinal Keith O'Brien, basing himself on his vast experience, considers the many ways in which we can meaningfully connect the Gospel with contemporary European and global concerns. Lorna Gold focuses on ways in which the work of Trócaire relates to the mission of the Church.

I sincerely hope that you will find this collection useful and informative. I also hope that it will inspire you, wherever you are, to bring good news to those around you. We have enough bad news anyway. This book is a collection of talks that were given at the Second Summer School held at St Patrick's College, Thurles, Co. Tipperary, from Monday 18 July to Thursday 21 July, 2005. The aim of the Summer School was to give participants an opportunity to reflect on the Gospel mandate to proclaim the Good News to the whole world and ascertain ways in which it can be accomplished meaningfully in our contemporary times. The Summer School was a success and those who attended it enjoyed it thoroughly.

Summer Schools and books do not fall from the skies. They are the result of the hard work of a number of people. I would like to take this opportunity to thank them all – the authors who have contributed articles, those who helped with the organization of the Summer School, those who chaired the various sessions, etc. A special word of thanks to Fr Tom Fogarty, President of the College, and to all the members of the Summer School Committee: Fr Joe Collins, Catherine Harty, Kevin Maher, Catherine McCormack, Therese Meehan and Alice Roche. Thanks to Veritas publications, in particular, Donna Doherty, commissioning editor, and Ruth Garvey, managing editor, for their help, cooperation and efficient execution. Thanks also to Bernie Bergin, Marian Gleeson, Seamus Kennedy, Mary Murphy, Kay Skehan, Mary Troy and all the other members of the staff for their support and encouragement.

Joseph Putti, Editor
Director of Development, St Patrick's College, Thurles.

The Changing Face of Ireland Today

Canon Conor Ryan

Introduction

It is impossible to sum up the way a whole society has changed in a short piece such as this. There are so many institutions that are involved and such a variety of ways in which they have changed that it is not possible to discuss them all adequately in an article or even in a whole series of articles. Furthermore, changes in institutions influence the behaviour and thinking of individual people in different ways. Books could be written on the changes to institutions such as the family, the workplace, education, the health services, recreation etc. and further books on how these changes have influenced people's behaviour and thinking, or vice versa. I have decided to confine myself to discussing those changes in Irish society which have most repercussions for religion and for the life of the Church in Ireland. In describing change, the length of time chosen in which change has taken place (100, 50, 20 or 10 years) and the perspective in which this change is viewed (Ireland alone; or Europe, the Western World or the entire globe) can have a major influence on the conclusions that can be drawn from these studies.

The winds of change have whistled through practically every dimension of Irish life.

Demographic Change

We will begin with demography and look at the trends in population change. We have over a million more people in the Irish Republic today than we had even 50 years ago. Instead of a gradually declining population, which was the norm from the Famine to the mid-1960s, we have had since then a gradually increasing population. Also, the days of mass emigration are gone.[1] Emigration had been a sad feature of Irish life but also a safety valve against high unemployment and the demands for radical change. The greatest increases are in the cities and particularly the commuter belts servicing the biggest cities. We now have almost full employment and even a shortage of trained employees in some key areas, i.e. nursing and some high-tech sectors, and also a shortage of people willing to work for the legal minimum wage. We have seen an influx of immigrants from Eastern Europe and Third World countries that have brought with them different cultures and religious beliefs. Even when they are Catholic, their preferred patterns of worship and beliefs may not be those to which we are accustomed. These changes put pressure on Church structures and at least call into question the easy assumption that the Republic of Ireland is Catholic and homogeneously so. Some people go much further than this and call for, not only equality for all religions, but also equality for diverse moral beliefs, i.e. morality being the concern of the private life of the individual and therefore not the business of the state.[2]

Economic Change

The second major change in Ireland is the rise in living standards and expectations, often described as the Celtic Tiger.

The Celtic Tiger has brought great benefits, which show themselves in better housing, better nutrition, greater availability and enrolment in higher education, better health-care, longer life expectancy and a more varied social and recreational life. The fact that our expectations in these regards soar even higher does not take from the very real advances that have been made. Undoubtedly there is a downside; for example, both parents having to work and leaving child rearing to child-minders, long commutes to work leading to frustration and stress etc. With more widely available higher education – presently over half of our young people go to some type of third-level institution – people are better educated, better trained to reason and think for themselves, and less likely to accept direction from any authority unless accompanied by reasonable argument and participatory discussion.[3] While 50 per cent attend third-level educational institutions and most get well-paid jobs, the gap between the comfortably well-off and the less well-off is widening. There is a danger that increasingly the working class (less well-off) will reject religion, which they will see as merely one of the conceits of those better off.[4]

Urban Lifestyle

The third change observable in Ireland since the late 1960s is a shift from a rural lifestyle to an urban lifestyle. This is not primarily a question of where you live; it is more a question of social behaviour, assumptions, attitudes and beliefs. In this sense, Ireland has become gradually more urbanised over the last fifty years. The technical application of the word 'urban' used to be 'areas administered by an urban council or commissioners'. Now in its technical meaning it is often applied to built-up areas with a population of 5,000 or more. However, the lifestyle we used to associate with the cities and larger towns has now permeated into the most remote rural areas. The distinction between urban and rural in terms of lifestyle is less significant as Ireland increasingly adopts all the trappings of a full-blown urban lifestyle. If there is a distinction to be made maybe it should be between the capital city, including its environs, and the provinces. This distinction may have a real basis in rates of religious practice. For example, urbanised people are more influenced by national media than local media; have a strict separation of home-life and work-life; socialise with people of common interest rather than geographical closeness; do not see religion as a cement of the local community as rural people do but as an activity which has to compete with shopping, sport, and other forms of recreation and is at best a significant factor in home-life only. In this context, religion is valued as a vehicle for passing on moral teaching and values to young people, and may also be seen as a source of private comfort or consolation, cheaper than regular professional counselling.[5]

Liberalism

The changes in Irish life mentioned above have made people more susceptible to different attitudes, thought patterns, value systems and beliefs, all of which directly impact on religious practice and belief. Many of these attitudes and convictions are a part of Western liberalism, but our increasing openness to them arises from our changing lifestyle and the changes in our thought patterns that this brings. Liberalism as a philosophy grows out of liberal democracy which argues that the citizens should be as free as possible in their beliefs and pursuits, with the only proviso that this freedom be exercised in such a way that all others can enjoy the same freedom. Increasingly Liberalism is wedded to a view of society modelled on the market place,[6] i.e. the strong will rise to the top and the proviso that the weak will be cared for by the state. It is not the business of the state to make saints of people and so the lowest commonly agreed denominator of moral values will be given legal expression. Religion, like all commodities in the market place, will flourish if there is a demand for it; otherwise it will become a museum piece to be studied by archaeologists and historians. Religion tends to be seen as irrational, i.e. not provable by reason. Moral values tend to be seen in the same way. There are no moral absolutes. There are exceptions, i.e. hard-cases, to every moral rule. Moral laws are then seen as subjective and relative. 'Relativists often assert that their position best safeguards human liberty by protecting people from having the truths of others imposed upon them', says Pope Benedict in his challenge to what he calls the 'dictatorship of relativism'. There is no absolute truth and no authority, whether Church or State, can manufacture it. This type of thinking is a direct challenge to the Church and its belief in objective truth and moral absolutes. The Pope argues that 'true liberty is not the freedom to do anything one wants but the freedom to become the creature God wants one to be, and in doing so to find fulfilment'.[7]

Individualism

We are all arbiters of our own beliefs and consciences. We have lost faith and trust in traditional authority. We have found them to be too human, i.e. flawed. Religious and moral teaching based its authenticity on the fact that it came from properly constituted religious authority. The conduit of truth was seen as a pyramid from the Pope and the Council down through the bishops, the priests to the people who received it in a spirit of obedience. The model of finding truth that is most used today might be described as the round-table model,[8] where everybody has his/her own bit to add and truth emerges as the sum of all the individual contributions, large or small, expert or simply opinionated. To see this model in action we need only to listen to phone-ins to the radio, or the text messages and e-mails to live television discussion programmes. Individualism is also seen in the answers to surveys where the 'ethic of authenticity', i.e. 'self-esteem', 'self-worth', 'being true to oneself', 'realising one's own potential' etc., score higher than 'determination', 'perseverance' or 'being willing to work for one's community'. In religion we see individualism manifested in the growing tendency to worship in private rather than in a church with the liturgical community. When there is little or, at best, diminishing community in urban life there is less incentive to worship as a community. According to the EVS and ISSP surveys, 'belief in God' is remarkably high, as is the number of those who 'pray sometimes'. The number attending church services, however, continues to fall. Dominant capitalism and excessive individualism breed off one another. Individualism thus leads to the point where one's home-life is separated from one's work, where one increasingly worships and prays in private and where one's opinions are formed according to popular consent rather than by any objective criteria.[9]

Instrumental Reasoning

Instrumental reasoning can lead to pragmatism where everything has a price. Everything must have an obvious and immediate function, otherwise it is dismissed. Questions such as 'Why should I?', 'What good does it do me?', 'Why should I go to Mass?' demand concrete practical answers. Instrumentalist reasoning shies away from ultimate questions such as 'What is the real purpose of life?', 'Why should I inconvenience myself to live by values that make huge and unreasonable demands on me?', etc. Ultimately instrumental reasoning leads to materialism, i.e. the belief that human happiness and fulfilment comes from possessing more material things. Material things are tangible and measurable. The more you own the happier and more fulfilled you will be. The same type of reasoning leads to secularism, where nothing matters except the 'here and now'. We should enjoy the goods of the world because they are all we have got. The belief in a God who cares but will ultimately judge us has no place in this scenario. The surveys show a relatively high incidence of belief in a 'Heaven' and a very low incidence of belief in a 'Hell'.[10]

Liberalism, individualism and instrumental reasoning have had a profound impact on the practice of religion in Ireland.

Religion – The Irish Situation

Religious Belief
We have seen the logic of the trend towards liberalism and individualism or modernity, as it is sometimes called. We can now ask how far this trend has taken hold in Ireland. To answer this we rely largely on the findings of various surveys. The most important are *European Values Study* (EVS) 1981, 1990 and 1999, and *International Social Survey Programme* (ISSP) 1991, 1998. These studies have done a remarkable job tracking the changing patterns of Irish beliefs, values and practices over the last twenty years. They also compare the findings for Ireland with those of other European countries.[11] As well as these we have national and local surveys of religious belief and practice. National newspapers commission occasional surveys, as does the Catholic Church.[12] *The Survey of an Irish Diocese – Archdiocese of Cashel and Emly 1998* by Irish Marketing Surveys is a good example. These surveys show a people with a very strong and widespread belief in God, as well as in an afterlife; a strong belief in Heaven but a declining belief in Hell; a surprisingly strong belief in the Real Presence in the Eucharist; and an almost universal acceptance of the right to life from conception to death. Furthermore, 'all the evidence points to the fact that while accepting many key tenets of modernity, the Irish remain a deeply religious people with an increasing sense of responsibility

towards themselves and towards others'. Again 'there is little if any evidence of the growth in the secularisation of Irish Society leading to a loss of a sense of the spiritual or to a decline in either the belief in traditional core Christian doctrines or a sense of the importance of God, religion or prayer in the lives of Irish people. One can also point to the rejection of extreme individualism that was observed in the surveys that suggests a continuing commitment to the core social character of Christian living'.[13]

Religious Practice
All the surveys agree that attendance at Mass and the sacraments, particularly Penance, is falling. Weekly Mass attendance varies from below 30 per cent in some parts of the capital city to above 70 per cent in some parts of the provinces but the numbers who totally abandon religious practice is less than 10 per cent. Irish people are easing off on Church attendance rather than abandoning it altogether, unlike in the European context where abandonment is becoming more widespread. Despite the scaling down of religious practice, however, the majority of people continue to believe in God, consider themselves religious and think that it is important to have religious ceremonies at births, marriages and deaths. The areas in the Irish religious profile that register the most serious decline over the lifetime of the surveys, apart from attendance at religious services, are belief in the moral authority of the Catholic Church and confidence in the leadership of the Catholic Church. The decline in the Church's moral authority is seen particularly in the changing sexual mores regarding questions like contraception, pre- and extra-marital sex and the number of children born outside wedlock (one-third to one-half of all babies). Loss of confidence in the Catholic Church started a full decade before the sex scandals. Other institutions, such as the State, Gardaí, etc., have been subjected to tribunals yet the Catholic Church has suffered the steepest decline in confidence. This may be due to a number of factors:

1 The influence and authority of the Church may have been abnormally high.
2 The fear of punishment in the after-life is less.
3 A liberal democratic culture prefers a participatory egalitarian society and authoritarianism is more noticeable in higher centralised authority and less in local clergy and the local church community, leading to the latter faring better in the surveys.[14]

> *Areas in the Irish religious profile that register the most serious decline are attendance at religious services, belief in the moral authority of the Catholic Church and confidence in the leadership of the Catholic Church.*

It is clear that modern society with its trends towards liberalism, individualism and secularism presents many challenges to religious belief and practice, but there is still a strong foundation of belief and practice upon which a rejuvenated Church can thrive again, with God's help.

Notes
1 Analysis of *Census 2002* population of the 26 counties as constituted at each census since 1841, www.cso.ie/census.
2 Even a cursory reading of the newspapers would bear this out.
3 See the article by Professor William Reville 'The Future of the Church in Ireland' in *The Irish Catholic,* 17 February 2005, p. 9.
4 Some evidence for this in *EVS surveys* cf. Bibliography.
5 See article by Archbishop Sean Brady in *The Voice,* 12 May 2005, p. 5; European Values Studies (EVS), 1981, 1990, 1999; and International Social Survey Programme (ISSP), 1991, 1998.
6 W. Ebenstein, *Today's ISMS,* pp. 139–209.
7 M. Kelly, Excerpts from Pope Benedict's speech to New Zealand's Ambassador in 'Letter from Rome', *The Irish Catholic,* 23 June 2005, p. 7.

8 See W. Reville in *The Irish Catholic*, Feb. 17th 2005, p. 9.

9 See Eoin G. Cassidy (ed.) *Measuring Ireland: Discerning Values and Beliefs*, Dublin: Veritas, 2002, particularly the articles Eoin G. Cassidy, 'Modernity and Religion in Ireland' and T. Fahey, 'Is Atheism Increasing? Ireland and Europe Compared'.

10 Ibid., pp. 33–40.

11 Most of the information concerning these surveys is from Eoin G. Cassidy (ed.) *Measuring Ireland*.

12 *Sunday Tribune*, May 2005.

13 Eoin G. Cassidy, *Modernity and Religion in Ireland*, pp. 17–45, and also T. Fahey, 'Is Atheism Increasing?', pp. 64–65 in *Measuring Ireland*.

14 Cassidy, pp. 40–44 and Fahey, pp. 64–65.

Bibliography

Breen, R., Hannon, D., Rottmen, D. and Whelan, C., *Understanding Contemporary Ireland* (Dublin: Gill and Macmillan, 1994).

Cassidy, Eoin G. (ed.) *Measuring Ireland: Discerning Values and Beliefs* (Dublin: Veritas, 2002).

Ebenstein, William, *Today's ISMS*, 7th ed. (Englewood Cliffs, NJ: Prentice-Hall, 1973).

European Values Studies (EVS), 1981, 1990, 1999.

Fogarty, M., Ryan, L. and Lee, J., *Irish Values and Attitudes: The Irish Report of the European Values Study System* (Dublin: Dominican Publications, 1984).

Giddens, Anthony, *Sociology* (London: Polity Press, 1989).

Greeley, Andrew M., *Religion in Europe at the End of the Second Millennium: A Sociological Sketch* (Brunswick: Transaction Publications, 2001).

Healy S. and Reynolds, B., *Ireland Today* (CMRS Office, 1985).

International Social Survey Programme (ISSP), 1991, 1998.

Irish Census 2002 with population returns since 1841, www.cso.ie/census.

Kelly, M., 'Letter from Rome', *The Irish Catholic*, 23 June 2005, p. 7.

Mackey, James and McDonagh, Enda (eds) *Religion and Politics in Ireland at the Turn of the Millennium* (Dublin: Columba Press, 2003).

Reville, W., 'The Future of the Church in Ireland', *The Irish Catholic*, 17 February 2005, p. 9.

Twomey, V., *The End of Irish Catholicism* (Dublin: Veritas Publications, 2003).

Wilson, Bryan, *Religion in Sociological Perspective* (Oxford: Oxford University Press, 1982).

Proclaiming the Good News:

Changing Perspectives and Emerging Trends

Joseph Putti

Introduction

Proclaiming the Good News has been an integral part of the mission of the Church from the very beginning. It was the desire to share that Good News with Jews and gentiles alike that gave the fledgling Church a sense of identity and purpose. And right through the ages the Church never lost this sense of mission. The discovery of the New World spurred the Church on to a new era of evangelisation in the mission territories. However, with the emergence of the modern world and the increasing secularisation of society in the West, the consciousness was forced on the Church that while it still had to be concerned with evangelisation in mission territories, it nevertheless had to turn its attention seriously to the loss of faith that was becoming increasingly common in the traditionally Christian West. It was Paul VI who, particularly through his Apostolic Letter *Evangelii Nuntiandi* and the Encyclical *Populorum Progressio*, both broadened the concept of mission by linking it with the total and integral development of the human person, and linked mission, not just with proclaiming the Gospel abroad, but also with invigorating the declining faith of people at home. The latter theme, often referred to as New Evangelisation, became central to the ministry of John Paul II and he repeatedly referred to the need to re-evangelise Europe. Pope Benedict XVI has already made this theme central to his papacy. By assuming the name

Benedict XVI - Benedict being the patron saint of Europe - he has given a clear indication that the overall health of the Church in Europe would be of utmost importance to his papacy.[1]

The Catholic Church is becoming increasingly concerned about the situation of the faith in the traditionally Christian West.

The concept New Evangelisation does not refer to the proclamation of a new message. While it is true that there are aspects of the message that may need to be rediscovered, re-emphasised and reinforced in response to changing needs and emerging contexts, the message nevertheless remains the same. The Church's mission is to proclaim the salvation that Jesus brought in and through his words and deeds, particularly his death and resurrection. However, the proclamation of the Gospel does not take place in a vacuum. It occurs in a specific context and is addressed to a specific people. The content of the message remains central, no doubt, but the importance of the context cannot be overlooked. It is vital, particularly in the secular society in which we live, that the proclamation of the living Word of God resonates with the real needs of people. It is necessary to connect the Good News with contemporary living. It is not the Gospel that is out of date. Its message is perennial. However, its relevance to particular contexts has to be brought out clearly. This is where the problem lies. People today tend to respond to religion, not so much on the basis of habit, custom or tradition, but individually and personally. It is necessary that the message is seen and heard, not so much as an obligation, a doctrine or a law, but as the Gospel of freedom that liberates, inspires and empowers. Causes that prevent people from listening and responding to the message of the Gospel and reacting to it positively need to be identified and analysed. It is this process that the term New Evangelisation generally refers to.

Jesus the Proclaimer

Jesus himself was the greatest evangeliser. He presented himself, right from the very beginning of his ministry, as a man with a mission. 'The Spirit of the Lord is upon me; because he has anointed me to bring good news to the poor. He has sent me to proclaim release to the captives and recovery of sight to the blind, to let the oppressed go free, to proclaim the year of the Lord's favour' (Lk 4:18). And this mission became the consuming passion of his entire life. 'But', he said to them, 'I must proclaim the good news of the kingdom to other cities also; for I was sent for this purpose' (LK 4:43).

The remarkable thing about the ministry of Jesus was his ability to connect with ordinary people in an extraordinary way.

What distinguished the Good News that Jesus proclaimed was that, unlike the message preached by many of the rabbis of the day which came across as dry, drab and lifeless, his words were experienced as refreshing and uplifting. He was a breath of fresh air. His word was no empty clatter, but emanated out of a profound experience of intimacy with his Father. And it became the source of life for many, saints and sinners alike. To a culture that had rendered God distant and remote, Jesus spoke of 'Abba, Father' and heralded God's homecoming. To a culture that had identified religion with the perfect observance of the minutiae of endless laws and regulations, Jesus presented a religion centred firmly on the love of God and neighbour. To a society that had segregated and stratified people, he brought the message of salvation to all and sundry, extending his arms to the pious Jew and the prostitute alike. To a culture where worship had become routine, empty and meaningless, he proclaimed a religion that would worship the Father in spirit and in truth. To a society where many were dedicated to the violent overthrow of the hated Romans, he spoke of the Kingdom of God, a kingdom of justice and peace. Jesus connected in a marvellous way with the people he ministered to, and that rendered his message powerful.

Proclaiming the Good News in the Early Church

It is possible to speak of three phases in the history of the proclamation of the Good News of the Gospel. The first phase coincided with the origin and development of the early Church and its establishment as the official religion of the Roman Empire. It began on the day of Pentecost, when the Apostles, in and through the power of the Holy Spirit, left the Upper Room where they had sought refuge for fear of reprisals by the Jews and went forth into the streets of Jerusalem to preach the Gospel of Jesus Christ in many tongues (Acts 2:5-11). Ever since, sharing the Good News became the driving force behind the early Church. This mission was not the prerogative of a chosen few. It was seen as a sacred obligation entrusted to the whole community. Roles, responsibilities and ministries were very flexible at the beginning. As the process of institutionalisation gathered momentum, there was an inevitable sedimentation of roles, but the focus on the community itself was never lost. The mission was given to every disciple of Jesus: 'Go therefore and make disciples of all nations, baptising them in the name of the Father and of the Son and of the Holy Spirit, and teaching them to obey everything I have commanded you' (Mt 28:19-20). Evangelisation was never understood in terms of proclamation alone. It is possible to identify at least five strands of ministries that were discernible in the early Church, namely *kerygma* (proclamation), *didache* (teaching), *liturgeia* (worship), *koinonia* (community building) and *diakonia* (service), all working in unison to proclaim, in word and deed, the advent of the Kingdom of God on earth in and through the ministry of Jesus.

It was the desire to proclaim the Gospel to Jews and gentiles alike that gave the fledgling Church a sense of identity and purpose.

These were certainly exciting and inspiring times in the history of the emerging Church. It was a time of saints and martyrs, when laying down one's life to bear witness to the Lordship of Jesus was seen as both an honour and a privilege. The many summers I spent as a guide in the catacombs in Rome brought home clearly to me the spirit of strength in adversity that prevailed in the early Church. The blood of the martyrs became the seed of the Church. And after the inspired Peter, during the First Apostolic Council of Jerusalem in AD 51, endorsed enthusiastically the need to take the mission of Jesus to the gentile land, the evangelisation of the Greco-Roman world became the singular goal of the early followers. And no one exemplified this new drive better than the Apostle Paul: 'Woe to me if I do not proclaim the gospel!' (I Cor 9:16).

The eloquence of Paul and Barnabas, and other inspired men and women like them, who gloried in the Cross, a stumbling block to the Jews and foolishness to the gentiles, played a decisive role in the success of the gentile mission. However, it was the daily witness of love that prevailed among the followers of Jesus that captivated an alien world and ultimately drew hundreds and hundreds into their folds. And this has remained so. With the conversion of Emperor

Constantine in 312 AD and the gradual emergence of Christianity as the official religion of the Empire, the first phase in evangelisation may be said to have been accomplished. We sometimes hear that bringing the Gospel to our secular society is a formidable task. No doubt it is so. However, it pales into insignificance when compared with the enormity of the challenge our early ancestors in the faith faced when confronting an alien and highly developed civilisation with the simple message of the Gospel.

The Evangelisation of the New World

The second phase in the history of the proclamation of the Good News may be said to have begun with the discovery of the New World. Motivated by adventure, glory and fortune for themselves and their empires, sailors and soldiers from Portugal and Spain were anxious to discover a sea route to Asia. They were interested as much in trade as in proclaiming the Christian faith to the New World. Pope Alexander VI in 1493 allocated all non-Christian lands to the east of a line drawn west of the Azores Islands in the Atlantic to the patronage of Portugal and all the lands west of this line to Spain. The aim of this arrangement was 'to bring to the Christian faith the peoples who inhabit these islands and mainland ... and to send to the said islands and to the mainland wise, upright, and virtuous men who will be capable of instructing the indigenous peoples in good morals and the Catholic faith'.[2] The Portugese and the Spanish were primarily traders, not colonisers, unlike the English, the French and the Dutch who came later on. The Portugese and the Spanish worked primarily for their empires, whereas the Dutch, the English and the French tended to work for individuals and groups. The alliance between the peso, the sword and the Cross that was forged during these times may surprise many today. However, in earlier days, it was not something that was frowned upon. And it worked well in certain ways, at least in the short term, but in other ways, it was a disaster. The Portugese were sailors, but the Spanish were mainly soldiers (*conquistodores*), who were interested in conquering new lands for the crown. The Portugese trading posts provided valuable bases for the Christian mission to China and India. The Spaniard Hernando Cortez, the conqueror of Mexico, was primarily a soldier, and quite cruel in his ways, but also doubled up as a preacher when the monks were not available. However, the desire to amass wealth was never far away. Cortez had no problem asking the representative of the Aztec king Montezuma for gold dust, explaining, 'the Spaniards were troubled with a disease of the heart, for which gold is the specific remedy'.[3]

To proclaim the Gospel effectively, it is necessary to make it an integral part of the local culture.

In spite of exceptional missionaries like Saint Francis Xavier, who were aware of and sensitive to the highly developed cultures in which they were called to proclaim the Gospel of Christ and often tried to present the Gospel in terms of native cultures, the missionary movement initially consisted, more often than not, in literally transporting to the new lands the Christian message couched in Western cultural terms. As the Catholic Church in the West, faced with the onslaughts of the Reformation, Renaissance and the Enlightenment, became defensive, reactionary and authoritarian in its presentation of the Christian message, the same occurred in missionary territories too. The stress was on preserving the purity of doctrine clothed in medieval terms, and in the process the Church alienated itself from much of the modern cultural and philosophical vision that was fast beginning to inform minds and mores in the West.

It was Vatican II, under the inspiration of the charismatic John XXIII, realising that while the Christian message had not lost its relevance, it was nonetheless becoming outmoded, initiated a movement of rapprochement with the modern world. And given the dehumanising poverty that existed in many of the poor nations in Asia, Africa and Latin America, and the realisation that injustice in the world was the result of structures that often originated in the Christian West, and under the impact of theological movements originating in the Third World, the stress in presenting the message began to move from an overly spiritual concern to save souls to action on behalf of the total and integral development of the entire human person. As *Lumen Gentium*, Vatican II's dogmatic constitution on the Church declares, the Kingdom of God is a kingdom of justice and peace as well as of holiness and grace.[4] The 1971 Synod of Bishops on *Justice in the World* spoke about 'how action on behalf of justice and participation in the transformation of the world were a constitutive dimension of the preaching of the Gospel'.[5] This was also the message of perhaps the best known papal document on evangelisation, namely *Evangelii Nuntiandi* of Pope Paul VI (1975).[6] It spoke of evangelisation as the proclamation of not just the Good News of future salvation, but also the Good News of the reign of God in our midst. Evangelisation is concerned with the whole human being, not just the soul. Evangelisation is liberation from sin and the evil one and from every form of economic, social and political oppression.

In the colonial era Christianity tended to be identified with the culture of the coloniser. The success of evangelisation was often identified with the success with which the culture of the coloniser penetrated and transformed the culture of the colonised. This strategy may have been successful, particularly in the Americas in the sixteenth century, but it also served to alienate the Christian communities in the new lands from their cultural roots and identify Christianity there with an alien culture. Bringing the Gospel to new territories continues to be a sacred obligation entrusted to the Church and all its members. However, in fulfilling this sacred obligation, it is necessary that the Church remains ever conscious of the need for inculturation. Christianity does not exist in a cultural vacuum. Wherever it exists, it exists in a culture, either the culture of the people among whom the Christian community lives or that of the evangelisers. Evangelising in a culture other than one's own requires special sensitivity. Too many times in the past progress in evangelisation was hampered by a failure to appreciate other cultures. There is talk today of reverse evangelisation. While in the past the movement in evangelisation tended to be from the centre (Europe) to the periphery (the mission territories), today it is from the periphery to the centre, and many new Churches are beginning to give witness and in their turn help to evangelise older Churches.[7]

New Evangelisation

Apart from the two phases we have already mentioned, it has become customary today to speak of a third phase in evangelisation. The third phase represents increasing efforts, sometimes sporadic and sometimes systematic, on the part of the Church to refocus efforts in evangelisation on the Christian West. This re-focusing is not by mere choice. It has been necessitated by a number of factors: the secular times in which we live, the changing world scene, the weakening influence of the Western civilisation, the deterioration of the life of faith in many of the established Churches of the West, etc. The third phase does not neglect or overlook the second phase, but opens a new front, so to speak, in the mission to evangelise. As such it is possible to speak of three dimensions to the third phase. The first is concerned with bringing the Gospel to peoples, groups and socio-cultural contexts that do not know Christ and have not heard of His Gospel. This is evangelisation in the traditional sense. We have already addressed this dimension.

One of the fundamental objectives of New Evangelisation is to fan into flame the dying embers of faith in many of the traditionally Christian countries of the West.

The second dimension refers to the ongoing pastoral care of the believing faithful. Such care is absolutely crucial today because the faith of even those who have been traditionally faithful is not safe and secure anymore. Many among them are experiencing confusion and darkness in their life of faith. Even in this country, many among the faithful ones are struggling to come to terms with the rapidity and the radical nature of change in society and Church. The traditional supports for the faith have either collapsed or are crumbling. Very often being a believer has become a lonely experience. The Church has the task, more than ever before, of confirming the faithful in the faith daily, through the proclamation of the Word, the celebration of the Eucharist and other sacraments, and commitment to the causes of justice and charity.

The third dimension is most often referred to as New Evangelisation. The term itself goes back to Pope Paul VI. 'The expression New Evangelisation was popularised in the encyclical of Pope Paul VI *Evangelisation in the Modern World*, as a response to the new challenges that the contemporary world creates for the mission of the Church'.[8] John Paul II made it the central plank of his entire Pontificate and returned to it again and again during the twenty-six years of his papacy.[9] 'I sense the moment has come to commit all of the Church's energies to a new evangelisation'.[10] Pope Benedict XVI has shown himself to be equally concerned with it, for even as Cardinal Ratzinger, he spoke quite extensively about it.[11]

New Evangelisation is an attempt on the part of the Church to come to terms with contemporary realities. The Western World has changed radically. This change has affected the situation of the faith profoundly. There is a deep decline in the practice of religion. The ranks of the faithful have dwindled significantly. Not simply the practice of religion, even the influence of Christianity in Europe has waned drastically. Pierre Cardinal Eyt, the Archbishop of Bordeaux, refers to the 'quiet apostasy' that prevails in Europe and admits that 'the European soul is no longer naturally Christian'.[12] Churches cannot stand idly by and let history take its course. They need to respond. If they do not, they either become irrelevant or dead. Pope Benedict XVI, when he was Cardinal Ratzinger, spoke of how a large part of today's humanity, particularly in the West, does not find the Gospel in the permanent evangelisation of the Church because of de-Christianisation and the loss of the essential human values.[13]

The role Christianity plays in the lives and consciousness of Europeans has changed dramatically. There are many who may have been baptised once, but who no longer consider themselves members of the Church. There are others who may be members of a Church, but whose experience of faith is at best fragmentary and occasional. It does not animate the totality of their experience. The past religious traditions hold only partial appeal. Many Christians who were baptised as infants have never made a personal commitment to Christ and the Gospel. As adolescents and adults, many of them have drifted away from the Church.[14] There are others in whose lives faith is absent altogether, and even though they may be Christians, they think and behave as if God does not exist. Then there are those who are so caught up in the intense pursuit of goals, dreams, possessions, entertainment and an endless list of new experiences that they have lost touch with their spiritual roots altogether.

The fact that people seem to have walked away from the Church does not mean that the Church should stop proclaiming the Gospel to them. Whatever the reasons people may have turned away from religion, they still deserve to hear the Good News of the Gospel and come face to face with its life-giving power and transforming message. The Church today has the task of moving beyond the ranks of the faithful and reaching out to those who have strayed. Jesus was never satisfied with catering to the needs of the faithful ones. He actively sought the sheep that may have strayed for whatever reason.

New evangelisation does not mean the proclamation of a new message. There is but one Gospel of Jesus Christ. There is one Lord, one baptism and one saviour. Therefore, the newness is not newness of content, but 'newness in ardour, methods and expression'.[15] New Evangelisation focuses not just on individual non-believers or non-practising Christians, but reaches out to entire cultures.[16] New Evangelisation is about quality rather than quantity. It is about building with patience, not looking for spectacular or instant success. New Evangelisation is modelled on the parable of the mustard seed and must avoid the temptation of large numbers (Lk 4:26-29). It is not a question of immediately attracting the large masses that have abandoned ship by sleek advertising or glitzy marketing. When and how the mustard seed will grow is something we must leave to God. The scriptures bear ample witness to the fact that God does not count in large numbers. Outward appearance is not the sign of His presence. It was David the youngest son who was chosen to be the future king of Israel. It was the weak and impetuous Peter who was chosen to be the rock. It was the virgin from Nazareth who was called to be the mother of the Messiah. Jesus himself had to avoid the temptation to worldly success (Mt 4:9). Today, it is crucial, as Benedict XVI insists, that we let the mystery of the mustard seed seep into our consciousness. Perhaps, in the past, our evangelisation efforts missed out a little on this important consideration.[17]

Building Blocks of the New Evangelisation

If New Evangelisation is the attempt on the Church's part to bring out the perennial relevance of the Gospel message to all sections of society, particularly those sections which, for one reason or other, have chosen to stay away, then what exactly are the elements around which this new appeal is to be built? As I have said above, these elements cannot be entirely new, because there is but one Gospel. What has to be done is to go back to the heart of the message in a refreshing and life-giving way, taking into account new realities and contemporary circumstances. What then are the constituent elements or the building blocks of New Evangelisation? Obviously, in a short paper like this, it will be impossible to do justice to all of them. I will attempt to merely outline, in a general sort of way, what I believe are the most important elements.

Awaken in People a Sense of God
New Evangelisation must begin with awakening in people a sense of God because what Europe has lost is not simply faith in organised religion, but in an even more basic sense, faith in the existence of a personal and caring God. As the German theologian John Metz has remarked, commenting on the decline of Christianity in Western Europe, the true problem of our times is the crisis of God, the absence of God, disguised as empty religiosity.[18]

> *What Europe has lost is not just belief in organised religion, but, in an even more fundamental sense, faith in the existence of a personal and caring God.*

There is indeed a hunger for spirituality today. People have not lost their sense of the spiritual. In fact, spirituality is a very popular subject today. Therefore, the source of the contemporary crisis is not spirituality as such, but the inability, on the part of many of the traditional guardians of the sacred, to connect their representation of the sacred with the spiritual yearning of people. Many of our traditional images of God do not communicate effectively any longer or communicate the wrong message. There seems to be a huge disconnect between where we are with our God and where people are with their concerns. The problem is not with God, but with our presentation of God. God is not the competitor in our life, but the guarantor of our greatness. He is not the enforcer, but the defender of freedom. The natural and the supernatural are not totally opposed to each other. While we must admit the reality of sin, we must nevertheless recognise that the natural is orientated towards the supernatural and that the supernatural does not swallow up the natural. Divine rights and genuine human rights are, ultimately, not contrary viewpoints. To defend God, we need not sacrifice man. We, as human beings, are open to transcendence.

New Evangelisation must help people to connect their yearning for the spiritual with their belief in God. It must begin with evoking in people a sense of the presence of God in their lives and in the world. However, the existence of God is not merely an intellectual question. To proclaim God is to introduce one to a relationship with God, to teach one to pray, to experience God. Only when we experience life with God does the evidence for his existence emerge. That is why speaking about God and speaking with God must go together. Religion cannot remain a slogan, but must become a celebration. Liturgy is an essential part of evangelisation. God is the centre of liturgy, not the minister.

If Europe were to look far and deep into its origins, it will discover, in spite of the prevailing attitude of pessimism and negativity, the fundamental role Christianity has played in shaping the various aspects of European culture. The task of New Evangelisation is to help people to sift through layers and layers of history, of European history, and discover afresh the presence of God imbedded there. To enable this to happen, the Church must first undergo metanoia, profound conversion. It must come to terms with the dark moments of its history.[19]

Waking up to the sense of God means becoming aware of His presence in our midst. Our world is not alien to God. It is not just a vale of tears. God is not a total stranger. Our earth is his home too. Evangelisation is not about bringing God into people's lives from an alien planet. It is helping people to encounter the One who is already there. As Kierkegaard says, 'God is the beyond in our midst'. Our world today is spent, tired and morally exhausted, having tried everything and found that none of it brings lasting happiness. Perhaps it is time to revert to God. As Einstein has remarked, 'We live in world of problems which can no longer be solved by the level of thinking that created them'.[20] Once we let go of God, all of our certitudes begin to unravel. He is the glue that holds all things together.

It is the sense of God that helps us to rediscover the inviolable dignity of every human person, that human beings are always a value in and for themselves. John Paul II, in his Encyclical *Redemptor Hominis*, criticises the view of man as an object of use, production and manipulation, with only an earthly destiny and therefore ignorant of man's irreplaceable supernatural destiny.[21] That human beings have a supernatural destiny means that success in life cannot be measured by criteria confined to this planet alone. To be able to assess human beings appropriately, we need to look beyond tomorrow. As the Apostle Paul tells his disciples: 'Our first citizenship is in heaven' (Phil 3:20). However, faith in eternal life does not make our earthly life insignificant. It rather enhances it. Only when the measure of our life is eternity, does our life on earth become great and its value immense.

Christ is at the Heart of New Evangelisation
Christ is at the centre of New Evangelisation because he is at the very centre of our faith. What characterised the confession of faith in the early Church was its absolute focus on the mystery of Christ. 'Evangelization will always contain - as the foundation, centre and, at the same time, the summit of its

dynamism – a clear proclamation that, in Jesus Christ, salvation is offered to all men, as a gift of God's grace and mercy'.[22] Only in Christ and through Christ does God become fully incarnate. Christ is Emmanuel, the God-with-us. New Evangelisation, therefore, must be centred on Christ. Being centred on Christ is the same as speaking the full truth about Christ. This truth is established ultimately, neither by historiography nor by any other scientific method. This is not to deny the contribution the scientific study of faith has made to the understanding and elaboration of the Christian faith in Jesus Christ. However, this faith is based, in the final analysis, on the testimony of the earliest followers of Jesus, particularly the twelve apostles. The apostolic testimony, borne eloquent witness to in the Scriptures, remains the bedrock of all Christian beliefs about Jesus Christ. Speaking the full truth about Jesus Christ means confessing that he is fully God and fully man at the same time. As Schillebeeckx would put it, Jesus is both the parable of God and the paradigm of humanity.[23] Whereas in the earliest times, particularly in classical Christology, in the attempt to highlight the divinity of Christ, his true humanity tended sometimes to be glossed over, today the temptation is to make Jesus a merely historical individual, a mere man. We must avoid the temptation to reduce Christ to our size. Speaking the full truth about Jesus means focusing on the sufficiency of Christ. Christ is the way, the truth and the life. There are many today who are turning to a plethora of spiritualities in their quest for meaning and salvation. For the Christian, however, he is the way to the Father. He brings the fullness of life.[24]

One of the central objectives of New Evangelisation is to proclaim the full truth about Christ.

Faith is not merely a thing to be known, a doctrine to be accepted, a law to be obeyed, a person to be loved and surrendered to. Accepting the salvation that Jesus brought is not simply a rational decision. It involves, as in the case of the Samaritan woman, as in the case of the disciples of Emmaus, as in the case of the drowning Peter, a personal and profound meeting with the Saviour.[25] It is not simply proclaiming Christ; it is also following Christ, *sequela Christi*. Following Jesus is not just imitating Jesus; it is to be assimilated into Christ, i.e. to attain union with God. All solutions beneath this level of divinisation are ultimately unsatisfactory. *Sequela Christi* draws us inevitably into the mystery of the Cross. The Cross belongs to the divine mystery. Whoever omits the Cross omits the essence of Christianity (1 Cor 2:2).

Building Communities of Faith

There is an erosion in the sense of community in Ireland today. Preoccupation with the individual has replaced the traditional focus on community. We are all too aware of the sense of isolation that many rural communities face. New Evangelisation must focus on the need to create genuine communities, communities of faith, bound not just by external ties, but also by a meeting of hearts which comes about as a result of clarity of vision, collaboration and communion. This is the language that won the early Church the allegiance of millions and it is the witness to community that will impress our age, steeped as it is in the worship of the individual.

Authoritarianism militates against the formation of genuine Christian communities.

That is why John Paul II has spoken of the urgent need to 're-make the Christian fabric of the ecclesial community'.[26]

Communities do not fall from the skies. They need to be built. Genuine communities promote a sense of belonging. Participation at all levels is the key. The Church needs to overcome the authoritarianism at all levels that has driven so many people out of the Church. Authoritarianism militates against the formation of genuine community. It promotes sycophancy and encourages passivity. Genuine communities are built on clear communication and transparency, not on the cult of secrecy and control. Community building happens at many levels. It happens at the level of the parish. The parish is the place where most Catholics meet God. However, it is necessary for parishioners to meet each other too and feel a sense of belonging. Priests need to share ministry with the laity and laity must take responsibility for the faith life of their community. Trust and openness wholly in accord with the dignity and responsibility of every member of the People of God must reign in Churches. It is not simply by sharing ideas, shouting slogans or believing in creeds that people become connected. It is, above all, by doing things together. 'The charity of works ensures an unmistakable efficacy to the charity of words.'[27] Evangelisation must also focus on the family, the first school of faith. The question that must be raised in this context is: How is it that when we were poor, we had no problem communicating the faith to our children and now that we are prosperous we find it difficult to talk to them about God?

Building the Faith of Individual Believers
It is necessary that the Church connects with people as individuals, because people believe as individuals. Faith is a personal decision. Freedom and faith go together. Days of fear, censure and excommunication are over. Our society is rooted in liberty, equality and freedom. As has been said above, evangelisation today is not about quantity, but quality. Quality evangelisation must seek to connect with people. It is necessary to encounter people where they are, since many of them no

longer go to church. God came to meet us where we are – in our own space, our own time. This is the heart of the mystery of Incarnation. As Jean Vanier once remarked, 'People are looking for a wisdom to guide their lives rather than a church to belong to'.[28] It is not that belonging to the Church is not important. However, if belonging to the Church does not promote the art of living, then, it comes across as pie in the sky, irrelevant to daily life. This art, as Benedict XVI remarks, cannot be construed by science, but can only be communicated by One who has life.[29] The Good News that has not lost its relevance. Its presentation has often become jaded, monotonous, routine and lifeless. The Church, therefore, is called to rise out of its lethargy and articulate the kind of vision that will give meaning to a confused and tired society. It is necessary to speak about the meaning, the full meaning of life, because our world is steeped in materialism and consumerism. Therefore, New Evangelisation must call people to conversion, personal conversion, i.e. questioning one's way of living, reflecting on one's priorities, searching for values, allowing God to enter into the criteria of one's life. There is a loss of the sense of afterlife in our world today. The sense of afterlife serves to affirm a sense of justice, accountability and personal responsibility in this life, a sense of what has traditionally been described as judgement by God.

Evangelisation of Cultures

The alienation between cultures and the Gospel is a growing reality today. Human beings, cultures and the Gospel exist contradicting each other. Paul VI said a long time ago that 'the split between the Gospel and culture is without doubt the drama of our time, just as it was of other times'.[30] As the vision for the New World was being hammered out in Europe, against the background of the fall of monarchy and the birth of democracy, the Church lost its opportunity to influence the same, by refusing to dialogue with the modern world. Instead, it gathered its people into a ghetto and followed a policy of entrenchment. That is why it seems to have so little influence today in shaping the direction of Europe to come.

Therefore, it is necessary to talk about evangelising culture today. Culture has crucial impact on people. It plays a decisive part in fashioning worldviews, philosophies and visions of life. Cultures influence behaviour, set trends and establish traditions. That is why John Paul II often spoke of the need to incarnate Christian values into European culture.[31] To do so effectively, the Christian faith may have to take on new forms and adopt new methods of evangelising and proclaiming the Gospel. Like many of the prophets of old, New Evangelisation would mean being the architect of a counter culture, judging critically and condemning values that run counter to the Gospel. Our culture is post-Christian and it therefore needs to be re-evangelised. This is precisely what Pope John Paul II did, when, speaking to the Church in America, he called for the restoration of soul to the secularised world, rediscovery of the hidden spirit and replacing with fervour the superficiality and lukewarmness with which, in many cases, divine things are treated.[32]

New Evangelisation is the Work of the Entire People of God
Proclaiming the Good News is the responsibility of every baptised person. Each parish, school and institution is called to engage in it.[33] This responsibility cannot be assigned simply to a group of people (bishops, priests, religious etc.), but must be assumed by the entire community, including in a special way the laity.[34] Lay men and women are called in a unique way to share in the work of evangelisation by helping to overcome the separation of the Gospel from life and by bearing witness to Christ and to his Church in the world.[35] As John Paul II says: 'No believer in Christ, no institution of the Church can avoid this supreme duty of proclaiming Christ to all the peoples.'[36] The Pope seems to go out of his way in exhorting that the mission of

evangelisation is the mission of not a special group of people, but of the entire Church, the People of God. This is not to diminish the responsibility of bishops, priests and religious, but to reinforce that of the laity. Above all, it means encouraging collaboration.

Methods of Evangelisation

New Evangelisation is not just about the content of evangelisation. It is also about the appropriate methods that should be used in the proclamation of the Good News. The methods employed must be in tune with contemporary human consciousness. Religious truth cannot be forced on people. It can only be communicated effectively in an atmosphere of freedom. Censure and excommunication are not going to work today. If we believe that the Gospel has a perennial appeal because it speaks about truths that are eternal, then, what is needed is to expose people to its appeal. In exposing people to this appeal, we must appeal not just to the intellect, but also to the imagination. The Gospel, in the final analysis, is neither a body of truths nor a set of laws, but an invitation to experience life and experience it in its fullness. The proclamation of the Gospel must be free. It should be pro-active rather than a reactive intervention to every type of crisis, heresy and scandal.

New Evangelisation is about both doing and being.

Our world is both wired and networked today. Communication technology has revolutionised contemporary existence. E-mailing and texting have become effective tools of communication. It is essential that we use the cyberspace in creative ways to proclaim the Gospel. However, whatever methods we may use, they are only means. They cannot be ends in themselves. All methods and modes of communication must ultimately be motivated by the good of the people and the glory of God. As Pope Benedict XVI says, we are not looking or listening for ourselves. We do not want to increase the power and the spreading of institutions, but wish to seek the good of the people and humanity, making way always to the One who is life.[37]

We must also keep in mind that Jesus did not redeem the world with beautiful words but with his suffering and death. The success of the mission in Paul's life was not the fruit of great rhetorical art or pastoral prudence; the fruitfulness was tied to the suffering, to the communion in the passion with Christ (1 Cor 2:1-5, II Cor 11:30, Gal 4:12-14). The mystery of the mustard seed rules here. What Tertullian said always holds true: the blood of the martyrs is the seed of the Church. We cannot give life to others without giving up our own lives.[38]

There is a saying in Latin which goes like this: *verba movent, exempla trahunt* (words move, but it is action that attracts). Evangelisation can never be just a way of speaking. It must become a form of living. It must embody a lifestyle. It must become a testimony. Just as it did in the early Church, even today it is the power of example that is the most powerful proclamation. And, ultimately, both word and action will be empty without the foundation of prayer. Jesus preached by day; by night he prayed. Evangelisers must become disciples first. Christian communities must become genuine 'schools of prayer' where the meeting with Christ is expressed, not just in imploring help, but also in thanksgiving, praise, adoration, contemplation, listening and ardent devotion, until the heart truly falls in love.[39]

Conclusion

John Paul II remains the greatest evangeliser of our times. The courage with which he was able to take the message to kings and queens, politicians and power brokers, as well as to the poor, the sick and the downtrodden remains a source of inspiration for all. With the force of his convictions and a great sense of freedom, he succeeded in crossing most boundaries. And he remains the greatest source of inspiration for all those who want to take the call of Christ to proclaim the Good News to the world seriously.

Notes

1 *Evangelii Nuntiandi* is Paul VI's well known Apostolic Exhortation, *Populorum Progressio* is one of his prominent social encyclicals; John Paul II has written extensively on New Evangelisation; *Redemptoris Missio, Christifideles Laici, Tertio Millennio Adveniente, Novo Millennio Inuente* are some prominent ones. While Benedict XVI does not have a formal encyclical on the subject, he has certainly spoken frequently about it.

2 Thompson, 1976, p. 81.

3 Thompson, 1976, p. 84.

4 *Lumen Gentium*, 39. All documents of Vatican Council II are taken from the volume edited by Austin Flannery.

5 The 1971 Synod of Bishops document *Justice in the World* by saying so moved papal social teaching to an entirely new level. This document is cited from the Gremillion collection.

6 The best known encyclical devoted to evangelisation in the modern world.

7 *Redemptoris Missio*, 34. Buhlman's book is very helpful in assessing the changing priorities with regard to mission in the developing world.

8 John Paul II, Crossing the Threshold of Hope, p. 114.

9 *Redemptoris Missio*, 3; *Novo Millennio Inuente*, 40; Nodar, p. 1.

10 *Redemptoris Missio*, 21.

11 Ratzinger, 2000.

12 Pierre Cardinal Eyt, 'The European Synod', *The Wanderer*, 14 October 1999, p. 9, cit. in Martin, Ralph, *Give to God What Belongs to God*, www.christlife.org/jubilee/essays/C -givetogod.html, p. 6.

13 Ratzinger, 2000.

14 *Evangelii Nuntiandi*, 52, 54, 56; *Redemptoris Missio*, 36.

15 *Novo Millennio Adveniente*, 29.

16 *Redemptoris Missio*, 33, 37.

17 Ratzinger, 2000.

18 cit. in Ratzinger, 2000.

19 Ratzinger, 2000.

20 cit. in Richard Carlson, *You Can Be Happy No Matter What: Five Principles for Keeping Life in Perspective* (London: Hodder & Stoughton, 1997), p. 167.

21 This is the central theme of the first encyclical of John Paul II, namely, *Redemptor Hominis*.

22 *Evangelii Nuntiandi*, 27; *Redemptoris Missio*, 44.

23 For an expansion of this theme, see Schillebeeckx, Edward, *Jesus: An Experiment in Christology* (New York: Seabury, 1979).

24 Ratzinger, 2000.

25 *Redemptoris Missio*, 44; *Evangelii Nuntiandi*, 27.

26 *Novo Millennio Inuente*, 29; *Christifideles Laici*, 34; *Redemptoris Missio*, 3, 36, 51; *Evangelii Nuntiandi*, 52, 54, 56.

27 *Novo Millennio Inuente*, 43, 45, 50.

28 cit. in Colm Kilcoyne, 'The Present Crisis: A Way Forward', p. 155 in Denis Carroll, *Religion in Ireland: Past, Present and Future* (Dublin: Columba, 1999).

29 Ratzinger, 2000.

30 *Evangelii Nuntiandi*, 20.

31 *Redemptoris Missio*, 31, 37, 51, 52; *Novo Millennio Inuente*, 40.

32 'Ecclesia in America', Address of John Paul II to the Church in America, 22 January, 1999: *Redemptoris Missio*, 51, 52.

33 *Lumen Gentium*, 16-17; *Christifideles Laici*, 34; *Redemptoris Missio*, 63-76; *Evangelii Nuntiandi*, 14; *Ad Gentes Divinitus*, Vatican II's *Decree on Church's Missionary Activity*, 2, 23, 35.

34 *Redemptoris Missio*, 63-76.

36 *Christifideles Laici*, 15, 34; *Lumen Gentium*, 31.

37 *Redemptoris Missio*, 3.

38 Ratzinger, 2000.

39 Ibid.

Bibliography

Buhlmann, Walter, *The Coming of the Third Church*, Slough (England: St. Paul Publications, 1976).

Dorr, Donal, *Option for the Poor: A Hundred Years of Catholic Social Teaching* (Maryknoll, New York: Orbis Books, 1992).

Gremillion, Joseph, *The Gospel of Peace and Justice: Catholic Social Teaching since John XXIII* (London: Orbis, 1979).

John Paul II, *Novo Millennio Ineunte* (London: CTS, 2001).

John Paul II, *Tertio Millennio Adveniente* (London: CTS, 1994).

John Paul II, *Christifideles Laici* (London: CTS, 1988).

John Paul II, *Redemptoris Missio, Encyclical Letter on the Church's Missionary Mandate* (London: CTS, 2003).

John Paul II, *Crossing the Threshold of Hope* (New York: Knopf, 1994).

John Paul II, 'Internet: A New Forum for Proclaiming the Gospel', 36th World Communications Day, 12 May 2002.

MacLaren, Duncan, *Mission Impossible: Restoring Credibility to the Church* (Milton Keynes, UK: Paternoster, 2004).

Murray, Donal, *The Soul of Europe and Other Selected Writings* (Dublin: Veritas, 2002).

Nodar, Dave, 'What are Characteristics of the New Evangelization?', 2000, http://www.christlife.org/evangelization/articles/C_nreevan.html.

Paul VI, *Evangelii Nuntiandi, On Evangelisation in the Modern World* (London: CTS, 1975).

Ratzinger, Cardinal Joseph, *Address to Catechists and Religion Teachers*, Jubilee of Catechists (Rome, December 2000).

Thompson, Alan, *Church History 3 AD 1500–1800 New Movements Reformation-Rationalism-Revolution* (London: SPCK, 1976).

Vatican Council II The Conciliar and Post-Conciliar Documents (Bombay: St Paul Publications, 1987).

Connecting the Good News with Contemporary Living:
Irish Perspectives

Donal Dorr

Introduction

The following chapter is divided into four sections. In the first section I will look at how we in Ireland came to be where we are at in relation to spirituality. In the second I shall speak about the rich spiritual vision which was made available to us by the Second Vatican Council forty years ago. In the third section I shall try to indicate why this rich vision has not really caught on here in Ireland. In the final section I shall suggest ways in which we can connect with the Good News in our daily lives.

How Did We Get Here?

The crisis in the credibility of the Church as the main carrier of spirituality is one of the most significant developments in the religious ethos of Irish society.

'I don't know who is right or who is wrong, but they'll have neither luck nor grace if they go agin the bishop.' That was a remark I heard a Mayo woman making in the 1940s regarding a dispute about an appointment of a school principal in Ballina. It gives an insight into the authority and respect in which church leaders were held in Ireland at that time.

CONNECTING THE GOOD NEWS WITH
CONTEMPORARY LIVING

Over the past fifty years there has been an erosion of this authority and respect. The controversy in 1950/51 about Noel Browne's 'Mother and Child Scheme' might be seen as the start of this process. A second key moment was the famous 'bishop and the nightie' affair in 1966 when Bishop Tom Ryan rang up the *Late Late Show* to complain. In the late 1960s the intransigence of the Pope on the issue of contraception led many people in Ireland to make up their own minds on the issue. Then came the Bishop Casey affair, followed by the Brendan Smyth scandal and many other cases of clerical abuse, then Goldenbridge, the Magdalene laundries and 'Cardinal Sins'.

Meanwhile the popular *Father Ted* TV show reduced the clergy to figures of derision, which is a most effective way to undermine their credibility and authority. The most widely read newspapers in Ireland – the *Sunday Independent* and the *Irish Independent* – moved from being very clericalist to being indifferent and at times quite anticlerical in tone. The bishops contributed to the undermining of their authority by their hard-line stance in relation to the first abortion referendum, their mixed messages at the time of the second abortion referendum and their unclear message at the time of the 2004 referendum about changing our Irish constitution in relation to citizenship. While all this was going on, the Irish 'Celtic Tiger' encouraged people to devote their time and energy to earning and spending money rather than engaging in a search for a deeper meaning in life or for any kind of spirituality.

The result of this development is that the credibility of the Church as the main carrier of spirituality in Irish society has been very seriously dented. Very many people no longer look to the Church to provide meaning and guidance in their lives. Many people now make a sharp distinction between religion and spirituality; they reject religion but still see spirituality as a good thing. In fact, there is nowadays in Ireland a real hunger for a rich and meaningful spirituality.

The Rich Spiritual Vision of Vatican II

Just at the time when the Church in Ireland was beginning to lose its authority and credibility, the Vatican Council in Rome was forging a radically new spiritual vision, which should have been very attractive to the kind of modern people we were becoming. The key documents that emerged from the Council between 1963 and 1965 represent a huge shift in the self-understanding of the Church. At present I see seven major aspects of this shift:

1   The realisation that the church is above all the People of God rather than an institution where the focus is on the hierarchy and clergy who staff the institution.

2   There is a clear break from the dualism that had characterised Catholic spirituality in the past. In referring to dualism I have in mind the fact that prior to the Council our spirituality distinguished sharply between the body and the soul, and put all the emphasis on the soul. I also have in mind the sharp contrast we made between this world and the next world. Before the Council we saw ourselves as 'poor banished children of Eve ... mourning and weeping in this valley of tears'. The council encouraged us to adopt a rich humanistic agenda, in which the 'vertical' and other-worldly religious dimension of the Christian faith is fully integrated with the 'horizontal' and this-worldly moral–political dimension.

3   The realisation that the church does not just *have* missions but that the church *is* mission. This involves a move from a fortress or even a ghetto outlook to a cosmic vision in which the Church is a community which sits at the heart of the world, a willing agent of God working to transform the world from within.

4   The Council paved the way for the recognition by the Church of the reality of multi-culturality. Ever since then we are invited to abandon the assumption that the Western culture and Western version of Christianity are superior and normative and that civilisation, human development

and our Christian faith are to be understood in Western terms.

5 The Council became an invitation to Christians to recognise that central truths about the human social situation can be found not merely in the Christian tradition but also in non-Christian religious traditions. The consequence of this recognition is that the Christian mission can no longer be seen solely in terms of 'bringing Good News' to others and teaching others 'our' truth; the mission of the Church must also include learning from other traditions and working with people of other religions and philosophies to understand and transform the world.

6 The Council opened the door for the emergence within three or four years of liberation theology and the concepts of basic Christian communities and of an option for the poor.

7 The Council documents provided a context in which Catholic thinkers began to take serious account of developments in humanistic psychology. The new approach is already indicated in the first four words of *Gaudium et Spes* (GS), focusing as they do on human feelings. What emerged in the 1970s and 1980s was an integration of spirituality and humanistic psychology. This has transformed our Christian spirituality in a very radical way – to such an extent that the spirituality with which Catholics of the pre-Vatican II vintage were brought up is now seen to be hopelessly out-dated.

People Are Not Buying Into the New Vision

The radically new spiritual vision that emerged from the Second Vatican Council has not really taken root in the Church in Ireland.

I hope what I have sketched out so briefly about the Council has indicated that there is now available to the Christians of Ireland a very rich spiritual vision. But the sad reality is that most people in Ireland are not aware of it. It would, I think, be more accurate to say that they do actually accept and respond to quite significant parts of this overall vision, but they are not aware that this has anything to do with the Church. Indeed for many of them the parts of that vision which enliven and inspire them often seem to them to be quite the contrary to what they imagine the Irish Catholic Church stands for.

This raises an interesting question. Is this primarily a failure of communication on the part of us committed Church people to witness to and speak of what we really stand for? Or could it be that much of the official Irish church, especially the bishops and priests, have not really taken on this post-Vatican II vision, haven't really internalised it or given it a central place in our lives? My own view is that this second explanation is pretty close to the mark. Many of us committed church people have not made the radical break with the past which is called for by Vatican II.

By way of example, I recall a time when I preached on Pentecost Sunday in my home village in Co. Mayo. I spoke about the gifts and fruits of the Spirit. In passing I said, 'If we do not experience joy in this life it is hard to see how we can expect to be joyful for ever in Heaven'. A few days later the local curate said to me: 'The congregation misunderstood you last Sunday; they thought you were telling them that if they are not joyful in this life they won't be joyful in the next life.' It never even occurred to him that that was more or less what I had said – because he took it for granted that this life is a valley of tears where our suffering earns us the joys of Heaven. We were two priests from the same background with only about twenty-five years of an age-gap between us, but we were living out of two very different Christian spiritualities.

I think we need to probe further to find why relatively few Irish people have bought into the new vision. I think it is because the new vision, despite its importance, is only one part of what Christian faith is about. Vision without energy goes nowhere. The vision as I have expressed it here and even as it is expressed in most of the Council documents and in the huge *Catechism of the Catholic Church* is too rational, too cerebral, too much in the head. Quite frequently it does not come alive, it lacks an experiential quality.

I think this helps to explain why so few people are finding in the mainstream church the spiritual nourishment they are looking for. The result is that a certain proportion of people are looking for their spirituality to Asian religions or New Age practices. Some of those who have remained with the Church have taken up devotional practices which I would see as quite marginal in relation to the central truths of our faith; they are devotions which give a major place to dire warnings about hell or which focus on visions, signs and wonders.

I want to suggest a fundamental reason for the lack of life energy which would make our new vision life-giving and inspiring. It is that the vision has not been linked to an experience of relationship with the living God. And this brings me on to the fourth and final part of my talk.

A Spirituality That Is Experiential and Alive

Over the past three years I have facilitated up to fifteen spirituality workshops with groups. The participants were drawn from a wide cross-section of Irish society. I could not claim that they were a random sample of Irish people but I believe they were quite representative of those who have a keen interest in spirituality. I invited them to indicate which of the various aspects and dimensions of spirituality were the most significant for them. What emerged was that the relationship with *nature* was very important for a large number of these spiritual searchers. Another key aspect for many of them was *guidance* – the sense of being somehow led or directed in their actions and decisions. Two other key notions for many of the participants were *personal integrity* and concern for *justice in society*.

It was quite striking how few of these searchers linked any of these central features of their spirituality with the Christian faith. That seems to me a great pity. It represents a great loss for these people, almost all of whom came from a Christian background and many of whom were practising Christians. I think it indicates a failure on our part to show the rich potential of the Gospel to throw light on all four of these aspects of spirituality – and not just to bring light but also to be a source of life-energy and inspiration.

For this reason I want to devote the remainder of this chapter to a brief presentation of what I see as the three fundamental and life-giving aspects of our Christian faith. These are our relationship with the three persons of the Trinity. In fact these are the very heart of our faith – the three features that distinguish our faith as Christians from the faith of Muslims, Jews and people of other religions. But they have been neglected in the way most of us picked up our Christian faith – either that or they have been presented in such a dried-out form that they lost much of their life-giving and inspiring quality.

The Life-Giving Spirit

I begin with the Holy Spirit. It would seem that many Christians, including many preachers and teachers, assume that because we have Jesus we don't really need the Spirit. But the Spirit is God's primary way of being in active dialogue with us today.

Jesus lived 2,000 years ago in a culture that is very different to ours. The Spirit never took flesh in any particular place or time. This means that the Spirit is equally available to people of every age and every place: 'The Spirit blows where it chooses ...' (Jn 3:8). The only snag is that the action of the Spirit remains elusive and mysterious: '... you do not know where it comes from or where it goes' (Jn 3:8). We need to invite the Spirit to speak and move in our hearts, sometimes 'with sighs too deep for words' (Rom 8:26). The Spirit is the one who enables us to 'read the signs of the times' in the world around us.

If we wish to be in touch with the Spirit we have to be in touch with the true depths of our hearts. We can never be quite sure that what we are hearing or sensing is an undiluted communication from the Spirit. The message may have become distorted or even corrupted by our lack of sensitivity or our self-centred preoccupations.

Our faith tells us that the Spirit is the love of God poured out into our hearts. This is a love that we can at times *experience* – it warms our hearts. In fact we pray that the Spirit will 'enkindle a fire' in us. We should normally expect to have some awareness of the Spirit's presence and work in us. In recent centuries most of the Christian Churches played down this 'felt' aspect of God's love, mainly because they were suspicious of religious feelings. We should normally be able to experience the 'fruits of the Spirit', i.e. spiritual feelings of joy, inner peace, gentleness, patience and generosity.

The Spirit usually works in and through our human attractions. So when a person feels a strong attraction for some particular vocation in life, we may assume that this is an inspiration of the Spirit – unless there is some clear indication that it is not from the Spirit.

St Paul assures us that the Holy Spirit lives in us and gives us many gifts, including the gifts of guidance and discernment. The normal way this guidance comes is in the form of movements of inspiration, of consolation or of challenge. If we are following Jesus and are in touch with his Spirit then we can trust that the movements that well up from the unconscious into our conscious awareness are gifts from the Holy Spirit. For the New Testament assures us that the Spirit prays in us, helps us in our weakness, pleads with God on our behalf in sighs deeper than words, joins with our own spirit in declaring that we are God's children and enables us to grow in expectation of a new creation (Rom 8:9-27; I Cor 12:3-11). We need to dispose ourselves for all this, by taking quiet time for reflection and prayer and by developing the more intuitive non-rational aspects of our mind and heart, where there may be more room for the Spirit to do its work.

Of course the Spirit works also through the guidance of wise authorities, through the advice of others and through our rational faculties. But there is perhaps more room for the Spirit to work in the deep 'unconscious room of our hearts' of which the poet Kavanagh often speaks in his poetry. When we reflect on issues in a very rational mode we may have already decided that we know what is right for us; and so we may not be very open to hearing new and unexpected ideas or suggestions.

The Creator

I want now to speak briefly about our relationship with God as the Creator. I'm sure that occasionally, when you have stood by the sea, walked in the hills or looked up at the stars on a frosty night, you have had the experience of being transported beyond your everyday concerns and suffused with a sense of gratitude and freedom – an admiration for the wonder of creation and the power and generosity of the Creator. This applies especially to those of you who are of a more contemplative nature. You can spend timeless moments lost in the wonder of creation and communing with the Creator in and through the creation.

As Christians we believe that God is transcendent, i.e. beyond the world. But we also are asked to believe that God is immanent, i.e. present in the world. This sense of God in the world was a major feature of celtic spirituality, as we see in the ancient prayers, 'The Deer's Cry' or 'The Breastplate of St Patrick'. We can experience God in the 'light of sun, radiance of moon, splendour of fire, speed of lightning, swiftness of wind, depth of the sea, stability of earth, firmness of rock'.

Unfortunately, Christianity in more recent times has become rather one-sided, stressing the transcendence of God and playing down the immanent aspect of God's presence. It is not surprising, therefore, that many people who are looking beyond Christianity for spiritual nourishment have turned to nature. We

have some who see the Earth as a goddess and try to get back
to the ancient rituals of nature-worship. But as Christians we
can rediscover the presence of God in nature and nourish our
spirits in nature, while still holding on to the other crucial
aspect, namely, a warm personal relationship with God and a
sense of being cared for by God. We need to rediscover the
traditional Irish sense of God's providence: 'Is giorra cabhar Dé
ná an doras' – God's help is nearer than the door.

I experience God's Providence in my life almost all the time.
I have what I call a 'strong' faith in Providence, by which I mean
that it feels right to me to ask God to do me little favours. There
is a thrill of gratitude when my prayers are answered. These are
reminders of God's care for me. They bring home to me that
God wants to be intimately involved in the everyday details of
my life.

I believe that my prayer often plays a part in bringing the
answer. My prayer and God's answer together form an act of co-
creation. God allows me to play an active part in shaping the
world. Sometimes this requires some action from me; other
times my part is simply to set my intention clearly and firmly on
what I am asking for.

Jesus

---

*Among the three fundamental aspects of our
Christian faith are belief in the presence and action
of the life-giving Spirit, belief in God who is
immanent and belief in Jesus as the human face of
God.*

I turn now to our relationship with Jesus, the word of God who
came to share our human life and lead us to the one whom he
called 'Abba', 'Daddy'. Jesus is the origin and centre of our faith.
The most important thing about Jesus is that in him there is a

link between spirituality as a personal relationship with God and spirituality as our relationships in the world – how just we are, how loving we are, how we respect the environment and how we maintain our personal integrity. The heart of this link is the title Jesus gave himself. The usual translation is 'the Son of Man', but this is a misleading and sexist translation. A more accurate translation is 'the Human One'.

What is meant by this title 'the Human One' which Jesus used of himself? It means that he is saying that he is one of us, in solidarity with all other humans in the world. It also suggests that Jesus is a model for what it means to be human. Furthermore, it indicates that the way he is showing us to come to God is though living human life to the full.

By using this title Jesus is telling us that the way to come close to God is to live authentic human lives rather than escaping from this world or running away from everyday human issues. This means that to be his followers we must commit ourselves to the values of justice, respect, personal integrity, ecology, and so on, since these are key ways of living an authentically human life. In doing so we can live in conscious imitation of Jesus and in an ongoing dialogue with him. So our living out of ethical and political values is fully integrated into our personal relationship with Jesus.

In his way of living Jesus challenged patriarchy, legalism and religious authoritarianism. I do not have time here to spell out the detail of all this, but he took the side of the poor and the marginalised, for example those afflicted with leprosy, which at that time was the equivalent of AIDS in our world. He didn't just heal them; he made friends with them. His 'option of the poor' involved standing up for them against those who were pushing them to the margins of society.

There is so much more to say about the way Jesus showed us how to live human life to the full, but I will focus on just three further points. The first is his use of power. He stepped fully into his own power, but at the same time he absolutely refused to use that power to dominate or captivate others; that is the heart of the account of his temptations.

The second point I want to mention is the ability of Jesus to discern when it is right to hold on and when to let go. For three years he found ways to continue his ministry, despite all the opposition he aroused. Sometimes he went to Jerusalem to challenge the oppressive authorities in the seat of their power. At other times he withdrew to Galilee or across the Jordan. But then, while he was still in the prime of his life, he knew that 'his hour' had come. He realised that the only authentic human response to his situation was to accept that, from a purely human point of view, his mission had failed. His struggle in the garden of Gethsemane was about letting his human powers go and accepting death, as he entrusted himself utterly into the hands of God (Mk 14:36 '... not my will but yours be done').

This shows us an important aspect of our spirituality. When we find ourselves up against intractable difficulties we need, like Jesus, to discern when to continue the struggle and when it is better to give up and let go. 'Letting go' can mean different things. It could mean giving up a job which has become too stressful, walking away from an abusive relationship or no longer trying to control the lives of our partners or our grown-up children. Eventually it involves facing death. At that point, 'letting go' means trusting that the darkness of death does not empty our lives of all meaning. It means rather following Jesus by entrusting ourselves to God, trusting that God's love will prevail in ways which we cannot predict, or even imagine.

There is one final point I want to note about the spirituality of Jesus. He was willing to call on his friends for support when he faced up to his death in the agony in the garden. He asked Peter, James and John to 'watch with' him during those hours of struggle (Mt 26:38). He was willing to let them see his human vulnerability. This suggests that we, the followers of Jesus, should not think in terms of mastery, independence or rigid self-control. We should rather be in touch with our own vulnerability and allow others to see us in our weakness. Vulnerability lies at the heart of an authentic Christian spirituality.

The Changing Shape of the Family in Contemporary Ireland
Challenges to Faith

Cathy Molloy

Introduction

The aim of this chapter is to present briefly some aspects of the changing shape of the family in contemporary Ireland, consider some of the challenges posed by this change and outline some suggestions for meeting these challenges.

On July 11 the United Nations commemorated the 18th annual World Population Day, celebrated under the theme 'Equality'. The family of the world contains nearly 6.5 billion people. (French Institute for Demographic Studies.) Of every hundred people, 61 live in Asia, 14 in Africa, 11 in Europe, 9 in Latin America, 5 in North America and less than one in Oceania. At its longest, life expectancy is 82 years in Japan and 80 in Switzerland and Iceland. The lowest, between 30 and 40 years, is found in the African states of Zimbabwe, Zambia and Malawi, mainly as a result of the AIDS epidemic. So as we contemplate the changing shape of Irish families and the ageing population of Europe, we need to remember that this is not the case in Malawi, for example. As we consider the situation of fewer children per family in Ireland and elsewhere, we need to remember that it is not simply a matter of family planning by whatever method that makes for fewer children in families in some other parts of the world, but rather such issues as the lack of clean water and basic medicines. As we contemplate the increase in single parent families, whatever the reasons may be, we might remember that the AIDS epidemic and resultant deaths are the biggest cause in some other countries. As we rightly and necessarily concern ourselves with the welfare of the many children who suffer the effects of their parents' separation or divorce, we might do well to remind ourselves that not having a living parent is the lot of so many children in many parts of the world.

> It is crucial that the Church understands and appreciates the many shapes and forms in which family exists in our contemporary society.

The Changing Shape of the Family: Challenges to Faith?

Ann Francis and Michael Ryan in *Spirituality for our Times*,[1] the collection of papers from the 2004 summer school at St Patrick's College, Thurles, treated the issues of the family as a school of spirituality and the impact of changing family structures, especially on the young, respectively. Ryan's excellent analysis of cultural change in Ireland and its impact on young people, for example, in the area of marriage or partnership breakdown, and the current research into its effects on children and young people, indicate that this is an area where massive support is needed and will continue to be needed. The recent Government announcement of an increase of €8.3 million in allocation for family support work is a welcome move in this direction. What the role of the Church might be in this area is one of the issues this chapter will try to raise.

The notion that family relationships, whether traditional or changing, mirror the Christian experience of God as community of persons, interdependent, deeply connected and yet uniquely other, raises questions for the followers of Jesus regarding how they understand themselves as a group. This chapter will not address the changing family as a challenge to faith in the broad sense, namely, faith in God as the source of life, or faith in the Spirit that, for Christians, is so evidently active in our lives, or faith in the person of Jesus the Christ, whose life and death and resurrection have shown who God is for us. Rather, it will explore it from the point of view of how the changing shape of family brings new opportunities, new ways to understand the perennial challenge to faith, which is the challenge to love as Jesus commanded his followers to love. 'Love one another as I have loved you' (Jn 13:34). This is the challenge the changing shape of family brings to each and every member of the Church, and also to the Church as institution, the body of Christ, in the world and for the world. And so there is need for each generation to play its part in making the right connections between faith and life. This challenge involves openness to what love might mean in any and all of our relationships today, and, especially, renewed efforts towards an understanding of the meaning of human sexuality, the gift at the very core of our being, which is a means of expression of love and a way to understand something of God, while also having the potential to destroy both.

Some Research Findings

Several recent publications present the facts concerning the effects of change on the family in contemporary Ireland from different perspectives. Finola Kennedy, in *Cottage to Creche: Family Change in Ireland* (2001), considers the links between family change and economic change. The Department of Social and Family Affairs' report by Mary Daly of Queen's University, Belfast, which coincided with the 10th anniversary of the International Year of the Family, was published as *Families and Family Life in Ireland* (2004). It was the result of a wide consultation and was intended to stimulate a nationwide debate on families and family life and contribute to an integrated strategy for strengthening families. The Céifin Centre and its director, Fr Harry Bohan, also commissioned research into family relationships. The subsequent 2003 report, *Family Well-Being: What Makes a Difference?*, authored by Kieran Mc Keown and others, was based on a representative sample of parents and children in Ireland. The Combat Poverty Agency report, *Lone Parent Families and Poverty* (2004), dealt with family change in Ireland and focused on the needs of children and parents in one-parent families, whose number, as is known, has increased by 20 per cent in the last ten years. Last week's figures from the Central Statistics Office (*Irish Times*, 14/8/05) give further indication of the changing shape of the family, showing that one-third of all births are now outside marriage.

> *The challenges that the institution of the family poses are manifold. Therefore, the solutions proposed cannot be simplistic.*

Each of these, in its own way, points out the wide variety of perspectives that exist in understanding what or, more correctly, who constitutes a family. According to Finola Kennedy, 'there is no single common understanding of the term. The concept has evolved from a broad notion of a household under a common head, to that of a nuclear family based on life-long marriage, to a wide diversity of family forms, including solo parent families, and families that have been reconstituted following the breakdown of an earlier family' (Kennedy, 2001, 7). She points out that family change in Ireland has followed a path similar to other European countries.[2] The survey already referred to, of families with children under 18, shows that two-thirds of families are comprised of two-parent married families. 8 per cent involve two-parent cohabiting families. A further 5 per cent include remarried as well as cohabiting parents following separation. Of all families with children, 21 per cent contain only one parent.

Whatever the causes of the change may be – the rise in individualism, better education, greater interaction with the wider world, changing roles of women and men, economic and social policy, waning influence of the Church as source of moral teaching – there is agreement about the fact that the shape of the family itself has changed radically in a relatively short period of time.

Among the most significant changes are the decline in the number of marriages and the marked rise in births outside marriage. These are accompanied by a sharp increase in marital breakdown. Young people are postponing marriage and parenthood, and many parents have adult children living at home well beyond what would have been usual in the relatively recent past. The birth rate has halved since the early seventies. It is projected that the biggest change to come will be in the numbers living alone. The ageing population is increasing and couples may have many years together after their children have left home. With fewer children per family and the huge increase in women working outside the home, the burden on individuals of caring for dependent family members will be considerably greater.

The fact that materially improved standards of living are accompanied by previously unexperienced levels of stress involved in commuting to work for so many, with babies and young children having to be left in crèches for long hours, is an increasing cause for concern. The current debate about child-care and what is in the best interests of infants and children is inevitably fraught with emotion, but this is not a reason for failing to pursue it rigorously. The effects of stress on marriage and partner relationships are all too obvious in the breakdown statistics. There is much evidence to suggest that the mechanics of material survival, albeit of a higher material standard, leaves parents with less energy for dealing with the everyday problems of couple relationships and child rearing. Many parents are unhappy about leaving children with carers for long periods. The tendency to try to compensate for this in other ways is natural, and no one would want to return to some of the old ways of child rearing. However, the skills needed to deal with parent-child relationships at their various stages and in new situations are often not in evidence or are in short supply. The needs of all concerned in these new situations seem to be more complicated than in more traditional environments.

The situation of lone parents (21 per cent of the total in McKeown's survey) is cause for particular concern. It is not just that many children are growing up without the presence of their fathers or, less often, their mothers, or that the lone parent has all the difficulties of managing alone. Research also shows that where these families are headed by women they face a particularly high risk of poverty.[3] Like England and the US, one-parent families, single and separated, are heavily concentrated in lower socio-economic groups. Here in Ireland, in the five years up to 2000, the top 10 per cent of households in income terms spent on average over twice the national average expenditure for all households and for the lowest 10 per cent of households the expenditure was less than a quarter of the average for all households (*After the Celtic Tiger*, Clinch, Convery and Walsh, 2002).

A small minority of families comprise gay or lesbian couples, with or without children, who are seeking recognition of their commitment to one another by Church and state. And, in recent years, many families of different faiths and cultures, newly arrived in Ireland, also pose challenges to the churches in terms of inclusion and integration into Irish society.

Challenges to Faith

The challenges to a faith and practice that upholds marriage as an indissoluble sacrament and the only basis for founding a family, indeed, the only right context for sexual relationship, forbids divorce, continues officially to oppose contraception, considers homosexual relationships to be fundamentally disordered, are a legion in the light of the above account. However, I believe that in the teaching and tradition of the Church, and in theological reflection, we have the resources to meet the challenges, bearing in mind that the Church, like the men and women who comprise it, the people of God, the body of Christ, is not static but dynamic, constantly changing and developing.

> *Respect for the dignity of the individual and the right of all to a fair share of the resources of the universe are two fundamental planks on which the social teaching of the Catholic Chruch rests.*

The two fundamental planks of the Catholic social teaching are, firstly, that all human persons are equal in dignity because each one is made in the image of God, and secondly, based on that inalienable dignity, that each and everyone has the right to share in the goods of the earth. Sometimes we can overlook the fact that this includes not only material goods, but also emotional, psychological and spiritual goods, which are so needed in order for each one to become the person he/she was created to be. All forms of Christian relationships are founded on this basic teaching.

Marriage

In a 1999 study, the Creighton University Center for Marriage and Family notes that changes in religious, marital and familial structures in the United States are dramatic and are 'creating contexts and concerns and needs that earlier generations never encountered.'[4] This study shows that there is a relationship between religion and marriage, that religion can impact both marital stability and satisfaction, and that marriage can impact the choice, practice and experience of religion. There is no reason to suppose that things in this regard are different in Ireland or elsewhere, and so there are important implications, arising from the above study, that might need to be considered carefully.

Coming from an almost exclusive consideration of marriage as institution, described as a contract, the major shift in Roman Catholic theology at Vatican II was to describe it as a covenant – an intimate partnership between two persons. The post-Vatican II teaching's recognition of the centrality of love in marriage is reflected in its description of marriage as 'a community of love', as an 'intimate partnership of conjugal life and love' based in a 'conjugal covenant of irretrievable personal consent'. This new emphasis on the personal reality of marriage is based on the biblical notion of covenant. The retrieval of texts such as the *Song of Songs* has also contributed significantly to a change of direction in theological reflection on marriage. While being an allegory for the soul seeking union with God, it is more fundamentally a celebration of love between a man and a woman, including the sexual expression of that love.

God is Love. Where love is, there is God.

Karl Rahner was among the first Roman Catholic theologians to reflect on the meaning of love in post-Vatican II Roman Catholic teaching. He understands the love of husband and wife for one another as from, of, and oriented to God, as acquiring fresh roots through grace and uniting the whole of humanity.[5] Love of God and love of neighbour mutually condition one another. For Rahner, all of creation is God's self-communication, and God is primarily recognisable in personal interrelationships. Because it is God's love that sustains creation, gives humans life and love and draws all to God through it, the love between two people can lead them to reach one another at the deepest level of their being. The personal love, which manifests itself in marriage, is a saving love through its source in God and intends God, not only in transcendence, but also in the nearness in which God's self is revealed: the innermost life and mystery of the human person. In short, Rahner is saying what we hear so often – where love is, there is God.

The wide significance of Rahner's contribution, which has enormous implications for how we respond to the changing shape of the family in contemporary Ireland, is based on his belief that all of creation is 'graced', that is, animated by God's own self-communication. All human love, therefore, in so far as it is a going out of self and a reaching towards another, is a reaching for God, and even a making present of God's love in our world. A welcome aspect of this understanding of Rahner's is that love need not, indeed perhaps should not, be split immediately into categories. God is present in all love. Perhaps a challenge here to faith is to recognise that we humans do not have a patent on the understanding of love; that to be human is to get it wrong sometimes, and that we must hold back a bit from rushing to judgement on the truth of love in the many human relationships that are not marriage and are yet waiting to be included in the human view of God's saving love.

The new insights of Vatican Council II in relation to marriage, incorporating also developments in the human sciences and some reflection on the experience of married people, have led to new awareness of what marriage is, and what it could and should be. Consequently there is also new awareness of what marriage is not, of what it could not and should not be. Surely there is a role for the Church in confronting the behaviours that are a travesty of Christian relationship in any and all contexts, but especially in violent and abusive marital and couple relationships. There are small signs that this is happening already.

The Challenge Posed by Marriage Breakdown

With some notable exceptions, we as a Church, faced with the statistics on marriage breakdown, have failed to show even the minimum level of concern that might be expected of a Christian community towards those involved in marriage breakdown. In a Diocesan Women's Forum, participants felt that their difficulties are compounded rather than helped by the Church.[6] They felt angry and alienated and had no sense that the Church shared their pain. Reformulation of their lives often took place apart from the Church, which was experienced as unsympathetic: 'The church doesn't want to know us any more and we feel sad and lonely.' Because of exclusion from the sacraments, many saw themselves as being in limbo. In addition to having to bear the rejection of a failed marriage, they also had to experience rejection by the Church. Here it is good to remind ourselves that 'the biggest harm is to extinguish hope.'

There is a new emphasis on the personal reality of marriage in the Church's contmeporary teaching on the family.

The same experience of rejection, alienation and abandonment by the Church in which one believes and to which one wants and needs to belong, was recorded in the report of the Forum for Catholic Women in Belfast. Accounts of the experience of some women with the annulment tribunal make pathetic reading. Many of them spoke of long years of waiting for cases to be heard and of their very real sense of injustice at the hands of the Church which is otherwise so ready to preach to the world about justice. They felt that they were the forgotten ones, the marginalized. And let us remember that these are the voices of only those women who have just begun to speak. The injustice within the Church is compounded by the fact that too

many people have no voice. Many have neither the possibility
nor the capacity to become involved in lengthy, costly and
complex procedures due to lack of money, education, emotional
or psychological strength, stamina, or, most often, a
combination of all these factors.

Second Unions, Remarriage and the Call to Communion

In spite of the call of John Paul II in *Familiaris Consortio* for the
Church community to support and give much respect,
solidarity, understanding and practical help to people who have
suffered marriage breakdown, the sense of abandonment by the
Church is strong for many. It has been noted that '... priests, the
bishops and the Pope may well utilise a vocabulary of *service* at
the same time they continue to have behaviour patterns of
power'.[7] These experiences, alongside the genuine difficulty of
many people (within as well as outside the Church and as
explained in the papers of the International Theological
Commission), in 'accepting current church discipline that
tolerates the common life of a union after divorce but requires
that sexual intercourse be excluded', are another great
challenge both to faith in the Church and to the faith of the
Church.[8]

In his 1988 Apostolic Exhortation on the Vocation and the
Mission of the Lay Faithful, *Christifideles Laici,* Pope John Paul
II developed at length the concept of the Church as *communion.*
Baptism, he explains, is 'the door and foundation of *communion*
in the Church. The Eucharist is the source and summit of the
whole Christian life ... and is a sign and actually brings about the
intimate bonds of *communion* among all the faithful in the Body
of Christ which is the Church'.[9]

I believe that the understanding of the implications of the
Church as *communion* is only beginning. Can there really be
categories of *communion*? Can one be in *communion* and be
objectively excluded from communion at the same time? There

is a real challenge involved in exploring this concept in the context of those who are being excluded from full participation in the Eucharist because of the perceived status of their intimate relationships.

The reality of marital breakdown and the pain and conflict associated with it are at the very heart of the situation of the family today.

Where a new union or remarriage is concerned, people find it a heavy burden to be asked, or expected, to make a choice between two kinds of communion. There is the communion that is vital to Christian life: participation in the union of love between Christ and the Church, which is signified and effected by the Eucharist, and which their state and condition of life is said to objectively contradict.[10] And there is the communion that is participation in the union of love between the partners, which is signified and effected by sexual intercourse. Both kinds of communion can be occasions of graced experience. If God's love is present in all love, is it right that we seek to split that love, to divide and subdivide it? Could it be that in some instances, rather than contradicting the union of love between Christ and the Church, people who have divorced and remarried might rather be contributing to the sign of that love in the Church and in the world? The challenge is further exacerbated by the fact that many faithful people find it difficult, even impossible, to understand and accept what they see as excessively harsh treatment of people in second unions – whether after separation or divorce – alongside the acceptance and welcome sometimes afforded to people who have been, or may be, involved in serious exploitation of their fellow human beings.

The current absolute ban on remarriage in the Church would not have to be compromised by offering some welcome or asking for God's blessing on couples who sincerely want to belong fully and actively to their parish community. In many cases all the signs are that God's blessing is already present, and some formal recognition of this could be the basis for the strengthening of their family bonds. One can only imagine the new life it would bring to the Church as a whole. The fact that the exclusion of so many from full participation in the Eucharist is a *de facto* exclusion of their children is also another reason for seriously reconsidering the discipline. Assurances that they are part of the Church ring hollow when accompanied by the ongoing exclusion from the Eucharist, which many experience as rejection, however it is explained. In this context, some considerations from the theology of the Eucharist might bring further insights. Is participation in the Eucharist a reward for perceived good behaviour? Or is it precisely spiritual food for the journey of life towards God, intended by Christ especially for those who are struggling to love in the best way they can, according to their life circumstances and relationships, whether or not these are on the officially accepted categories of love list?

Cohabiting families

The increase in the number of young, and not so young, couples and parents in cohabiting relationships challenges the notion that true love and commitment only find expression in marriage. There are many reasons why this way of living is chosen by people today. Some are committed to marrying in the future, some see it as a trial marriage, some want to oppose the norm of society, and for some it may be a point of principle where the couple look on marriage as something banal.[11] Others may be unwilling or unable to obtain an annulment or a divorce, perhaps for reasons of non-cooperation of a former spouse. There are understandable problems with formalising commitment in a culture where so much is 'disposable', change happens so fast and uncertainty across a range of areas is the norm. It is understandable that couples who have experienced the pain of their own parents' separation or divorce would have serious reservations about marriage. There were other times, and there are other cultures, where marriage was and is a process involving several stages, and cohabitation may be part of this. It is important that distinctions are made between the various kinds of cohabiting relationships and that as Church we do not base our welcome or exclusion of people on the assumption that every incidence of cohabitation is to be dismissed as a casual, temporary and ill-considered 'living together'.

Cohabitating couples and couples in second unions often feel that they have been abandoned by the Church.

Liberation Theology as a Resource

Liberation Theology sets out to highlight, interpret and transform the situation of those suffering intolerable material conditions of poverty, injustice and oppression in Latin America. Without overlooking the specificity of its context, I would nevertheless like to suggest that some of its insights might be of help in addressing the situation of people in the many kinds of family in Ireland today, a situation that poses such a challenge to faith and to the Church. Among such people must be included those who feel discarded, rejected, marginalized or, even worse, just tolerated because of their marital situation. For many of these, not just their material poverty, but also the existential situation they find themselves in and the inherent conflict associated with it, lead to experiences of oppression and alienation both within and outside the Church. I refer to people whose relationship of love with their new partners, and perhaps also children, is precisely where they experience the love of God in their lives, and find that it is precisely this that precludes them from being full participants in the Church. What they experience as life-giving and would like to celebrate in their faith community is at best tolerated among the people of God, and sometimes not even that.

In *The Liberation of Theology*, Juan Luis Segundo notes that 'oppression usually does not reveal itself in barefaced fashion; it hides and hallows itself behind ideologies that obscure what is really happening in concrete human reality'.[12] But God's revelation shows up in a different light when God's people find themselves in different historical situations. For Segundo the Bible is not the discourse of a universal God to a universal human being. It must be seen as being addressed to specific contexts and such a line of thinking 'is justified because we must find, and designate as the word of God, that *part* of divine revelation which *today*, in the light of our concrete historical situation, is most useful for the liberation to which God summons us'. He speaks of those who 'tend to muzzle the word of God by trying to make one particular portion of Scripture the word of God, not only for certain particular moments and situations, but also for all situations and all moments'.

Liberation and Salvation

The relationship between liberation and salvation[13] (the Good News of the title of this summer school) is central to liberation theology. The Vatican II document *Gaudium et Spes* speaks about the relationship between temporal, earthly progress and the growth of the Kingdom.[13] The one is said to be of 'vital concern' to the other, in so far as it can contribute to the better ordering of human society. Gustavo Gutierrez affirms the 'global character of the gratuitous gift of God's love'.[14] This affects all areas of human life. We can and should distinguish between the natural and the supernatural, but must not lose sight of the fact that they are ultimately unified. There is only one real order of salvation; not one of the history of grace and a separate one of the history of nature. Christ brings us liberation from sin to a sharing in the life of God. Salvation is the completion of liberation, of communion with God and with one another. Gutierrez points out that the Kingdom of God is not reducible to human history or human progress, but without historical liberative events there would be no growth in the Kingdom. God's saving power is revealed through human events. Liberation includes every dimension of humanity, and salvation embraces all human reality, transforming and leading it to its fullness in Christ. *(Surely this is the 'Good News' that this Summer School is seeking to connect with contemporary living?)* The focus is on the presence of grace (accepted or rejected) in everyone.

Even though the context does not totally determine morality, yet it is crucial in evaluating morality.

Where is grace in this perspective? Simple questions direct the answer. Where is God to be encountered by human beings today, especially by those in the changing families in contemporary Ireland? Where is God to be encountered among the groups who are marginalized by their Churches? Does salvation begin now in our liberating, graced experiences? For some, perhaps many, their salvation begins through their re-finding of their self-esteem, of their capacity to go beyond self in loving a new partner, in loving and caring for the children of that union. This is not to imply that salvation can ever be complete in this life, but a question remains: do we cooperate with grace or do we block it? Of course we block grace by our personal sin, but it may also be true that as Church, we block grace by some of our structures and laws for dealing with internal problems, or by particular applications of those laws or structures. It may be that in some instances it is dis-grace rather than grace that is pushing people to the margins and leading to the kinds of experiences reported by some people in families whose shape has changed.

Suggestions for a Way Forward

Family poses a challenge to laity, clergy and religious alike. It is necessary to respond to this challenge creatively. I would like to suggest some creative ways:

• *Education*
Make a commitment to ongoing education. Explaining the teaching of the Church in whatever way needed/appropriate is important. The Church's teaching on *conscience* is often poorly understood, as is that on marriage and separation/divorce. Many wrongly believe themselves to be marginalized or excluded.

Remind people frequently that the right to judge is reserved to God and we cannot claim to fully know the mind of God.

Highlight the fundamental Christian call to love and the ongoing search that is necessary to discover what love really involves in any given context.

Seek a new language and new ways to make the Church's teaching on marriage meaningful for people today, whatever their context.

Challenge people to authentic faith; motivate them to strive for what is truly good; help them to comprehend one of the central messages of the Cross, namely, what looks like failure is not necessarily so.

Engage in action for justice in the area of social and economic policy as it impacts on families; for example, housing, supporting people with disabilities, mental illnesses, and addictions, employment policy, child-care, education, etc.

- *Pastoral*

Be inclusive. Do not just talk inclusive but be inclusive. Acknowledge the existence and presence of different kinds of families. Invite all families and make them welcome. *Acknowledge* the particular situation of lone parents and the courageous job they are often doing. Ask how the Church can help and respond to their real needs. For example, can the Church hall or parish centre provide an alternative place/space to separated fathers to be with their children at weekends?

Address the pressing needs of people in different situations. The rise in suicide, especially among young men, outlines the need to affirm all people and help them to be aware of the value and sacredness of each life.

Strive to help maintain faith in the 'sheer gratuity of God' – the image of the parent who waits, allows to develop; who waits, and welcomes, and lets go.[15]

Accept and articulate the fact that social sin is real, that it exists in the Church, that in being called to love we are being called to overcome this and to continually work for more just structures within and outside the Church.

Notes

1   See Francis, Ann, 'The Family as a School of Spirituality', and Ryan, Michael, 'Understanding and Relating to the Culture of the Young in Ireland Today', in Joseph Putti (ed.) *Spirituality for our Times* (St Patrick's College, Thurles, 2005), pp. 77-83 and 154-69.

2   Kennedy, Finola, *From Cottage to Creche*, (Dublin: Institute of Public Administration, 2001), p. 1.

3   See Combat Poverty Agency website: www.combatpoverty.ie. Lone Parent Families and Poverty.

4   Creighton University Center for Marriage and Family, *Ministry to Interchurch Marriages, A National Study* (Nebraska: Creighton University, 1999), p. 9.

5   Rahner, Karl, 'Marriage as Sacrament', *Theological Investigations, X* (New York: Herder & Herder and Darton, Longman & Todd, 1973), pp. 199-221.

6   Reports of the Dublin Diocesan Women's Forum and of the Forum for Catholic Women (Belfast) are unpublished to date.

7   Parent, Remy, *A Church of the Baptized* (New York: Paulist Press, 1987), p. 83.

8   Malone and Connery (eds) *Contemporary Perspectives on Christian Marriage*, (Chicago: Loyola Press, 1984). For fuller discussion see Cathy Molloy, *Marriage: Theology and Reality* (Dublin: Columba Press, 1996), Chapter 3.

9   John Paul 11, *Christifideles Laici*, 1988, n.19.

10 John Paul 11, *Familiaris Consortio*, 1981, n.84.

11 See Lawler, Michael, 'Becoming Married in the Catholic Church, A Traditional Post-Modern Proposal', in *Intams* Review 7 (2001), for an extended treatment of cohabitation in the contemporary West.

12 For what follows see Segundo, Juan Luis, *The Liberation of Theology* (Maryknoll, NY: Orbis Books, 1976), pp. 27-34.

13 *Gaudium et Spes*, 39, in Austin Flannery, OP (ed.) *Vatican Council 11: The Conciliar and Post Conciliar Documents*, p. 938.

14 Gustavo Gutierrez, *A Theology of Liberation* (London: SCM Press, 1974), p.177.

15 Robinson, Marilyn, *Gilead*, (London: Virago Press, 2005).

Nurturing the Faith through Religious Education

Joe Collins

Introduction

The topic for this chapter is so broad that, given the limitations of space, I can hardly do justice to it. Therefore, in this article I intend to outline some general ideas on religious education. Internationally, there has been a lot of debate in recent times regarding the precise relationship that exists or should exist between religious education and catechesis. However, this debate has not really touched the Irish shores because in Ireland, in the main, most schools have been managed by the Catholic Church.

> *The debate about the precise nature of the relationship between catechesis and religious education, popular abroad, has yet to reach the Irish shores.*

Religious Education and Catechesis

In discussions about the appropriate approach to faith education, some tend to stress the educational moment and others the catechetical one. Whether there is any direct relationship between the two and what precisely is the nature of this relationship remains a matter of some debate. Harris and Moran would see them as closely related: 'Religious Education has to include both academic instructions in religion and teaching people to practice a particular religious way of life.'[1] Others tend to make a more clear-cut distinction. Catechesis is seen as the maturing of faith and religious education as religious instruction in the faith. Whereas the former is often seen as an informal process, the latter is often referred to as the formal or the academic process.

> *Nurturing the faith must be seen as an integral dimension of religious education, however broadly it may be interpreted.*

For the purposes of this article, while recognising the validity of the debate, I nevertheless intend to intertwine the two terms because in the Irish context they remain very closely connected. Many would argue that Church and State in Ireland are like hand and glove, at least in the primary school sector.

A Brief Overview of History

Let me begin my comments with a broad historical sweep of the field. From a historical perspective, it is possible to talk about five key centuries in religious education, namely the first, fourth, sixteenth, twentieth and twenty-first centuries.

- The first century is central because it marks the beginning of the Church. In the early Church, conversion and the catechumenate were very much the order of religious education.
- The fourth century is significant because, during the reign of Emperor Constantine, Christianity became the official religion of the empire, marking in effect the end of adult

catechumenate. With Christianity becoming the religion of the empire, infant baptisms became the norm.

- The sixteenth century is important because it represents the post-Reformation era. It marks the beginning of the era of the Catechisms. Martin Luther published the first Catechism in 1529. As a response to Reformation, the Catholic Church convoked the Council of Trent (1545), out of which came the first Roman Catholic Catechism. The Heidelberg Catechism for the Reformed Churches was published in 1563. In 1598 Robert Bellarmine produced a Catechism that was approved by Pope Clement III. The English Parliament produced the Westminster Catechism in 1647. Closer to home, in 1795, James Butler, Archbishop of Cashel and Emly, produced the Butler Catechism. In 1885 the Maynooth Catechism was born. Subsequently this became the Penny Catechism and after that it became the Green Catechism.
- The twentieth century is important because of the Second Vatican Council.
- The twenty-first century is important because it is the century we live in today.

The brief look at the above five key centuries gives us a general picture of religious education in the history of the Church. From the sixteenth century onwards, with the birth of the Catechisms, religious education took a strict question-and-answer approach. Learning by rote was the order of the day. However, the question that needs to be asked today is: Is this what religious education is all about?

What Is Religious Education About?
Too often in the past, faith has been confused with belief and religion. Bishop Donal Murray describes the purpose of religious education thus: It '... is not to prepare unquestioning

and compliant cogs for the smooth running of society as it is. It is to prepare people to be constructively critical, to take responsibility, to recognise the need for change. It is to give people a vision of human dignity and human purpose against which the shortcomings of any society can be judged and in the light of which something more human can be pursued.'[2]

If religious education has to be meaningful, it must be approached holistically. It should connect the rational and the emotional creatively.

Oliver Brennan challenges us to see the *bigger picture*. He writes: 'The narrow understanding of the aim of religious education which confines it to that of nurturing the faith is no longer viable. This is but one, and only one, dimension of the important field of religious education.'[3] Donal Murray's definition is helpful as it is all encompassing and challenges us to engage seriously with all the aspects of religious education. Oliver Brennan, on the other hand, while making a valid point that religious education is more than catechesis, still seems to be caught up in the debate about the relationship between religious education and catechesis. However, both would agree that the catechetical moment is an integral part of religious education and that nurturing the faith is essential to religious education, even though it should be seen in the broader cultural context.

Why Nurture the Faith through Religious Education?

However one may interpret the relationship between religious education and catechesis, it is clear that in the Christian tradition, nurturing the faith has been at the heart of religious education, however broadly the latter may be understood. Let me point out a number of reasons why it has been so:

- The mission of the Church is to evangelise.[4] The Church has one mission, i.e. 'Go out and make disciples of all nations'.[5]
- Christian education is essentially, though not exclusively, the ongoing unfolding of Jesus' Gospel to believers 'teaching them to observe all that I have commanded you'.[6]
- Religious education is meant to contribute to the revelation and communication of God's love, 'an experience of the love of God flooding through our hearts'.[7]
- It should help us to respond to God with love and gratitude.
- It should lead us to respect the innate dignity of *every* human being by promoting respectful and inclusive attitudes.
- Religious education should inspire us to engage with our personal and social development by encouraging us to ask questions about humankind.
- It is meant to foster and deepen our faith.
- It must help in the understanding of the story of our faith community and in the connecting of this story with our own stories.
- It should assist in dealing creatively with the affective, active and cognitive dimensions of religious experience.
- It is meant to breathe new life and vitality into our lives.
- It should promote prayer and bring us into a deeper relationship with God.

Religion and Culture

While nurturing the faith is crucial, it is also important that faith is understood, not so much in an esoteric manner, but against the broader cultural perspective. From a brief look at the history of religious education, it becomes quite clear that from the fourth century on, virtually all writers agree that religious education must be in tune with culture and cultural changes. Culture is not something static, but changes perennially.

NURTURING THE FAITH THROUGH RELIGIOUS EDUCATION

A relevant and contemporary religious education must be in constant dialogue with culture.

We do not need to look any further than our own culture to realise this fact. The Irish culture has undergone a real transformation in the past few decades from a Church dominated culture to a radically secular one. So much so that many anthropologists today look upon Ireland as an excellent case study in the analysis of cultural change. Just think of the Church we were born into and the many changes that have occurred therein in our life span!

Let us think for a moment about Ireland during the 1950s and Ireland today. If you were to examine some examples from *The Irish Ecclesiastical Records* from the 1950s, you would get a clear idea of the transition I am talking about. Some examples from as recently as 1957 include:

- A priest from Achonry Diocese writes in asking about the kind of indulgences attached to kissing a prelate's ring.
- A Kilmore priest asks a question about the rightness or wrongness of attending dances during lent.
- A Cloyne priest asks a question about what type of priest should act as a confessor in charge of nuns.
- Another priest questions a husband's responsibility for a wife's pre-nuptials debts.

The above questions illustrate what the catechetical issues of the day were and provide an insight into just how unprepared the Irish Church was for the Second Vatican Council. The Second Vatican Council was a complete shock to the Irish Church. Archbishop McQuaid's famous comment, on arriving home from Vatican II, was, to say the least, very telling: 'Nothing has changed, nothing at all'. How wrong he was.

The Church into which many of us were born is simply disintegrating. This may be a painful fact, but needs, nevertheless, to be acknowledged. Let me point out just a few issues:

- The sexual revolution.
- The power of psychology. A lot of people are addicted to psychology today. Can psychology interpret the interior life in ways that theology/religious education cannot?
- The media and the internet. The capacity they place in our hands to access the world is simply mind-boggling.
- Changes in the family structures. These changes lead to various perspectives, sometimes radically differing, on the family, its role and place in society.
- Developing religious awareness. There seems to be a certain hunger out there for spiritual awareness. Yet, many people tend to distinguish spirituality from religion. Religion is seen as too closely linked to institutions and spirituality is sometimes confined to whatever one thinks it is. Does the split between religion and spirituality occur in developing countries too or is it just a phenomenon associated with the developed world? In many developing countries, this split does not seem to be there – just look at India, for example. In Ireland, we can say that even though the split began only recently, it has truly begun!

Inculturation

Inculturation is a key issue in religious education today. Where exactly does culture come in and what role does it play? The task of religious education and catechetical reflection is not so much to question or condemn culture, but to partake in dialogue with it and not miss it or let it pass by. Karl Barth, one of the greatest theologians of the twentieth century (incidentally a protestant theologian), once said: 'You preach the Gospel with the Bible in one hand and the newspaper in the other.' We have to know what is going on in the world around us.

If we take inculturation seriously, then, we must realise that what may be done in Sri Lanka could be quite different from what is done in Ireland. In this country catechesis/religious education is linked very much to schools and, as far as I can see, this situation is not going to change any time soon. It is very unlikely that it will be reversed. This is so because schools are absolutely central in our educational system. Schools, as far as governments in most countries are concerned, particularly primary schools, are the very way to turn bits of biology into new citizens. They form citizens. Countries everywhere invest heavily in primary schools. Lenin is reported to have once said: 'Give me a primary school and I'll give you a communist country.' Schools run far deeper in society than other institutions, such as banks. They are the key to the future and so it is crucially important to think through schools.

In Ireland, both North and South, schooling has always been critical historically. This is unusual because this is not true of countries everywhere, for example Poland. Polish Catholic peasants (peasants in the economic sense) will not go to school, believing in the idea that schooling undermines farming. This was never really the case here. During the 1830s/1840s Archbishop Cullen of Dublin and Archbishop McHale of Tuam had a huge debate as to whether national schools would destroy or save the Sate/the Church. Cullen won. From the 1830s onwards, national schools in the Republic became central to Irish education and consequently to the Church. And the Church, since the 1930s, has been heavily involved in them. It is difficult to see how this will change.

While what has been said above is true, nevertheless, it does not mean that it should be accepted uncritically. There are serious problems within the schooling system, particularly with regard to teaching religious education. Ireland is becoming more and more secular. Therefore, what about a teacher who comes from a non-faith background or a teacher who is illiterate in the faith? How does he or she fit into the close nexus that exists between schooling and religious education? Constitutionally, politically and legally, there are a host of problems here. There is a very definite change in our culture and a definite clash with our history.

Inculturation in the Irish context might now mean, for the first time since Vatican II, that attention may have to be turned away from schools, particularly with regard to religious education. Religious education has to be re-imagined. However, we must admit the fact that as things stand there is a close connection between religious education and schools. The Church has always seen schools as the focus of religious education. A huge amount of attention has been devoted to schools since the 1830s, but it is time to think new thoughts and seek new directions. This is difficult, as it involves energy, time and resources. Most of the qualified people involved in the area of religious education are all bound up in education, teaching, lecturing, working in teacher training colleges, etc. They do not have the time or luxury to sit down and re-imagine religious education. We need professionals and researchers to do that job. And they need to be paid properly so that they can think, reflect and plan professionally. Otherwise there will be NO CHANGE.

How then do we Nurture?

Religious education cannot be confined to schools alone. Therefore, we need a wider base for nurturing the faith. From where do we pick up our images of God? Is it from school? Is it from home? Is it from liturgies/participation in the Mass/local community? The quest for an answer to this question suggests a consideration of the three main agents responsible for religious education. The three main agents are the home, the school and the parish/community. In *Islands Apart*,[8] Martin Kennedy effectively argues that the *how* of nurturing religious education is breaking down. He sees a diminishing religious discourse at home. The level of religious experience in the local community is frequently low and schools are often the only agent where the child is exposed to some kind of religious experience.

His study contends that in order to nurture the faith, the three agents of home, school and community need to work together. Religious education begins at conception and is received through the family to which one belongs. As we grow older, the classroom becomes a predominant facilitator of religious education. Upon entering adulthood, we are expected to participate in the workforce, and as retired persons, we experience more time for rest and leisure. Thus home, school and community should be viewed as a life-long sequence – the most fundamental basis for a theory of education/religious education. Education then is a life-long process. Religious education is the same. Religious education that finishes with primary school is not enough. We need to pay an increased amount of attention to the home/school/community nexus.

For a religious education programme to be dynamic, it must engage the three agents responsible for faith formation, namely the home, the school and the parish/community.

How do we Nurture Faith at Home?

The home is the primary catalyst in the nurturing of faith. Parents are the *primary educators*. All faith development theorists argue that children's sense of the divine is related to the quality of their relationship with their parents/guardians. However, the notion of family has undergone drastic changes in recent times. These changes include the emergence of dual working parents, which often means less time with children/less influence and other agents – such as television, Playstation, etc. – filling the void; marital breakdown; single parent families and so on.

The home as religious educator engages in many forms of learning. Religious education within the home takes place in a unique manner and in a way that differs from the other agents. The home is a microcosm of larger society. Here it is that the primary models of human interaction are encountered, namely love/hate, trust/rivalry, the loci of a range of human experiences. Nurturing the faith in the home is possible through several different means:

• Education of children by parents;
• Education of parents by children;
• Education of parents by parents;
• Teaching by design;
• Teaching by modelling/performance;
• Teaching languages within the home;
• The home as moral educator;
• The home as prayer.

In short, the family educates by being a family and a community. To this end, the family accompanies its members towards psychological, social and religious maturity by showing them how to live and how to die. It facilitates the journey towards the Kingdom of God.[9]

Community as Religious Educator
The community/parish is the local Christian community that gathers for worship and whose members serve and support each other and reach out to the wider world. Pope John XXIII described this agent as the 'village fountain' where people meet while gathering life-giving water. Let me mention some examples of how the community can become an agent of religious education:

- Through being a religious body – life of prayer and service;
- Connections with homes/families;
- Connection with and involvement with schools;
- Liturgies – inclusive and participative;
- Involvement of its members;
- Educating people towards religious maturity – ongoing;
- Adult formation/religious education;
- Prayer groups, etc.

The School as Nurturer of Faith
Since the 1830s the Catholic primary school attached to the parish has had the responsibility for the task of providing for the formal religious education of children. With the advent of religious education as an academic subject at second level, the manner in which it is viewed has changed considerably. Teaching religion is now seen as an educational process where a person is shown how to use words and concepts so as to understand the field of religion. It is no longer primarily about teaching people a way of life. Some of the prominent aims and objectives of religious education at school are:

- Enable children to grow as people of faith;
- Organise the content in such a way that while it allows for clarity of thought and articulation, it also profoundly influences the whole approach to life;
- Engage with the child of today;
- Respect children as children – children are not miniature adults;
- Value children for what they are, not for what they can become;
- Include prayer – different experiences of prayer;
- Be open to new solutions/approaches;
- Have the capacity to engage the imagination;
- Use story – the Christian story and our own story;
- Include moral development;

- Provide resources to foster home/school/community connections;
- Include prayer services and community links;
- Have messages to parents in the pupil textbooks and worksheets;
- Allow for an experiential programme that would engage the spiritual;
- Connect with children's ability to wonder, to be spontaneous, to live in the present and to be creative.

The above list is, of course, very ambitious. This goes to show how crucial the role of the religious educator is: We *teach who we are*.

Challenges to Religious Education

We will now look at some challenges that nurturing the faith through religious education will have to face in the future. Firstly, some of the challenges relate to the Irish context. With the exception of Dublin where one-third of the population lives, Irish dioceses are too small to be able to offer appropriate services. If dioceses do not amalgamate for all purposes, then amalgamation at least for catechetical purposes is necessary. Dioceses will not be able to survive on their own. The Western dioceses could easily amalgamate.

Secondly, there are huge financial implications. Probably one of the greatest myths about the Catholic Church in Ireland is that it is very rich. It is not. It operates very much from hand to mouth. There are no reserves worth talking about. All we need to do is to examine the finances of parishes. The Catholic Church in Ireland cannot afford to employ catechists. Irish teachers are, by international standards, well paid. So if you expect them to work in the catechetical arena, the resources simply are not there to pay them. The only way this imbalance can be redressed is by long-term planning.

Thirdly, given the above limitations, it is very important to have clear and limited expectations. We need to set limited goals and try to reach them. Some people will say that if priests were to do more – for example, visitations, bringing Holy Communion, Confirmation, etc. – then there would be no problem. Perhaps there is some truth in this, but only some. However, with the stark, even staggering, decline in the number of clerics, the changes here in the next ten years will be massive and the role of the priest is thus necessarily going to have to change.

Finally, we still have the highest practice rate in the world (perhaps with the exception of Malta). In some areas we still have practice rates of between 40 per cent and 50 per cent. This is absolutely incredible by international standards. Irish ecclesial affiliation is still very strong. In the Irish context the practising people do matter. We need to focus our re-evangelisation efforts towards them.

Looking to the Future
Everyone agrees that in times of difficulty, it is always good to go back to the origins. Whatever the organisation – whether it is Fianna Fail or the GAA – everyone agrees that in moments of crisis you revisit the founders and return to the original ideology. You do not go back to the origins/founders to get answers to today's questions, as some of today's issues would not have been encountered then or by them. However, by going back to the origins you have an opportunity to get some of the energy that was there at the time of the origin. You can tap into the wellsprings that are at the root of the organisation. For example if you want to draw up a pastoral plan for the Archdiocese of Cashel and Emly or for any other diocese by just looking up at St Paul's writings, you are not going to find a blueprint for a pastoral plan, *but*, and this is the key, you might get energy and inspiration from, say, St Paul's Letters to the Corinthians. Everybody knows that energy is most in need; it is most in demand today in our

world. Energy is in short supply. When it comes to energy and the Church or energy and religious education, rushing back to the Law of the Church is pretty much irrelevant. Looking to Canon Law to solve our problems would be akin to Bertie Ahern saying that the 1948 Road Traffic Act, which was amended in 1967, is the answer to today's traffic needs.

Returning to the origins brings in the concept of journey. Journey is a very rich motif throughout the scriptures. The purpose of all journeys, whether we come from centre roads, back roads or even cul-de-sacs, is to enter into the inner journey. The same is true of Christian life and religious education. When I think of the future of religious education, the parable of the Sower and the Seed comes to mind. All Christian scholars agree that the correct and proper context for the interpretation of this parable is eschatological. The seed has been sown and it will never stop growing. It will grow sometimes where we least expect it. It will grow almost unnoticeably. We cannot often see the seed growing, yet we need to learn, we need to distrust our eyes, we need to accept that the seed of the Kingdom of God will keep growing.

We are all sowers of the seed. 'The Kingdom of God is close at hand – repent and believe'.[10] In Greek the word 'repent' is *metanoia*. It means turn around and look the other way. For example, you are walking along and someone shouts *Metanoia!*; you look back at where you have come from and you will probably see that the seed grew where you least expected it: in your life, in others' lives, in institutions, etc.

If we can only believe, then we will see the seed is growing and the seed will continue to grow. However, as in the Gospel, it will grow often in ways that we least expect. 'We are all sowers of the seed.' All we need to do is to prepare the ground. The challenge of nurturing the faith through religious education is to prepare the ground to sow the seed. Like any investment we will reap what we sow (or sometimes others will reap what we have sown) but in the world of existential faith, the rewards for the sowing are immeasurable. Let us begin.

NURTURING THE FAITH THROUGH RELIGIOUS EDUCATION

Notes

1 Harris and Moran, *Reshaping Religious Education*, p.168.
2 D. Murray, 'The Language of Catechesis' in D.A. Lane (ed.) *Religious Education and the Future* (Dublin: Columba Press, 1986), p.133.
3 Oliver Brennan, *Critical Issues in Religious Education* (Dublin: Veritas, 2005).
4 The Religious Dimension of Education in a Catholic School, 1988.
5 Matthew, 28:19.
6 Matthew, 28:20.
7 Romans, 5:5.
8 A study on Religious Education published by Martin Kennedy in 2000.
9 See F. Cunnane, *New Directions in Religious Education* (Dublin: Veritas, 2004).
10 Mark, 1:14-15.

Bibliography

Brennan, O., *Critical Issues in Religious Education* (Dublin: Veritas, 2005).
Cunnane, F., *New Directions in Religious Education* (Dublin: Veritas, 2004).
Glazer, S. (ed.) *The Heart of Learning* (New York: Crossraods, 1999).
Murray, D., 'The Language of Catechesis' in D.A. Lane (ed.) *Religious Education and the Future* (Dublin: Columba Press, 1986).
Norman, J., *At the Heart of Education* (Dublin: Veritas, 2004).
Topley, R. and Byrne, G. (eds) *Nurturing Children's Religious Imagination* (Dublin: Veritas, 2004).

Proclaiming the Good News to the Young

Gerard Gallagher

Introduction

We live in a time of considerable change. Change affects all of us, either directly or indirectly. It affects our decisions, thoughts and lifestyle. Change also touches our values and what we believe. Some of our certainties are now being questioned. Much has been spoken of and about change that has occurred in Ireland during the modern period. We have changed from a largely agricultural and traditional society to a modern, technological and progressive one. The traditional family has changed in its make-up. Ireland has changed from being perceived as a staunchly Catholic country to one that has more in common constitutionally with modern democracies. Our Church has changed too from being a dominant institution which permeated all aspects of life in Ireland to one that has been forced to change due to external analysis by the media and successive scandals. Our understanding of our Catholic identity has changed as a result. Without doubt, whether we realise it or not, change has impacted every aspect of our lives. As Bob Dylan summed it up, 'the times they are a-changing'.

In this article I will look at a number of aspects of how the Gospel is proclaimed to the young in this changed and changing context, such as:

- How our cultural landscape has changed;
- Some of the issues that face our young people;
- Some of my personal experiences of working with the young;
- Some areas where the Gospel is proclaimed in a meaningful way to young people.

Changing Ireland

Since the 1960s, several people in Ireland, including priests and religious, have commented on how Vatican II provided a catalyst for change within the Church. They have spoken of signs that indicated that traditional forms of religion might not prove sufficient in the future. Steps were taken in order to begin to offer fresh ways of presenting religion and the Gospel to young people. The early seeds of youth ministry were sown during this period.

It was the young people who were leading the social revolts around Europe, especially in France. Many priests, religious and lay people were able to read these 'signs of the times' and connect the Good News with the life of the young. They began to introduce a new way for young people to be involved in the life of the Church. They introduced new ways of praying such as Charismatic Renewal and its new music. Young people began to experience a new type of school retreat based predominantly on their personal faith experience. Several of the radical changes that the post-Vatican II era unleashed, and which often disturbed the comfort of many, served as catalysts for young people to rebel against an outdated Church.

Ministering effectively to the young in the changed context in which we live is one of the serious challenges facing the Church in Ireland today.

Ireland was affected, not just by changes in the Church, but also by changes in the wider society. Secularisation had a great impact on the practice of the faith. Statistics for mass attendance are still significantly higher in Ireland than in most other European countries. However, a number of surveys map how religious attendance has been changing over the years. In 1973 church attendance in Ireland was an amazing 91 per cent. An *Irish Times/MRBI* poll in December 1996 showed that only 66 per cent went to weekly mass. This was down from 79 per cent in 1991 and 85 per cent in 1986. In 1998 an *MRBI/RTE Prime Time* survey found that 60 per cent went to mass weekly. By 2002 a *Millward Brown IMS* survey found that only 48 per cent attended mass weekly.[1] A *Sunday Tribune/IMS* opinion poll in April 2005 found that a mere 34 per cent of those interviewed attended mass each week. Only one in four of the under-thirty described themselves as mass-goers. This is a big change in Irish culture and a challenge that the Church needs to address.[2]

During the 1980s, as one commentator noted, 'the large fidelity to mass-going is undoubtedly the greatest strength of the Irish Chruch; but this strength could rapidly become our greatest weakness'.[3] This scenario of weakness happened more quickly than people were prepared for. Similar trends from other countries were known, yet little or no contingency planning was conceived or undertaken in the years preceding the scandals. Given this situation, it was easy for young people to either walk away or just drift. There was nothing to keep them in and few invited them to stay. The younger generation was fast drifting out of the Church's orbit. The Church was losing its grip on young people. It was either insignificant or irrelevant to the lives many young people were living. Young people had abandoned a part of the traditional Irish culture that was universally important to their parents.[4] And the Church did little to address the situation. It was occupied with reacting and responding to scandals rather than offering the genuine leadership that was sorely needed. 'It was pretty familiar stuff for any Church in any European country, but it was not until the early 1990s that the Catholic Church in Ireland really alerted itself to the defection of the younger generation.'[5]

Change occurred rapidly in the Irish Church. In a period of just over ten years, its position in society, its status in family life and its moral voice have all imploded. The institution of the Church is now facing a great challenge on how to maintain a voice in modern Ireland and at the same time remain relevant to young people. One group of commentators made the following point. 'Young people have been less and less successfully socialized into institutional religion as Ireland has moved from a position of 'moral monopoly' to a de facto pluralism, where there is ready access to multiple media sources, values and lifestyles.'[6]

One of the greatest challenges that the Church in Ireland has to face up to is that without proper intervention and leadership it will continue to lose its youth. The exodus would continue as long as proper steps are not taken. What is needed is vision, a sense of mission and leadership. From the 1960s to the present, there has never been a long-term and well thought-out strategy in the Church in Ireland on keeping young people involved in the Church. It is almost by accident that so many young people continue to be involved over the years. Yet it is clear that a time of reflection needs to happen in order to create a path for the future of youth ministry and proclamation of the Gospel in Ireland.

Challenges Facing Young People

It is not easy being a young person today. Certainly we have progressed. But young people are being forced by external pressures to succumb to the pressures of the modern world. At a stage in life during which they are trying to form their own values and become themselves, they are forced to deal with issues on a scale that previous generations never had to. We have become a more addictive society. People drink more today across all age categories. However, among those under the age of twenty-five there has been a significant increase.[7] Alcohol abuse and misuse especially, if un-monitored, becomes a gateway into other unsavoury aspects of life such as drug abuse, civic violence and even death. This stark image is not portrayed in the glossy advertising.

Young people today have to make difficult choices. Yet if there is a lack of good local interaction in parishes, youth clubs or local civic organisations, young people can fall into the false security of doing what everyone else is doing. If young people are searching for happiness in such aspects of social life as drink, drugs, etc., they are not finding it. It is false happiness. Many lack the opportunity of being able to turn to someone for advice or being able to get involved in alternative leisure pursuits. Maybe this is why suicide has almost reached epidemic proportions among young people, averaging around 400 deaths per year and staggering alleged attempts numbering 10,000.[8] It is this void in youth culture that has to be challenged by practical responses. Young people and their culture need to be offered a new alternative. One young person told me that when her friends go to mass, it is usually only for a funeral of a peer. This is the reality faced by all our young people. This dark side of youth culture and the void it leaves needs to be filled by a spiritual and faith-based alternative.

It is not easy being a young person today. While young people today have possibilities that their peers even a generation or two ago could only dream of, they are faced with dangers that their peers hardly ever had to contend with.

The challenge of presenting the Gospel to young people in Ireland may be hard, but one cannot assume a defeatist attitude. There is hope and often it comes through those who continue to spend time with young people and to explore issues and present faith to them in a credible and meaningful way. It boils down to how imaginative and creative we are when it comes to thinking about the future. It is about how we offer a real, tangible experience of Christian community. They certainly lack a real sense of Christian community – and if they don't have a role in community or a sense of participation in the wider group, then they will easily give up a commitment.

Recently, the Ombudsman was quoted as saying that as people 'tiptoe' back to the churches, they are doing so on the basis that there is something deeper on offer in them than in secular society. If this is the case, then what is on offer needs to be relevant to them. [9]

Personal Experience of Young People in the Church

Since the early 1990s I have worked with young people full time on behalf of the Church. The experience has been extremely challenging, and yet a privilege. For most of that period I worked with Catholic Youth Care in Dublin. I have said above that it is not easy being a young person in the Church. It is even harder being a youth worker! Yet the challenge serves as a good motivating factor. The last fifteen years, as has been said above, have been some of the most difficult that the Church in Ireland has had to face in recent times. Yet, throughout that period, ministry to young people has continued to evolve and change. I have fantastic memories of being a young person in the Church and was proud to be a young Catholic. Young people today have a right to a similar experience.

I believe that a great number of young people in Ireland, the next generation, would be deprived of a rich faith experience if we fail to find new ways of proclaiming the Gospel – or, even worse, if we fail to try. The faith of many young people is almost an optional add-on with no depth. The challenge to people working with youth is to make their faith grow deeper and research, design and find ways of achieving it. I am reminded in this context of Paul VI's great encyclical on evangelisation and of the need to discover new methods, means and language to proclaim the Gospel.[10]

Today, too few parishes have youth ministry programmes for young people. They also probably have nothing for young adults. Youth ministry is often something occasional. One priest told me that youth ministry was something that he tried, but it didn't work. Even though efforts are being made to create structures for youth ministry to happen, we have to face the fact that many priests find it very difficult to work with young people. Some priests tell me that they are not in active contact with any young person. Others say that their youth ministry consists of not much more than signing a cheque book in order to pay for a young person to do something such as a course or participate in a pilgrimage. Cheque book ministry is not youth ministry. It is a sign that parishes have forgotten how to do youth ministry. Some priests have given up working with young people totally. It is up to people involved in youth ministry around the country to present the challenge to priests as to why they should involve young people in the local parish. It is also the task of the bishops to give high priority to getting young people involved in the ministry and life of the Church.

During this period of change, we need to be clear about what has worked and what has not. In the past youth ministry was more about numbers and programmes. This will not suffice for the future. In the past, most of the youth ministry programmes and opportunities presumed a faith based on knowledge, experience and commitment. However, today some of the young people who participate in Church-related events may have received a full school-based catechetical programme, yet know little or nothing about the basics of the faith. Many are ignorant of the basic tenets of Christianity and the rubrics of faith. I have met young people representing their parish at diocesan or national events who are on one of two extremes. They are either very positive about their faith and experience, but yet would not have made the same faith journey someone of a similar age would have made a generation ago; or they are well-intentioned young people coming from well-known families in the parish, but lack, at the same time, even such basic skills as knowing how to pray, how to talk about faith and so on.[11]

The Church in Ireland needs to audit what it offers young people with regard to faith development. If what we are offering and investing in is not working, then, it seems fair to look at other options. We need to look at the ethos of Catholic schools and the declining numbers of young people challenged by faith that are emerging from them. We need to reflect on what is offered to young people in our parishes and find out what would work. We need to examine what is the most effective programme or event at present. We need to look into the future and realise that we all have a responsibility to proclaim the Gospel, but we need to find the correct method and means. There is no point continuing to maintain something if it is not effective. That does not make sense.

Radical Young People in the Church

Some of the most radical young people I know are young people who have made a personal faith journey, asked searching questions along the way and tried to develop knowledge of their faith and a relationship with God. I personally know young people who have participated in programmes and opportunities provided by Catholic Youth Care and who can say humbly that participation in a World Youth Day or an Alpha Course, School of Faith, etc., 'changed their lives'. Few jobs can humble a person. I know that the young people I work with, befriend and challenge are on a journey of personal self-discovery. I know that they may not have the full skills to debate Church matters, intellectualise on a matter of faith or spirituality. The starting points for them and for me and possibly you are different. They are radical because they have come out of a culture in Ireland where faith, over the years, has gone through a profound crisis. Nothing culturally supports them in their faith anymore. Young people participate in CYC because they can meet friends who understand, share an experience and make it okay to be Catholic. Yet they have equal parallel friendships with friends who do not support their faith commitment, but understand and accept them and are not hostile.

Effective ministry to the young must begin where young people are rather than where we expect them to be.

CYC works with the poor and disadvantaged young people in Dublin. A new category of poor are the young people who have been deprived of an authentic proclamation of the Gospel and the experience of a living Church. In my work with young people over the years I have been struck by how, once they are presented and challenged by the Gospel and faith, their lives become more meaningfully balanced. I have also noticed that on pilgrimages to Taizé or World Youth Days young Irish Catholics are amazed by the commitment, zeal and pride with which young people from around the world live their faith. This is an eye-opening moment. Their poverty of experience is then translated into a rich meaningful encounter of faith. This is the universal Church when it really is working – presenting the universal message of the Gospel in a simple idea.

Peer Ministry – World Youth Day

Around the world at present, hundreds of thousands of young people representing hundreds of countries have just returned from pilgrimage to World Youth Day (which took place in Cologne from 15–21 August 2005). Why has WYD been so successful? Millions of young people have taken up this initiative that the late Pope John Paul II began in 1985. Many turned up at his funeral, to the puzzlement of observers. The simplicity of their presence was remarkable and hopefully will remain a legacy of the late Pope. John Paul II saw the value in the Pope meeting the young people in an urban setting. He saw the value in young people going on pilgrimage. He had a clear vision – he was a model icon pointing the way for young people. WYD is an event and an entry point into faith. Young people were able to sample the Church, receive a new understanding of faith, meet the Pope and minister to each other. The Pope saw his role as a continuation of the Gospel imperative to go into the world and proclaim the Gospel. The Pope probably was the greatest youth minister in the Church's history simply on the basis that he met with and challenged more young people with the Gospel than anyone else I know. Young people who have gone on this experience have told me that it helped to change their lives and often overturned many of the decisions they were making. The grace of WYD is hidden and it is only afterwards that we notice the hand of God guiding young people. We need to replicate this courage in our entire ministry with young people and not be afraid of inviting young people and challenging them with the Gospel.

Peer ministry is the ideal ministry for young people.

Approximately one-third of the young people who attended WYD in 2002 and 2005 were there by a personal invitation from of a friend.[12] WYD is perhaps the most successful youth ministry initiative in Ireland today. The Pope challenged the young with the Gospel. He asked them to go home and tell their friends of what they had experienced. He felt that the recounting of such experiences could bring joy and enthusiasm back to the local Church. I know many young people who say that WYD changed their lives. The Holy Spirit is certainly present and active through the many people involved in this event. When people say that the Church is no longer relevant to young people, I can reply by pointing out to the millions of young people touched by the Gospel. WYD has become a new way for young people to be involved in the Church.

A Challenge to the Church

The Church needs to accept that young people today present themselves for sacramental moments with no real understanding of the doctrine of faith. They see themselves as cultural Catholics and not really people who sign up to all aspects of faith - simply because they are either not familiar with them or ignorant of them. They do not feel compelled by the Church's teaching - yet they are also equally at home in the modern world embedded in secular ideals and values. Their values are confused. The Church in my experience of working with young people needs to present its alternative message - despite modern attitudes and cultural changes. The Church needs to believe in its message and hold firm. Young people want certainties - not something loose and vague. Think of those young people who loved Pope John Paul II, listened to his challenging words. He did not condemn or judge them - he challenged them with the Gospel message, even if their lives and values were quite different to what he was inviting them to.[13]

The Challenge of Evangelisation and Young People

The proclamation of the Gospel needs to be the central element in our work with young people. It needs to be a lived message, a relevant message. It needs to be a challenging message too, if young people are to sit up and take notice of it. It also needs to be a way of living for which youth leaders and the wider Church take responsibility. We knew how to be Christian when we were poor, under-educated and culturally marginalised, but we are struggling to be Christian when we are affluent, educated and have a full place in the culture. We know what to do for someone who comes to Church – but we don't know how to get someone to come to Church!

Life After the Young Church

One of the laments I have heard from successive young people who were involved with the Church while they were young is that they have no vehicle for involvement in the Church once they move into full adulthood. There is no outlet for them as a late twenty-something or thirty-something. They move from a Church that is happy and friendly to one that is not prepared to accept them. There is no middle ground in the Church, they would say. The Church sometimes acts like an older person who won't accommodate fresh blood. As a result of this lack of understanding and accommodation, there is a silent schism in the Irish Church in the young adult age profile. Apart from a period of high involvement in sacramental preparation for children and families after confirmation, a possible flirtation with some youth programmes or pilgrimages and the regular mass, there really isn't anything that would interest or challenge them.

New Ways of Involving Young People

The Church needs to create new spaces for involving young people outside of existing structures. Most parishes do not really suit modern living. Most people travel more or are prepared to. Maybe the Church needs to be more community based. Maybe what is needed is the establishment of new types of Church communities. There is a lot of speculation about changing pastoral landscapes, with some parish boundaries being redrawn as a result of the decline in the number of available priests. Maybe the time is ripe to offer new types of Christian communities building on the strengths of young people around music and liturgy, in order to invite and explore new ways of being Catholic in the modern world.

It is imperative that the Church constantly reaches out to the ever-changing culture of the young.

Shortly after becoming Pope, Benedict XVI told the Italian bishops that for young people to be able to accept the demanding message of the Gospel, they must feel loved by the Church, especially by bishops and priests. Young people are the hope of the Church. 'Therefore they need to be helped to grow and mature in faith.'[14]

International

Over the last year through my work in Dublin I have encountered a new development in the Church. I have met a different category of young people who are interested in their faith and want to participate. They are emigrants living in Ireland. Some are from the Eastern and Orthodox tradition. Others are from countries where the Church is vibrant among the young. They come from countries such as the Philippines, India, Nigeria and China. Some of these nationalities have priests who meet with their new communities for mass and offer some type of pastoral support. We need to find new ways of offering these immigrants to Ireland ways of interacting and getting involved in the local Church. One Indian priest told me that when his community members want mass they text him on his mobile. New forms of technology are being used to form new communities. This is a concrete example of a new way of presenting the message of the Gospel.

Through my work I have discovered that you have to be familiar with the technology of young people in order to contact them. Most of the ongoing ministry that I am involved in co-ordinating is organised through the use of e-mail or text message. It can get a direct response. The Church should not be afraid to embrace new technology as a method of being able to transmit its message.

Many groups around the world have responded to the call for a 'new evangelisation'. This revitalised proclamation of the Gospel has not been fully taken up by the Church. One of the key elements in many of these new renewal movements is that they offer clarity for people who wish to be challenged by the Gospel. The role of the new religious communities, mainly European, such as the Focolare, Emmanuel or the Neo-Catechumenate, is to offer people a way of life, based on the Gospel, an extended community of friends who wish to live the message of the Gospel in a more committed way. These movements are close to the centre of the Church. In some places they have revitalised the Church. 'Mission to the City' was an idea of a number of bishops in Vienna, Paris and Lisbon to bring on board some of these movements to offer a city-wide mission. It has involved an intense and joyful proclamation of the Gospel to people outside the Church. Church structures are prepared to invite and come up with new ways of inviting people either back to the Church or to help people become Christians. This is the new evangelisation at work in some of the older cities of Europe where Christianity is less vibrant than before. Young people are also attracted to groups that offer a blend of music, fun and faith. It would appear that where the Church is less powerful young people can identify with it in a clearer way. In the USA, Lifeteen and Youth 2000 are quite successful at this, offering a parish-based opportunity for young people to be involved in a big youth movement. In Germany, Youth 2000 would be one of the biggest youth movements. Many of these groups grew out of World Youth Days during the late 1980s/early 1990s. They are based on the pillars of mass, Marian devotion and personal prayer. In Ireland at present they are probably the largest non-diocesan youth groups and in some cases have replaced diocesan and parish youth ministry altogether. The Gospel is still relevant. Where gimmicks are used, young people are less interested.

What is our Challenge?

As people who work with young people, or desire to work with young people, we need to sit down and look at what we are doing well and resource it fully. Also, we need to look at what we are not doing that works elsewhere and consider a strategy that can begin it in our area. Youth Ministry begins by taking the first step. If you don't dream, then you won't lead young people anywhere. If our faith means anything, we must be ready to get involved and find new ways of involving young people in the life of the Church. If the Gospel means anything to us, we won't hold it for ourselves – we have the responsibility and mandate to find ways to pass it on to younger generations.

The evangelisation of young people needs to be a priority of all believers. Just because young people do not seem interested or appear indifferent to what is on offer, we cannot soft-pedal the obligation to present the Gospel to them. In CYC we have over the years attempted various ways of presenting young people with the Gospel. During the late 1990s and early 2000 Cardinal Desmond Connell symbolically presented young people with the Gospel and invited them to read it. Through WYD and other initiatives we have attempted to offer help to young people who wish to learn how to pray using the scripture.

This is a difficult type of work to get right. Presenting young people with the Gospel needs to be followed through with action. We need to offer them signposts suggesting ways they can live the Gospel and ways they can do this with others. As a result of parishes having little or no outlet for young people, the diocese through CYC has had to create new ways of gathering young people who wish to be involved in the Church. This is a new diocesan community of young people with few personal experiences of parish life. It is through such new communities that we can challenge and invite young people to take more responsibility for their faith. These new communities are examples of a young Church with no boundaries; a young Church that involves young people in friendship with each other. This is a space where we in CYC can challenge young people to live the Gospel and use their talents for the building up of the local Church.

Youth ministry of the future will be a ministry to young people who seek alternative ways of living.

Such a ministry needs to be clear about what it stands for. It needs to offer young people a challenge and an experience of Church that will either be new or deeper than what has been on offer to them previously. Religion in the future needs to engage people, especially young people, about the story of their faith, capture their imagination and provide opportunities for them to explore what it means to believe in the modern world.

Much depends on how we resource youth ministry. If the concern is the greying age profile of the Church, then steps need to be taken to redress the balance. It might be a case of involving more young people in parish life, liturgy and music. We need to provide them with a message of hope and reason for living their life within the Church based on the Gospel. Young people when challenged with the Gospel might find it strange at first, but when they are surrounded by people who will walk with them and explain things to them, they will in turn make a personal commitment to the values of the Gospel. Maybe we need to consider deeply what the Gospel means to us first and then begin to see how we can communicate that vision to those young people we know either in our lives or through our ministry.

Notes

1 A summary of these statistics can be found in *The Irish Times*, Friday 20 September 2002, in an article by Patsy McGarry.

2 *Sunday Tribune*, 24 April 2005. This survey was published after the election of Pope Benedict XV.

3 M.P. Gallagher, SJ, *Help my Unbelief* (Dublin: Veritas, 1986), p. 36.

4 Brennan, p. 76.

5 Philip Fogarty, *Why Don't They Believe us?* (Dublin: Columba Press, 1993). This book raises some questions as to why young people find it difficult to make a faith commitment to the Church. It also echoes a concern of many parents as to where they went wrong in passing on the faith. Also, see Tanner, *Ireland's Holy Wars* (London: Yale University Press, 2001), p. 386.

6 C.T. Whelan and T. Fahy, 'Religious Change in Ireland 1981–1990', in Eoin G Cassidy (ed.) *Faith and Culture in the Irish Context* (Dublin: Veritas, 1996), p. 110.

7 *The Irish Times*, Editorial, 17 August 2001, highlighted the consequences that alcohol has on other aspects of living such as social dislocation, road carnage, drug abuse, violence, etc.

8 Statistics taken from *The Irish Examiner*, 8 August 2001.

9 Talk given at Céifin Conference 2004, *Imagining the Future*, by Emily O'Reilly, quoted in *Irish Independent*, 4 November 2004.

10 'It must constantly seek the proper means and language for presenting or representing God's revelation and faith in Jesus Christ.' *Evangelii Nuntiandi*, 56. Also *Novo Millennio Inuente*, 2001. This encyclical makes similar points especially for people engaged in ministry post the Jubilee Year of 2000.

11 Quoted in *Anyone for Alpha?* p. 83, from R. Bibby, 'Going, Going, Gone: the Impact of Geographical Mobility on Religious Involvement', *Review of Religious Research*, Vol. 38, No. 19 (1977), p. 172.

12 'The young should become the first apostles of the young, in direct contact with them, exercising the apostolate by themselves, taking into account

their social environment.' *Apostolicam Actuositatem, 12*. Youth ministry works best when it is young people who are driving it.

13 Shortly after confirming that he would attend World Youth Day in Cologne, Pope Benedict XVI said the following about young people: 'They are tossed to and fro and carried about with every wind of doctrine. Therefore they need to be helped to grow and mature in the faith, this is the first service they must receive from the Church ... Many of them are not able to understand and accept all the Church's teaching immediately, but precisely for this reason it is important to reawaken within them the intention to believe with the Church, the belief that this Church, animated and guided by the Spirit, is the true subject of faith.' (Vatican City, May 31 2005).

14 www.Zenit.org; refer to the quotation above.

Bibliography

Brennan, Oliver, *Cultures Apart? The Catholic Church and Contemporary Irish Youth* (Dublin: Veritas, 2000).

Cassidy, Eoin et al. (eds) *Faith and Culture in the Irish Context* (Dublin: Veritas, 1996).

Flannery, Austin (ed.) *Vatican Council II*, The Conciliar and Post Consiliar Documents (Dublin: Dominican Publications, 1988).

Fogarty, Philip, *Why Don't They Believe Us?* (Dublin: Columba Press, 1993).

Gallagher, Michael Paul, *Help My Unbelief* (Dublin: Veritas, 1983).

Knights, Philip and Murray, Andrea, *Evangelisation in England and Wales – A Report to the Catholic Bishops* (London: Catholic Communications Service, 2002).

Lynch, Seamus, *Cast Out Into the Deep, Attracting Young People to the Church* (Dublin: The Liffey Press, 2004).

Novo Millennio Inuente, Encyclical of John Paul II.

Renewing the Vision, A Framework for Catholic Youth Ministry, National Conference of Catholic Bishops (USA, 1997).

Tanner, Marcus, *Ireland's Holy Wars: A Struggle of a Nation's Soul* (London: Yale University Press, 2001).

The Parish as an Agent of Change

Clare Slattery RSM

Introduction

'A person is a person with others.' This African proverb holds a truth that underpins the title of this paper. To be an authentic human being one must interact with others. It is impossible to develop one's full potential by living in complete isolation. Indeed the word 'person' is a communal word coming from the Greek *prosopon*, 'turned towards the other'. Our word 'idiot' is also derived from the Greek and literally means, 'one who stands alone'.[1]

> *When we talk about the parish we are talking about something that is relational at its core.*

The parish is not primarily a geographical area, a combination of buildings or structures of any kind. As the Latin American Bishops make it clear:

[The parish] is not principally a structure, a territory or a building, but rather the family of God, fellowship, afire with a unifying spirit. The parish is founded on a theological reality because it is a Eucharistic community. The parish is a community of faith and an organic community, that is, constituted by the ordained ministers and other Christians who live and work deeply within the fabric of human society and in close solidarity with its aspirations and problems.[2]

The heart of the parish is in the hearts of the people of that parish. To say, 'this parish is dead', is to say that the relational aspect of life is missing there for whatever reason. Is the parish a symbol of hope for Irish society today or merely the geographical location of certain people?

The parish, especially what happens within and among its people, is pivotal to its being an agent of change. So let us take a look at the parish and see how it can become an agent of change, change in the service of evangelisation, mission and conversion.

Parish the Place of God's Grace

To see anything for what it is is to see the goodness of it, the love of God for it, God's grace in it. The challenge is to see things as they are, as God sees them. 'That which is always and everywhere, that is, God's grace, must be noticed, accepted and celebrated.'[3]

Parish, then, is a place of God's grace. It is the leaven in society that has the potential to be an agent of change. It has the possibility of radiating the dynamism of the Kingdom, the living out of the values of that Kingdom. To parishioners we need to say the words of the hymn:

You are the salt of the earth, O people,
Salt for the Kingdom of God.
You are the light of the earth, O people,
Light for the Kingdom of God.

It is ultimately God's grace that brings people together into a parish, inspires them to proclaim and live the Word, challenges them to speak out against every form of oppression and knits them together into a dynamic community.

What are the ways in which the parish is a place of God's grace? The parish is the local church housing, sheltering, nurturing and witnessing to the domestic church – the family – in mutual evangelisation. Most significantly the parish is the local agent, as it were, of catechesis. Remembering that, according to the General Directory for Catechesis, the goal of catechesis is to put people in touch, in communion, in intimacy with Jesus Christ it follows that the parish is the most important place where formation for the faith takes place. This is where 'people become aware of themselves as a community of God, a welcoming and warm home. Here is where faith is born and nourished'.[4]

The Challenge of Parish Catechesis Today

It is necessary for us to listen with our eyes and think with our hearts. We need, urgently, to open the call of baptism and respond to its essential depth. If we could take this call seriously parish would then take on a whole new sense of worth and meaning. At the end of Matthew's gospel we read, 'Go, make disciples of all the nations; baptise them in the name of the Father and of the Son and of the Holy Spirit and teach them to observe all the commands I gave you'. (Mt 28:19-20) Jesus is sending the disciples on a mission to the world. Note the sequence of commands: Make disciples – Baptise – Teach. Have we ignored the wisdom of the Lord? Look at what we have done: Baptise (infants) – Teach – Make disciples (hopefully this will happen down the road, if at all). The parish is impoverished when we do not take seriously the ministry of catechesis.

THE PARISH AS AN AGENT OF CHANGE

According to the GDC

What does the ministry of catechesis at parish level involve? Obviously, there are a number of elements that make up the ministry of catechesis. The suggestions made by the GDC are pertinent:

- Adult catechesis must be given priority;
- Next comes announcing the Good News to those who are alienated or indifferent about their faith;
- The development of small Christian communities is highly recommended;
- Then and only then do we come to the catechesis of children and young people as a necessary element.

Educating adults in the faith is one of the most serious challenges facing the Church today.

This is not to decry in any way the significance of the role of the Catholic school in catechesis, but merely to keep it in context. I am suggesting that for the parish to be an agent of change, it must be an agent of catechesis. Inasmuch as we neglect making adult catechesis a priority the parish fails to be an agent of change.

Nurturing Adults towards Maturity of Faith

Different forms of catechesis for adults are necessary if the faith of parishioners is to be nurtured towards maturity. Included would be:

1 Sacramental theology, where the sacraments, especially the sacraments of initiation, would be explained and allowed to give new impetus to the faith of the people;

2 Simple study of the Bible – its origins, its inspiration and guidance for daily life;
3 Social teaching of the Church to help form and inform the conscience of parishioners in their moral decision making;
4 Liturgical catechesis, offering an understanding of symbols and gestures. The importance of participation cannot be overstressed. (Why is taking part in the offertory procession often seen as an imposition? Reading as reading and not as proclamation? Eucharistic ministry as 'helping the priest?' The ministries are not understood properly);
5 Spiritual direction is an excellent way towards spiritual growth.

All the above dimensions need to be activated at parish level or at cluster parish level in rural areas if a parish is to be alive and active.

Harnessing the Gifts
The parish that does not use the gifts of its parishioners finally loses them. There is talent, knowledge and skill in abundance all around us, but too often we fail to harness the gifts that we know we need. We know we need to change and, in truth, we can change through a certain partnership of priest and people. This partnership, like any relationship, needs to be worked at: will it be worked at though, unless and until priests and people see themselves, in the words of Enda Lyons, as 'Companions All'?[5]

Parish Pastoral Councils
The parish, through its Pastoral Council, can lead the people, in cooperation with the local clergy, towards becoming a community of communities. In fact Pastoral Councils are there specifically to direct change. Their ministry is Pastoral Planning, as John Flaherty suggests in *Four Ways to Build More Effective Parish Councils*: 'The most important role for all of us as

Christians is to evangelise the world and transform the world of economics, politics and technology by the witness of our lives. The Pastoral Council is the elected local church body that is called to be prophetic and challenging to parishioners about what the Church teaches, about walking in the footsteps of Jesus of Nazareth.'[6]

We have yet to discover the potential Parish Councils have for building dynamic Christian communities at local level.

Pastoral Councils lead parishioners to:

1 Look for the lost sheep;
2 Place one's trust in God;
3 Believe in the guidance of the Holy Spirit;
4 Heal divisions, seek peace;
5 Become aware of the mission of the Church – evangelisation.

Parish Councils are called to build up the local community, a task that needs knowledge and skills as well as faith, hope and love. They need ongoing education to fulfil their ministry.

Small Christian Communities
In an age when individualism and consumerism have turned life into a ladder rather than an interdependent road forming groups of families into small communities, Small Christian Communities are not just needed, they are essential. As Michael Paul Gallagher observes, 'The village world is gone'. We have decided 'bigger is better', not 'small is beautiful'.[7] And the cost, to ourselves, is huge. However, I believe that it is within the *Small Christian Community* that the love of God can become a

reality, because it is here that roots can really sink in. I do not want to believe that 'the village world is gone'.

Small Christian Communities can be a powerful antidote to an era steeped in individualism, materialism and consumerism.

Working in South Africa and seeing the Small Christian Communities (SCCs) – 30 to 40 families who meet weekly to pray, listen to the Gospel Reading, share their words, their worries and their blessings as a Community – has certainly convinced me that we in the Irish Church need to grasp the nettle on this one. Have we told ourselves that our people are not capable of, or not interested in, forming SCCs? I find it extraordinary that the leadership of the Irish Church has never set up a dialogue with our returned missionaries, male and female, religious and lay, and invited them to help spearhead SCCs in Ireland. We have never acknowledged their wisdom, gifts and understanding of mission itself and this, I believe, is to our impoverishment.

Thurles Seminary closed. Many people believed that's it, it's all over. But here we are gathered this evening in a building that has been given a rebirth through prophetic imagination. This place is humming with hundreds of students doing various programmes. This September a Certificate Programme in Pastoral Ministry, masterminded here, is having an outreach in Nenagh – a new cooperative venture between the Archdiocese of Cashel and Emly and the Diocese of Killaloe.

Thurles has shown us what change can do, that crisis is opportunity to change. One is reminded of Deuteronomy 30:19: 'I put before you life or death, choose life.' Will we 'choose life' at parish level and form Neighbourhood Christian Communities, given the significance of that word 'neighbour' in our Irish context and its possible potential for including our immigrant population?

Lesser Agents of Change
Within the parish when you listen with your eyes you notice the lesser but significant agents of change. For example, take the familiar and taken-for-granted ministry of the Eucharist minister. If seen as 'helping Father' the meaning is lost. If seen as mediating the Body and Blood of Christ to their sisters and brothers, then how different is the reality? As a Eucharist minister, I offer you, your Lord. If my heart is in the right place, I will have prayed a blessing on you and yours. I will have humbly acknowledged my servant ministry to the Lord and in the process stand before you as a bridge to your God.

As reader I proclaim the Word of God. If I understand my ministry as 'proclaiming', I will know that there is a difference between proclaiming and reading. Reading is getting myself heard accurately and with some sense of meaning. Proclaiming is:

- Calling those present to listen to the reading;
- Calling them to a new awareness of the Word, alive and active in them;
- Calling them to respond in their hearts and minds to the Word being spoken to them;
- Calling those present to conversion, inviting them to growth.

If a reader reflects on this, then they will feel a need to prepare well, to look up a good commentary or be part of a group that studies and prays the Sunday readings. Pray and Play or Look – the engagement of small children during the Eucharist is certainly creating a readiness for being agents of change in our children.

Other Parish Groups
The other faith-inspired groups that exist in the parish have valuable contributions to make if they are properly integrated and made to feel part of the parish family. How come we are

fairly at home with Taizé music but have small contact with Comhaltas? What is the parish participation expected of devotional groups like the charismatic and other prayer groups? Cell groups? Padre Pio prayer groups? Youth 2000, etc.?

Since all parish groups should be at the service of mission, one wonders how to integrate the above into a parish vision with a sense of belonging and meaning, a sense of mission in the local church. They are needed within the local church, not as a sideshow, however spiritually attractive that show might be! It is time to create new parish conversations that would call all the above into the liturgical life of the parish in a more participative way, to the enrichment of all.

The Family as Agent of Change

I referred already to the parish as the shelter for the domestic Church, the family. In the *Declaration on Christian Education* we read: 'It is through the family that they [the children] are gradually introduced into civic partnership with their fellow human beings and also with the People of God. Let parents then clearly recognise how vital a truly Christian family is for the life and development of God's people.'[9]

This Declaration is clearly stating that the family, the domestic Church, is called to participate in the transformation of society. The prevalence of new social problems arising from capitalist and socialist economies, relentless materialism and the ensuing poverty is a reality for many people today. How can the Christian family in the parish participate in the transformation that is needed? To quote Pope Paul VI: 'While very large areas of the population are unable to satisfy their primary needs, superfluous needs are ingeniously created. It can thus rightly be asked if in spite of all our conquests, [we are] not turning back against [ourselves] the results of [our] activity. Having rationally endeavoured to control nature, [are we] not now becoming the slave(s) of the objects [we make]?'[10]

Can we take a more reflective look at family life within the parish and ask ourselves, 'Are we slaves of the objects we make? Do we think that objects can provide us a sense of identity, can give us companionship? Offer us intimacy? Is our mindset focused on getting more and more? Do we slavishly soak in the adverts and in personalising the object, objectify the person?' In 1977 the Bishops of Applachia had this to say to their people:

Many times before, outside forces have attacked the mountain's dream. But never before was the attack so strong. Now it comes with cable TV, satellite communication, giant ribbons of highway driving into the guts of the land. The attack wants to teach people that happiness is what you buy – in soaps and drinks, in gimmicks and gadgets and that all of life is one big commodity market. It would be bad enough if the attack only tried to take the land, but it wants the soul too.[11]

The Family Needs to Recover its Soul
A person is a person with others. They need to hear the Gospel challenge to justice, peace, sharing, in the midst of a grasping society and be empowered to respond to the call of the Spirit to walk another way. Family is where reconciliation and forgiveness is experienced at depth. Family is teacher of right and wrong and nurtures moral maturity. Conscience is respected, formed and informed in the kitchen. Life-long conversation and story begin in the family. It is in the family that we learn to love and be loved. Sadly, in difficult family situations much of the above cannot and does not happen. But we would hope that in a parish no family is left in the loneliness of isolation, since a core family value is outreach to other families. Family will recover its soul in communion with other families.

> *The parish can create a space for families to come together to recover their soul.*

It is of the highest importance that families come together and devote themselves directly and by common agreement to transforming the very structures of society. Otherwise, families will become the first victims of the evils they saw being committed, but stood aside in silence or indifference.[12] It belongs to the laity, without waiting passively for orders and directives, to take the initiative freely and to infuse a Christian spirit into the mentality, customs, laws and structures of the community in which they live.[13]

It is possibly true that many families do not participate in the social mission of the Church because they have not made the connection between their faith and its expression in social action. The need to open the baptismal call to transform the world through transforming the local neighbourhood is a priority in the parish. This would call for Baptism to be celebrated at weekend Eucharist rather than privately so that the local community hears its call to live out Baptism in daily life.

Abuse of the Earth's Resources Affect the Family

Family life is being severely affected by the abuse of the world's resources. We are called to be stewards of creation (Genesis 17), not its destroyers. But today our very planet is threatened by our greed. In an unpublished article on the Eucharist and the Cosmos, Sean McDonagh SSC, quotes a preface written by ICEL in 1984 which describes beautifully the interrelatedness of all creation:

Blessed are you, strong and faithful God.
All your works, the height and the depth, echo the silent music of your praise.

In the beginning your Word summoned light; night
withdrew and creation dawned.
As ages passed unseen, waters gathered on the face of the
Earth and life appeared.
When the times had at last grown full and the earth had
ripened in abundance,
You created in your image humankind, the crown of all
creation.
You gave us breath and speech, that all the living might
find a voice to sing your praise.
So now, with all the power of heaven and earth, we chant
the ageless hymn to your glory.[14]

The question for us is: Do we want to have serious
conversations about these things? Can we even try to connect
our faith with our living and vice versa?

Parish on a Vision Quest

Clearly parish has the potential to be an agent of change. Should
parish see itself as an agent of catechesis, then, education in the
faith would lift all boats and the parish would build community
in ways people had never thought possible. Here the Parish
Pastoral Council, in Partnership with Parish Clergy, has a
crucial role to play as leader and planner of change.

Some years ago, while studying in the US, I had the privilege
of spending some time with the Lakota Indians in South
Dakota. These are people at one with creation, people who, at
regular intervals, take time out to go on a 'Vision Quest' when
they pray, meet with their guide and search for wisdom. What is
our Vision Quest for the parish? Is this not a kairos time when
we must stop, look, listen, reflect and decide on values that are
for the common good? Questions we might ask include:

- What was your most life-giving experience in your parish this
  year?

- What do you value most about your parish?
- If you could transform your parish what two things would you do to improve parish life?

Let me offer some suggestions for change in this area, so that we may better serve the needs of our people in the context of catechesis, evangelisation and community building.

1 My first suggestion is storytelling in small neighbourhood groups in host homes. A person is invited some weeks beforehand to write his/her story, or to just have headings to help tell it. Helpful guidelines could be given. I see this storytelling as a marvellous community builder – posing no threat, perpetuating no inequality and offering great possibilities for bonding and acceptance within a group.

   When we really listen to the story of another, when we enter as fully as possible into the world and experience of someone we presume to be a stranger, we will be changed. And even if we are not changed, our vision of the human has been expanded by every story we hear. We may discover in the end that the strange is not dangerous: empathy is.[15]

2 Following the above could come a session on 'Jesus, the Storyteller of God'. Meetings could be organised where the parables are explored and people make links and find wisdom and courage in his story. This is done simply. People hear the Word and are challenged to live out their baptismal call to build the Kingdom in their own milieu.

3 We need to stop having parents' meetings simply for First Communion and Confirmation. Much more necessary are meetings of parents and children beginning in First Class, where we can create a forum for family conversations that parents themselves do not seem empowered to initiate. We must survey parents and children when inviting senior classes for possible topics. A core group of parents and parish teams could be responsible for these gatherings.

Transition year students could facilitate the children's small groups. This generational mix will make a big difference. And don't forget the grandparents!

4 Same at post-primary level.
5 Eucharistic ministers and readers.
6 Sacred space for Advent/Lent.

Change is difficult for all of us. We all resist it. However, if we do not change, we die. This is the law of life. Let me outline some basic observations about change:[16]

1 All reality exhibits a pattern of life, death and rebirth. The process of life (growth) and death (breakdown) are always at work in every system or relationship.
2 Change is inevitable. Systems that do not consciously address changing conditions will be at the mercy of the agenda of others. Denying the existence of negative forces is a waste of energy.
3 Energy spent keeping something from happening is not available for positive use.
4 A focus on problem solving assures the generation of new problems.
5 Energy used in trying to restore what is breaking down is energy that is not available for building something new.
6 Persons are of supreme value.

At parish level one can easily detect stages of change. Let us outline four such stages: firstly, there is the identity search: people wonder who they are, what their identity is. Secondly, there is the value search: people begin to look at what is meaningful to them. Thirdly, they focus on what they need to achieve what is meaningful to them: the strategy search. Finally there is the method search: they concentrate on how they can achieve what they need to achieve.

Leadership

Paulo Freire in *The Pedagogy of the Oppressed* suggests that all persons have to be empowered to name the world and change it. I suggest that Pastoral Councils as local leaders, as agents of change, have to set up a dialogue in the local Church. This dialogue allows people to encounter each other and address experience and problems and possible changes out of their united reflections and action. Dialogue then becomes an act of creation. However, Freire insists that dialogue is not possible without the presence of a 'profound love for the world and for people'.[17] Without this love, we cannot enter into true dialogue and we will surely fail in courage and commitment to others. There will be little or no change. Humility, i.e. the acceptance of oneself as a learner, is sorely needed if one is to grow in trust through dialogue. Out of this trust, as Freire indicates, will emerge the birth of critical thinking linked to action without fear of risks or consequences.

> *Priests and people must work together, and not be afraid of each other, in order for a parish to become a community.*

Here we have exciting possibilities for Parish Pastoral Councils in partnership with parish clergy.

- Gather the people;
- Set up a dialogue;
- Encourage the formation of Neighbourhood Christian Communities;
- Be humble and truthful in your approach;
- Listen, reflect and make decisions with the people, not for them;
- Allow aspiration and inspiration to flow, but make sure that you catch and hold it;

• Take action with the people, not for them or in spite of them.

This is a mammoth task and will not happen overnight. But many, especially young people, are waiting for this kind of dialogue to begin. Are we going to let people walk away in indifference or will we, with a new respect, coax them to new conversations? Have they not a right to be a voice in the story of the local community? Do they not have a right to a deeper sense of belonging, a right to be part of the transformation that we all hope for? Haven't our youth a right to a youth Pastoral Council instead of a token voice on an adult one, or perhaps none at all?

So we have no right to read these suggestions and go away without taking any action. Let us go away with our heart focused on setting up a conversation in our parishes about how the community spirit can be improved. Let us go away intent on nourishing our own faith by learning more about it, reflecting on how it can be deepened, how we can reach out to others and how we can meet Christ.

May we meet God many times – at home, in our workplace, in our neighbourhood and among our friends. And may we have wonderful, challenging, maybe dangerous, conversations with Him so that our parish may come fully alive and truly be an agent of change.

Notes

1 Groome, 2003, p. 112.
2 Proceedings of the Santo Domingo Conference of Latin American Bishops, n. 58.
3 Michael Hines, cit. in M. Fischer and M.M. Raley, 2002, p. 90.
4 General Directory of Catechesis, B. Huebsch, 2001, pp. 257–8.
5 Enda Lyons, 1993, p. 20.
6 Fischer, M. and Raley, M.M., 2002, p. 128.
7 Michael Paul Gallagher, 2003, p. 171.
8 Brendan Kenneally, 'Salvation', *The Stranger Collection*.
9 Vatican II, *Gravissimum Educationis, Declaration on Christian Education*, n. 3.
10 Pope Paul VI, Octogesima Adveniens, n. 9.
11 Pastoral Letter of the Bishops of Appalachia, n. 20.
12 Lineamenta: The Role of the Christian Family, n. 44.
13 Octogesima Adveniens, n. 48.
14 Unpublished article. Cited with author's permission.
15 H. Anderson et al., 2004, p. 107.
16 M. Fischer and M.M. Raley, 2002, p. 62.
17 Freire, 2000, pp. 88–9.

Bibliography

Anderson, H. et al., *Mutuality Matters, Family, Faith and Just Love* (New York: Sheed and Ward, 2004).
Darcy-Berube, F., *Religious Education at a Crossroads* (New York: Paulist Press, 1995).
Fischer, M. and Raley, M.M. (eds) *Four Ways to Build More Effective Parish Councils* (New Haven, CT: Twenty-Third Publications, 2004).
Freire, P., *Pedagogy of the Oppressed* (New York: Continuum, 2000).
Fuellenbach, J., *Church Community for the Kingdom* (New York: Orbis, 2002).
Gallagher, Michael Paul, *Clashing Symbols* (London: Darton, Longman and Todd, 2003).
Groome, T. and Horrell, H.D., *Horizon and Hope, The Future of Religious Education* (New York: Paulist, 2003).
Groome, T., *What Makes us Catholic, Eight Gifts for Life* (New York: Harper Collins, 2003).
Huebsch, B., *Directory of Catechesis in Plain English* (New Haven, CT: Twenty Third Publications, 2001).
Lyons, E., *Partnership in Parish* (Dublin: Veritas, 1993).
Roberto, J. (ed.) *Growing in Faith: A Family Source Book* (New York: Don Bosco Multimedia, 1990).

Good Celebration of Liturgy:

A Primary Source of Evangelisation

Seamus Ryan

Introduction

When this topic was suggested to me by the editor, I spent a long time thinking about it and wondering about a possible approach. I had just been reading Fr Diarmuid O Murchu's book *Our World in Transition* where he boldly endeavours to make sense of our Christian faith in a changing world. He sees our traditional faith as too cocooned in a narrow ecclesiastical mould and appeals for a greater attention to what the creative Spirit of God is doing in the midst of creation and in the lives of all peoples. Our spirituality needs to be more creation-centred, as our old Celtic spirituality undoubtedly was, with its almost playful sense of joy in the numinous presence of Christ suffused throughout all creation.

> *We must arise from our cocooned existence and come to an awareness of what the creative Spirit of God is doing in the midst of creation and in the lives of all the peoples.*

While I was mulling over this, I thought of an old friend of mine, John Normoyle, a carpenter farmer from Lissycasey in Co. Clare, who used to offer a few profound words of advice to members of his family when he saw them burdened by something: 'Stand back from it!' So, taking those wise words to heart, I begin with a few preliminary reflections which I offer as a kind of backdrop to our main subject.

I am encouraged in looking at this wider context of the Eucharist by some words of John Paul II in his encyclical on the Eucharist. He is reflecting on the many locations in which he has celebrated the Eucharist in his various trips around the world. Yet he is always aware that even in the humblest of places, Mass is still celebrated 'on the altar of the world'. The Pope is significantly echoing the poetic language of Teilhard de Chardin SJ, who saw evolution as God's ongoing work of creation. In the bread and 'fruit of the vine' he found a deep cosmic dimension to the Eucharist, and helped open our eyes anew to an earth and heavens full of God's glory.

The Altar of Planet Earth amid the Immensities of Space and Time

I would ask you to capture in your mind's eye that extraordinary photograph the American astronauts took of our world back in 1969: planet Earth rotating against the blackness of space. It is a picture of great evocative power, stirring deep emotions in the human heart; compassion for our vulnerable world hanging there amid the immensities of space; thoughts of interdependence and a sense of belonging with all those who share with us our common home; recalling those early verses of Genesis (recited by one of the astronauts) in the joyful conviction that God no less now than then acknowledges that our world is good, indeed very good, and delights in all that was made (Gen 1:31).

I like to look at that shimmering blue planet that holds everything so precious to us, recalling that a much later book of the same Bible begins consciously with the same words, 'In the beginning ...', and goes on to tell us that 'God so loved this world that he gave his only Son' (Jn 3:16) and that the same Jesus gave his life 'to gather together into one the scattered children of God' (11:52). It gives us a sense of perspective when we remember that some of those 'scattered children' walked on this earth five million years or more before Jesus came among us. The same prologue of John's Gospel sees every man coming into the world as connected with Jesus, 'enlightened' by him, and goes on confidently to proclaim: 'All things were made through him, and without him was not anything made that was made' (1:3). Our universe, whose connectedness with Jesus is affirmed here, has been around, or so the scientists tell us, for 46,000 million years!

It is not that long ago since Dr James Ussher, Protestant Archbishop of Armagh, and a reputable scholar, proudly defended his thesis that the world was created by God in the year 4004 BC at nine o'clock in the morning! How differently we see things now just a few centuries later.

Incarnation: Homo Capax Dei (Men and Women the Creatures God could Become)

'Stand back from it'. Forty years ago when I was involved in post-graduate work in Germany I gained a fresh perspective from the great Karl Rahner SJ, who over a semester enthralled his audience with his insights on issues relating to Creation and Incarnation, especially in the context of an evolving world.

> *Men and women are more than the rational animals of Aristotle's thinking. They are the creatures God could become.*

He took as his starting point the old Latin axiom: *Bonum est diffusivum sui* - Real goodness always wants to share itself. It is God's plan to share the wealth of divine nature with creatures. God will do it (perhaps in the only way it can be done) by becoming a creature himself. And so God arranges for a creature to emerge in the process of evolution over long aeons of time, until at last there stands upon the earth a creature with the capacity to know and to love, a creature who is called to respond lovingly to the Creator and to his fellow creatures, but also a creature who is free and might not so respond.

I remember Rahner recalling a piece of sculpture he had seen in some old cathedral in Europe that showed the Creator fashioning the head of Adam. But the divine sculptor is not looking at the face of Adam at all as he fashions his subject. No, he is looking across the room at a figure of Jesus. What the Father is fashioning, says Rahner, is a creature that God can become (*Capax Dei*), a creature that God in fact one day did become - Jesus of Nazareth. Men and women then are more than the rational animals of Aristotle's thinking. Could this be who they are - the creatures God could become? Is there some hint of this in the first page of the Bible when it tells us that 'God created man in his own image; male and female he created them' (Gen.1:17)?

Our faith has always told us that God is present somehow in every created thing: in the rock, the tree, the mountain and the stars. But God could never become a rock, a mountain or a star. Yet we can point to a human being and say, 'There is God'. God took on a human face in the child born in Bethlehem. But our Christian faith also hints at some kind of *ongoing* incarnation in the human race. Because of Christmas, because of Easter, is it the wish of the risen Lord to be birthed in every human heart, so that we can say in some very real sense that Jesus looks out through the eyes of every child, every man and woman (Matthew 25)?

Called to Share in the Joy of God

At the heart of the mystery of God there is this mutual joy of the Father in the Son, and the Son in the Father. As disciples of Jesus we are caught up into that same mutual delight which is often described by the saints as being beyond words. In the final discourse of Jesus at the last supper we read those remarkable words: 'As the Father has loved me, so I have loved you. Remain in my love ... I have told you this so that my own joy may be in you, and your joy may be complete' (Jn 15:9-11). Later in the great priestly prayer John records Jesus speaking directly to the Father: 'I have given them the glory you gave to me, so that they may be one as we are one, with me in them, and you in me ... And I have loved them as much as you have loved me' (17:24).

Jesus had a delight in people, finding a joy in their very existence.

The joy that the Father found in Jesus at his baptism ('This is my beloved Son in whom I delight' Mk 1:11), Jesus finds in all those whom the Father has called into existence, made in his image and likeness. It is clear from the Gospels that Jesus had a delight in people, finding a joy in their very existence. He worked his first miracle to help sustain the joy of a little couple in the country church of Cana and is so often found in the midst of all kinds of festive occasions sharing food and drink with people. It is God's delight to be with the children of men, a delight that Jesus showed in the company of saint and sinner.

This must have been a most attractive feature of his life, the easy spontaneity of his love. You never get the impression that Jesus loved people because he felt obliged to or because it was expected of him, as might be our reluctant kind of moralising. Think of him standing with the woman who had been so mercilessly caught in the very act of adultery, facing down her accusers. Or on the side of the poor man with the withered hand being used as a pawn by scheming lawyers more withered in heart than any hand could be. We are not told the experience of Jesus' love to which the woman of ill repute in the house of Simon the Pharisee was responding. It is good to imagine that for once maybe even Jesus was outdone by her spontaneous gesture of loving gratitude. Though judged and despised by the company around her, she washes his feet with her tears, kisses them, dries them with her hair and anoints them with ointment. Those who waited for Jesus to show embarrassment at her sensual indulgence waited in vain.

I like to tell people that God smiles on them, has a joy in them, even laughs at us that we might learn to laugh at ourselves! Sadly too often their own life's experience gets in the way of allowing them to think of God in any such terms. There are few things that give me greater comfort than coming across an old man or woman who has grown through life into the strong conviction that they are truly loved by God. Fr Brian Greene shares with us an experience from a recent prayer meeting: 'An old lady in her eighties told us that life for her was becoming happier every day. We asked her why. And she said very simply, 'Because I have come to realise that God loves me. For most of my life I thought I had to do things for God. Now at last I see that the starting point is in letting God do things for me. He is teaching me more and more to love myself.' That shut up everyone'.[1]

There is no denying that genuine sanctity is consistently marked by a joy that can only be a gift of God. 'A sad saint is indeed a sorry saint' – a remark attributed to Francis de Sales. Timothy Radcliffe OP reminds us that, according to his fellow Dominican, Thomas Aquinas, 'happiness' is one of God's names. To be touched by God's joy is something beyond human definition. He quotes the closing words of GK Chesterton in *Orthodoxy*:

There was something Jesus hid from all men when he went up a mountain to pray. There was something that he covered constantly by abrupt silence or impetuous isolation. There was some one thing that was too great for God to show when he walked upon our earth; and I have sometimes fancied that it was his mirth.[2]

GK Chesteron and Ronald Knox, converts and contemporaries in the first half of the twentieth century, were in different ways literary giants in the world of religious writing of their time. We have seen how Chesterton, in the closing lines of *Orthodoxy*, voices his own conviction about the joy that is at the heart of God. In a similar vein Ronald Knox, in the final lines of his well-known work *Enthusiasm*, a study of the phenomenon of ecstasy in religion, comes out unambiguously to identify enthusiasm and its spontaneous joy as one of the most attractive traits in a religious person, or indeed in any human being.

If there is a lack of vitality in our Sunday worship, could it be that many in the assembly do not have that joy in God so evident in the old lady in the nursing home? Is Fr O Murchu right in thinking that our traditional faith is too cocooned in a narrow ecclesiastical mould that cannot do full justice to the ineffable mystery that is God? If many of our young people are absent from the Sunday Eucharist, could one reason be the evident lack of a shared enthusiasm? And as for spontaneity in our worship ... not much place for that, or even room, amidst the pews. Yet maybe, just maybe, an attractive lady with abundant tears and kisses descending on the hapless parish priest of St Matthew's with her flowing locks and exotic ointments might yet stir our 'frozen' people!

John Paul II and the 'New Evangelisation'

But it is time to return more immediately to our theme: liturgy and Evangelisation. Pope John Paul often referred, particularly in the decade leading up to the millennium, to this dimension of liturgy when he sounded a clarion call for New Evangelisation. In *Redemptoris Missio* he envisages three different contexts in which the Gospel is preached:

1 Where the Church's missionary activity addresses people or groups where Christ and his Gospel are not known ... this is *missio ad gentes* in the proper sense of the term.
2 Christian communities where there are adequate and solid ecclesial structures. They are fervent in their faith and in Christian living. They bear witness to the Gospel in their surroundings.
3 There is an intermediate situation, particularly in countries with ancient Christian roots, and occasionally in the younger Churches as well, where entire groups of the baptised have lost a living sense of the faith, or even no longer consider themselves members of the Church, and live a life far removed from Christ and his Gospel. In this case what is needed is a New Evangelisation.[3]

The struggle of faith goes on within people and not just between them.

Most commentators would agree that the two last categories, a people fervent in their faith and those who have lost a living sense of faith, are found to co-exist in Ireland and generally in our Western World. People who are committed Christians and people who are indifferent or have drifted from the Church can be found in the same villages and even in the same families. Describing the religious situation in Ireland back in 1983, Fr Liam Ryan had this to say: 'Conflicting values and beliefs are held even by the same person. The struggle of faith goes on within people and not just between them.' Around the same time Michael Paul Gallagher was contending that 'the main danger to religion in Ireland is not unbelief but shallow belief, a religion without challenge and without depth, on the margin of life'.[4]

The evidence of some recent surveys suggests that there may still be a strong measure of faith in most Irish people, even without total fidelity to Church doctrine or laws. Many who do not belong may still believe. What is undeniably true is that on the fringe of almost every congregation at Sunday Mass there will be a number of those who find themselves somewhere along the spectrum of John Paul's categories above ... outsiders, seekers and latecomers ... not too unlike the Magi of old![5] They may even outnumber the loyal faithful at Christmas time.

Some commentators have expressed surprise at John Paul's explicit linking of evangelisation and liturgy: 'The total evangelisation I have in mind will naturally have its highest point in an intense liturgical life ...'.[6] They argue that evangelisation is about bringing people to Church; it is not what takes place in Church. Writing about the US scene Thomas Rausch SJ says that it is not uncommon for people to 'shop' for a parish that meets their needs. He quotes Archbishop Weakland as saying that those who represent the largest group in his archdiocese of Milwaukee are looking for vital parishes with good liturgies and preaching and programmes to help introduce their children to the riches of the faith.[7] Of course, as Rausch points out, in the United States of fifty years ago Catholics had a great loyalty to their neighbourhood communities, strong ethnic enclaves in which they grew up, lived and died. Those neighbourhoods are gone now and that kind of social cohesion has long disappeared.

'Shopping for a parish' that suits one's needs is not unknown in Dublin and elsewhere, though it may not be as common in urban areas in Ireland due to the strong identity that is still found in many places between the local parish and the old neighbourhoods. Rausch points out that the liturgy in these 'select' parishes in the US may take at least an hour and a half. If a Dublin parish were to opt for extra time of that kind, my intuition tells me that, no matter how good the liturgy might be, the 'Dubs' would be marking it down as a Church to be avoided on a Sunday morning!

Witnesses to the Faith: The Front Line of Evangelisation

It remains undoubtedly true that the front line of evangelisation will be found beyond the walls of the Church in the many ways that people share their faith with others. The Gospel is above all proclaimed by witness, as Paul VI stressed in a memorable passage in *Evangelii Nuntiandi:*

> Take a Christian or a handful of Christians who, in the midst of their community, show their capacity for understanding and acceptance, their sharing of life and destiny with other people, their solidarity with the efforts of all for whatever is noble and good. Let us suppose that, in addition, they radiate in an altogether simple and unaffected way their faith in values that go beyond current values, and their hope in something that is not seen and that one would not dare to imagine. Through this wordless witness these Christians stir up irresistible questions in the hearts of those who see how they live: Why are they like this? Why do they live in this way? What or who is it that inspires them? Why are they in our midst? Such a witness is already a silent proclamation of the Good News and a very powerful and effective one. Here we have an initial act of evangelisation.[8]

It is necessary that the Church becomes more resourceful in seeking out new and imaginative patterns in pre-evangelising.

One is reminded of the directions Francis of Asissi is reported to have given to his early friars as he sent them out to evangelise: 'Go out and preach the Gospel. Use words only if they are needed.' The *Tablet* reported recently on a move to seek the beatification of Charles de Foucauld. From his lonely hermitage in Tamanrasset in the Sahara he sought to pioneer a novel presence of the Gospel in the harsh environment of the desert, a modern version of the Baptist seeking to prepare a way for the Lord in a milieu decidedly hostile to Christian influence. In this post-modern age where we have become increasingly secularised (at least in the West) there is undoubtedly a greater need than ever for the Church to be more resourceful in seeking out new and imaginative paths in pre-evangelising.

Faith and Friendship

There are many devout parents who continue to be loyal to their Sunday Mass, and agonise over their grown-up offspring who no longer come to Church. It may happen that their son or daughter has a good experience at the occasional liturgy they attend (a Christmas Mass, a baptism, a wedding, a funeral) and begin to frequent the Church again. Perhaps the first step may not be through the doors of a Church. Their greatest need may be some form of *pre-evangelisation,* perhaps along the lines of friendly contact with people of their own age or young parents like themselves whose quality of faith and life is deeply impressive in the way Paul VI described above, and they find their own lives gently questioned. It shows the importance of fostering small faith communities in every way we can in our parishes. Many of the groups are there; they can be helped by catechists and other lay leaders and priests to grow into the mature faith needed today.

Liturgy as Evangelisation

The Constitution on the Sacred Liturgy of Vatican II spells out the importance of liturgy for evangelisation in its opening paragraphs:

> For it is through the liturgy, especially the divine Eucharistic sacrifice, that the work of our redemption is exercised. The liturgy is thus the outstanding means by which the faithful can express in their lives, and manifest to others, the mystery of Christ and the real nature of the true Church ... Day by day the liturgy builds up those within the Church into the Lord's holy temple ... At the same time the liturgy marvellously fortifies the faithful in their capacity to preach Christ.[9]

Sunday Mass must be a priority focus for the energy and resources of the parish.

Few will question that the main exposure of the 'faithful' to the Gospel remains the Sunday Mass. For the regular faithful it is an opportunity to hear the word of God and celebrate the Eucharist, the source and summit of the Church's life and activity. The Eucharist, particularly when it is celebrated well, can strike a chord with the occasional people on the fringe of the assembly, perhaps awakening in them a yearning for greater depth to their lives. Those for whom the Church is quite marginal are sometimes to be found at a funeral or wedding, where personal involvement is more easily presumed.

It comes as no surprise that Donal Harrington in his recent book, *The Welcoming Parish*, argues persuasively that the Sunday Mass should be a priority focus for the energy and resources of the parish. Before we make this investment in the enrichment of our Sunday Eucharist, he requires one indispensable precondition: 'We ourselves - meaning the familiar faces who regularly attend - *must transform our own way of seeing the Mass.*'[10]

We must Transform our Way of Seeing the Mass

A bold statement! He goes on to explain. The most common name for the Mass amongst the first Christians was 'the breaking of bread'. They did not 'go to Mass'. They gathered to 'break bread together'. Above all, the Eucharist was an action that the people did *together* in memory of Jesus as he had asked them to do. Vatican II strove mightily to recover this sense of our Sunday Eucharist as worship that was done together. Unfortunately we have become accumstomed over generations to speak of what we gather to do on Sunday as 'getting Mass' or 'hearing Mass'. People will enquire from the sacristan: 'Which of the priests is *saying* the funeral Mass?' Here our language betrays the hidden measure of our clericalism and the liturgy reduced to something that can evidently be 'said' or 'read'.

How long is it going to take before the baptised truly own their sharing in the priesthood of Christ and come to accept that they are truly offering themselves with Christ in the Eucharist?

The Council of Trent (1545-1563) provides an interesting example of the dominant role of the priest in the celebration of Mass at that time. A number of bishops came up with an extraordinary proposal: Would it be better, they suggested, if the laity just stayed at home and let the priest say his Mass without the distraction of a congregation? The proposal was rejected, but it does show how far the Mass in appearance had strayed from the Eucharistic assembly of the early Church when priest and people came together to listen to the Word of God, and join in the 'breaking of bread' in memory of Jesus. People forget, if they ever knew, that prior to the liturgical movement of the past half-century, the priest celebrated the great Easter Vigil on his own (or with a solitary server) in a locked Church on Holy Saturday morning, eventually opening the doors when the people came for Mass.

The Sunday Mass is still popularly referred to as our 'Sunday obligation' where the accent falls on Mass as a duty, a far cry from the joyful *sursum corda* of the preface of the mass. Even the great colourful feast-days of Catholic tradition became known as 'the holy days of obligation'. It was widely accepted that you had 'done' what you were obligated to do if you arrived for the Gospel, even if you left before the communion.

Today, forty years after Vatican II, many are still in thrall to that culture and its language. People are familiar now with the word 'liturgy' but unaware that the original word *leitourgia* is made up of two Greek words (*laos* – people and *ergon* – work) and literally means 'a work done by the people'. 'Liturgy,' says Gabe Huck, 'is not done *for* people, or *to* people, or merely *in the presence of* people. The people do it.'[11] The Eucharist is not something that is done by others before an audience; it is the kind of human activity that does not allow for a division into 'those who do' and 'those who are done to'. Eucharist is simply an action that the people do together. But how long will it take for this to penetrate into the hearts and minds of the faithful if the Eucharist, as they experience it, is not something they are doing together? How long will it take until the baptised truly *own* their sharing in the priesthood of Christ, and come to accept that they are all truly offering themselves with Christ in the Eucharist?

To the question: who celebrates the Eucharist? There is only one answer: The body of Christ, the faith community assembled together. As St Paul reminds us, the body has many parts:

energies, voices, hands, feet and so on to do the body's work. So the assembly as *the primary minister* needs many specialised full-time and part-time ministries; bishops and priests who preside, deacons, ushers, readers, Eucharistic ministers, cantors, choirs, musicians ... people for the many tasks which will require talents and training. But how long will it take until this will become the mindset of the assembly – that they are in a real sense con-celebrants, and that the ordained minister or priest is the one who presides?

Nobody has cared more passionately about the Church at worship than Robert Hovda, who has written most eloquently about this dimension:

> Ritual tradition assigns different texts, gestures and actions to different participants – to the congregation, to the presider, to various other roles, and to the assembly as a whole. A good presider will resist the temptation to do everything, as will other leaders. And all the leaders will see their roles as enabling the assembly to celebrate ... This flourishing of different and many roles of leadership is a great accomplishment – part of the monumental task of making our Sunday celebration again the people's *own*.[12]

Full, Conscious and Active Participation – Vatican II
The great seminal statement of paragraph 14 of *Sacrosanctum Concilium, The Constitution on the Liturgy,* puts it so well: 'The Church earnestly desires that all the faithful be led to that full, conscious and active participation in liturgical celebrations which is demanded by the very nature of the liturgy. Such participation by the Christian people, as 'a chosen race, a royal priesthood, a holy nation, a purchased people' (I Peter 2:9), is their right and duty by reason of their baptism'.

> *The aim to be pursued, before all else, in the prioritising of a good liturgy is the full and active participation by all the people.*

Full, conscious and active participation! It can be taken as a kind of a code for the whole document: it is *the nature of the liturgy* to be done by the people. All this is rooted in our baptism; if we have been 'christened', if we have put on Christ, then celebrating the liturgy as our full, conscious and active work is a right that cannot be taken away from us. It is something in our bones we want to do. The same paragraph 14 continues: 'In the restoration and promotion of the sacred liturgy, this full and active participation by all the people is the aim to be considered before all else; for it is the primary and indispensable source from which the faithful are to derive the true Christian spirit. Therefore through the needed programme of instruction, pastors of souls must zealously strive to achieve it in all their pastoral work.'

There you have it: *the aim to be pursued before all else* in the promotion of good liturgy is 'the full and active participation by all the people.' And why? Because full and active participation by all the people in the liturgy '*is the primary and indispensable source* from which the faithful will derive *the true Christian spirit'.* Enabling the faithful to catch the 'true Christian spirit' will always be a high priority for evangelisation. But how do we make this happen in our Sunday liturgy? I list what Gabe Huck singles out as four of the most important tasks for any parish interested in promoting public worship of a consistently high standard:

1 Build and renovate buildings that will allow for the 'full and active participation' of all the assembly. If the worship space says 'audience', most congregations will be likely to act like an audience, i.e. like spectators.

2 Make sure that all those who exercise a liturgical ministry, priests especially, understand themselves to be members of the assembly exercising a service to the assembly and to the Church, which in turn is a service to our Lord for the life of the world.

3 The crucial importance of music and song. 'Liturgical action is given a more noble form when sacred rites are solemnised in song ... with the active participation of the people'. Music and song 'express prayerfulness, promote solidarity, and enrich sacred rites with heightened solemnity.'(*Sacrosanctum Concilium*, n.112). Today, forty years after the Council, there is a much stronger call for congregational singing, and an important role for the cantor. The choir remains at all times an important part of the assembly with its own distinctive liturgical role. 'It should never displace, or dominate the rightful song of the assembly.'[13] Some liturgists insist that the singing of the assembly is the most important music that ever occurs in worship. This is what Robert Duggan has to say: 'As long as large numbers of Catholics remain mute when the liturgy calls for the assembly to sing, true liturgical renewal will elude us. No single element will make as much difference as the empowerment of the faithful. We need a better repertoire, better training, better song leaders.'[14]

4 Seek the primary objects before the secondary: a worthy book, worthy vessels, bread that is bread to every one of the senses, and wine that is wine for all.[15]

It is time to turn our attention to particular moments of Mass where the evangelising dimension of our Sunday Eucharist can be greatly enhanced.

A Team to Plan and Help with each Weekend Mass

In our parish we have not had a happy experience with a liturgy group over the years. In the planning for a clearly defined occasion like Christmas or Holy Week we seem to manage quite well. But the group foundered with the nigh impossible task in 'ordinary time' of coping each weekend with the variety of Masses (traditional choir, folk Mass, children's Mass, quiet style of Mass), and especially with the variety (and idiosyncrasies!) of three different celebrants.

We are experimenting at the moment with a small *liturgy group* which has a kind of overseeing function over a number of *teams*, each of which helps to plan and coordinate with the presiding priest one of the six Masses over the weekend. When we appealed for volunteers to make up these teams more than sixty people offered to help! As was expected people signed up for the Mass which they normally attend, with the result that some Masses were oversubscribed. We are in the process of dealing with the inevitable teething problems, but on the whole the venture has been very well received and many people have been delighted to see and hear a great variety of faces and accents instead of the all too familiar few.

It is essential that the individual celebrant is actively engaged with the team and all be committed to the principle of 'full and active participation'. The fact that the event was over-subscribed has turned out to be the greatest blessing. Each group is still small enough to generate a sense of ownership of the venture, while the many new faces help to convey to the whole assembly that they (the people) are all responsible for the quality of the celebration.

Our experiment has led us to the helpful insight that the primary responsibility of the *parish liturgy committee* is not a *hands on* involvement with a particular Sunday Mass or other liturgical occasion. This should be left to the group who have a connection with that Mass as mentioned above, and usually include a member of the committee. The liturgy committee itself has a different focus – the full range of the parish's liturgical life. This will include long range planning, evaluating liturgies, promoting the formation and education of liturgical ministers, shaping the environment for a particular liturgy, budgeting for future needs etc.

At parish level we are slow in facing up to the hard fact that all this will require training in the leadership skills required. Liturgy is an art with the power to transform hearts, lives and communities. Art needs artists, and we need to identify in the community those with artistic skills in music, ritual movement and environmental art. We could begin by looking at the talent available today in the drama departments of our schools.[16]

There is no reason why the importance of a *team* should not apply beyond Sunday to occasions like a funeral or wedding Mass. The team can be quite small, maybe no more than two people with the priest involved. I am thinking of the debacle I personally experienced at a recent funeral, when members of the bereaved family tried unsuccessfully to play a song from their own CD player at the end of the Mass. About four members of the family raced up to the sanctuary in succession, and the ensuing chaos effectively robbed the liturgy of its inherent power to help a family cope with the pain of grief. There is nothing more vital to good liturgy than adequate preparation, and this is best assured where we work together as a team with attention to detail and to quality.

A Welcoming Assembly

Donal Harrington, in his aforementioned book, finds the most life-giving initiatives in parish life today around the issue of *welcome*.[17] Many of the children and parents who come to new programmes for baptism, communion or confirmation are not Mass goers, but the programme links them with parish at very special moments in their family life. Their experience of Church is not 'being told what to do' as if the journey to the sacrament were a kind of obstacle course to be negotiated, but hopefully an experience of joy, welcome and warmth.

The most life-giving initiatives in parish life today are found around the issue of welcome.

The priests of my generation are often hesitant in acknowledging the merits of contemporary catechesis and products such as the *Alive-O* programme. Sometimes we carry a lot of unhelpful baggage from the past. I desperately want to belong to the new style of welcoming Church I see emerging, but I surprise myself when acting out of the more authoritarian Church in which I grew up as a child, a seminarian and a young priest. It is hardly surprising that many people experience our Church as giving out contradictory signals. We are slow learners. We forget that the Eucharist was the last of a long line of suppers ('the *last* supper') to which Jesus insisted on welcoming the sinner as well as the saint.

And so we are learning again that a sense of welcome should pervade the whole Eucharist. The way people are welcomed is itself evangelising. It will be there from the start in the friendly face that meets them on entering the Church and helps provide the missalette or the hymn sheet. When somebody else other than the priest introduces the Eucharist, it is another gentle hint that this is not just 'Father's Mass' but something we do together.

A procession through the Church should be the norm, helping to draw people into the celebration. It must never be forgotten that liturgy calls for the engagement of our bodies as well as our minds and hearts. 'We have to help the faithful to overcome a legacy of passivity', says Robert Duggan. 'They need to be 'stretched' in their ritual repertoire of gestures, processions and other elements that call for the engagement of our bodies ... ordinary Catholics need to know in their bones that their full participation in the ritual action is crucial for its succcess. You will know this is working when more people arrive on time and fewer leave early.'[18] A reminder that we have yet a long journey to travel.

But a beginning has been made. It is to be hoped that simple acts of welcome by designated members of the assembly plant a seed of community in us. Gathering and welcoming are not just preliminaries to the real work of worship; at the heart of all genuine hospitality in the assembly lies an attentivess that acknowledges the 'worth-ship' of each individual. Pope Paul VI makes it a requirement of good liturgy that we recognise the presence of the Lord not only in the priest but also in the people to whom he ministers. This offers the best antidote to thinking of the sacraments as something the priest 'brings' with him; sacraments cannot be 'brought', they can only be celebrated with those in whom the liturgy already recognises a presence of the Lord.

The Liturgy of the Word
It will be evident that proclaiming and preaching the Scriptures lies at the heart of the evangelising power of the liturgy. The words of Karl Barth still carry a great deal of wisdom: preaching should be done with the Bible in one hand and the daily newspaper in the other, i.e. attending to the Scripture text and the context of people's lives in a way that engages at a deep level the attention and faith of the people.

> *Attending to the Scriptural text and the context of people's lives in a way that engages at a deep level the attention and faith of the people is crucial for a relevant liturgy.*

Apart from the Sunday Mass the homily can be a significant moment for the *New Evangelisation* at weddings and funerals where the congregation will include a fair number of the not so faithful, the outsiders, the seekers, many of those people on the margins for whom Jesus had a particular welcome. The General

Instruction on the Roman Missal alerts us to the pastoral possibilities of such occasions: 'Pastors should, moreover, take special account of those who are present at a liturgical celebration or hear the Gospel only because of a funeral. These may be non-Catholics or Catholics who never or rarely share in the Eucharist or who have apparently lost the faith. Priests are, after all, ministers of Christ's Gospel for all people.[xix]

American liturgical scholar John F. Baldovin SJ recommends two spiritual qualities for all those who have some kind of leadership role in the Liturgy of the Word at our Sunday Eucharist: *humility* and *reverence*. If the ministers of the Word are not humbled by the fact that Christ is really present in his word and that God is actually speaking to the assembly through them, can we expect others to appreciate God's Word as the most fundamental source of our faith? Readers of the Word should bring to their ministry a kind of 'enthusiastic humility'.

Secondly the General Instruction makes it clear that one of the ways in which Christ is present here is in the midst of the gathered assembly. This implies that the priest and other ministers need to show *reverence* not only for the liturgy but also for their fellow members of the body of Christ. The priest has a very delicate role in the liturgy: he represents Christ to the assembly (which is the body of Christ), and he represents the body of Christ to God. During the liturgy of the Word when the priest is not speaking, he should lead by listening. If he does not turn attentively to face the reader, or otherwise show that he is listening (John Paul was an outstanding example), he is sending a subtle lesson to the rest of the assembly that it is not important for them to listen either.[20]

The Homily: Three Tips from the Liturgist

In conclusion, the professor of liturgy at the Jesuit School of Theology in Cambridge (USA) offers a few wise words about preaching:

I offer here only three points. First, it is important to remember that the liturgical homily is a way to connect a particular assembly's experience with God's living word. Second, this means that the preacher must have a good 'feel' for each assembly. He is not merely offering an exegesis or explanation of the Scriptures – although that prior work needs to be done in his office and in his prayer. Third, there is no substitute for being an interesting person. Preachers need to read (fiction, non-fiction and poetry); they need to go to movies and concerts and watch television; they need to listen to music of many sorts. In other words, they need to be thoroughly engaged both in reflection on Scripture and theology, and in the culture in which they live. They should have something significant to say.[21]

The Homily: Three Insights from the Scholar

Timothy Radcliffe sees a way forward for our preaching at Mass in the close bond which theology forges today between the presence of Jesus in Word and Eucharist. Each belongs to what Karl Raher calls 'the one whole Word of God.' Radcliffe sees three moments in the story of the Last Supper that need to find a clear echo in our preaching at Mass. I hope my brief summary does him justice.[22]

1 'Jesus reached out to the disciples in their individual puzzlement and confusion.' We must reach out to humanity in its distance from the Gospel. We must face their doubts, their questions, often found in our own hearts too. This has to be the beginning of our preaching.

2 'He gathers the disciples into communion.' This begins with a commitment to telling the truth. There is no love without truth. The preacher must be able to tell the story of Jesus in

a way that enables the congregation to recognise in it their own joys and struggles, victories and defeats, agony and ecstasy. Our words must be born of a conversation, a love-making, a language which resonates with their life. There is no truth without love. Only this kind of preaching can gather into communion.

3 'He reaches beyond community for the fullness of the Kingdom.' The community gathered around the altar is a sign of the Kingdom. But not yet the Kingdom ... at every Eucharist we are challenged to reach out for the Kingdom by taking down the defences we erect to exclude people, to keep out the stranger. Jesus stretches forward to the Kingdom which is glimpsed but always lies beyond the grasp of our words. The preacher lives within that space, begging for the enlightening word or image. 'We have too many words with too much noise in them, we could use fewer words with more silence in them.' (*Barbara B. Taylor*). We need poets and artists, those singers of the transcendant, to bring us to the edge of what can be said.

A Preacher's Recipe for a Homilist: Poet, Lunatic, Lover

I recall something a celebrated Protestant preacher wrote half a century ago; 'the religious man or woman,' he said, is a 'queer mixture' of three persons, 'the poet, the lunatic, the lover'.[23]

It takes a fair measure of *lunacy* in a preacher to seek to bridge the gap that separates so many of our contemporaries from the Gospel amid the near disappearance of a Christian culture. There is something of the foolishness of the Cross in reaching out to humanity in its distance from the Gospel. The doubts we have to face are also within ourselves. 'True preaching is like *making love* to the congregation, and to every soul in it.' I like that quotation from John Donne, Anglican poet and preacher: 'Every Eucharistic prayer when it moves into the narrative of institution begins with some equivalent of the old

Roman Canon: *Qui pridie quam pateretur* (on the day before he suffered)'. They all in turn echo the words with which John begins his account of the Last Supper and the Passion: 'It was before the festival of the Passover ... they were at supper and Jesus knew that the hour had come for him to pass from this world to the Father. He had always loved those who were his own in the world, and now he would love them to the end.'(Jn 13:1) It would be a fitting prayer in the heart of the priest as he moves into the Eucharistic prayer to have that same love of Jesus, that 'recklessnes of the loving heart' (Buechner), for all those who share this celebration with him.

In the New Testament there are almost 150 references to the Kingdom. The more Jesus talks about it, always in parables – a hidden treasure, a precious pearl, a fishing net, a great banquet, a wedding feast – the more we become aware that the Kingdom is a reality which is beyond our words: 'what no eye has seen, nor ear heard, nor the human heart conceived, what God has prepared for those who love him' (I Cor. 2:9). *The poet must find a place in us.* The poet reaches out for a fullness of meaning and communion that is beyond what words can say ... an alternative way of living that is only glimpsed wherever a community begins to be 'stretched out' to embrace all of humanity. We need poets and artists, singers and musicians, 'singers of the transcendant', as Timothy Radcliffe calls them, to enliven our preaching, and bring us to the edge of what can be said.[24]

The Prayers of the Faithful

Providing a space for the assembly to voice its prayers is a welcoming gesture. This promising liturgical initiative of Vatican II is not always well done. Too often the prayers have little or no local reference and sound hackneyed and cliched, as though they were being lifted out of some book or manual of several years' vintage, which is often the case. Since

Advent 2005 the Jesuit website at Gardiner Street, Dublin, has been offering samples for each Sunday, which give one a good kick-start but which still need some kind of local rootedness. It is a ministry of prayer for which people need to be well prepared, so that we catch in their delivery, and in the response of the people, something of the power of prayer. I find that the prayers capture the attention of the assembly more effectively when they are shared by two people, preferably by a man and a woman.

> *Providing a space for the assembly to voice its prayers is a welcoming issue.*

The famous words of St Augustine may have a particular relevance for this unique moment of the congregation at prayer: 'bis orat qui bene cantat' (a prayer has twice the value when it is well sung). I think of the powerful effect of Liam Lawton's *Alleuia* and *Verse* ('Speak Lord, your servant is listening ...') when sung by a whole assembly. I wonder if it might not be possible, at least occasionally, to have a *trio* involved in this prayer of the faithful. Each prayer is said by the appointed reader; in a short form of sung words suitable for the occasion the cantor then invites us to pray; and finally the cantor leads the assembly in full voice of song. Where it is done successfully it bears strong witness to the conviction that Catholic liturgy is indeed a team game!

The same Augustine tells us that the rafters of the church in Hippo used to shake at the vehemence with which the congregation responded with their final AMEN to the Eucharistic Prayer! Before any tremor is discernible in the rafters of our beloved church of St Matthew's in Ballyfermot, we need a wider repertoire of suitable chants and, most important of all, a profound conversion of hearts! A conversion to the belief that the singing of the assembly in unison is the most important music that can be found in worship. Song is an essential way to lift our voices in prayer as a chosen race, a royal priesthood, a community of the redeemed.

The Liturgy of the Eucharist

The General Instruction of the Roman Missal distinguishes three parts: the preparation of the gifts, the Eucharistic prayer and the breaking of the bread (Communion). Members of the assembly bring forward the bread and the wine in procession to the altar. It seems best that the gifts are placed directly on the altar by those who bring them. It is a reminder that from earliest times the altar has been venerated as a primary symbol of Christ, and that the gifts of bread and wine represent the people of God and their willingness to offer themselves with Christ.

The Eucharistic Prayer

A few things must be said. Even a cursory examination of the prayer (which begins with the preface) reveals that the great early verbs 'we give thanks', 'we offer', 'we pray' make it clear that the priest is speaking not only in his own name but also in the name of the entire assembly. His words, in the first place, are not addressed to the assembly or directed at the bread and wine. It is the prayer of the entire assembly, addressing God the Father through the ministry of the priest who acts both as a representative of Christ (*in persona Christi*) and speaks in the name of the assembly (*in persona ecclesiae*).

To engage the assembly more actively in the great central prayer of our Sunday liturgy demands more refined skills on the part of priests.

Even when it comes to what we traditionally call the 'consecration', the celebrant reminds the Father of what Jesus did on the night before he died, and takes up the gifts into the same great prayer of praise and thanks to the Father which Jesus offered at the last Supper. The change in the bread and wine is not wrought through any magic form of words, but in being taken up into the great memorial prayer recalling and making present what Jesus did on the night before he suffered.

The Eucharistic prayer should not be heard in the same way that the readings are heard in the Liturgy of the Word. Here we have two different situations. The readings are proclaimed to be listened to by the assembly. God is speaking to them through the ministry of the lector. But the Eucharistic Prayer is a *prayer* in the first place, proclaimed in praise of God the Father who listens. The whole assembly, through the ministry of the presiding priest, is the speaker. Caesare Giraudo, SJ, Professor of Liturgy in the Pontifical Oriental Institute in Rome, sums it up as follows: 'There is a qualitative difference between the receptive listening of the assembly to the proclamation of the readings through the ministry of the lector, and the active listening they are called to during the proclamation of the Eucharistic prayer through the ministry of the presbyter. In the former they listen ... in the latter they speak to God.'[25]

All this demands more refined skills in priests, especially if they are to engage the assembly more actively in this great central prayer of our Sunday liturgy. First, and most important of all, they will need to be prayerful. Eye contact will be an important aspect, and body language will communicate more effectively than any words. In the faithful the most important requirement will be 'active participation' at the deepest level, i.e. an interior awareness of who they are as the body of Christ, offering themselves with the priest in the great sacrifice of thanksgiving and praise that is the Eucharistic prayer, 'the source and summit of the liturgical action'.[26] Virginia Sloyan writes 'from the pew' about her hopes around the Sunday assembly: 'Sunday after Sunday ... we come to this setting to hear the sacred story and pray the great prayer with sisters and brothers, hoping to feel enlarged, expansive, full of praise, better than we are, knowing this is the way God sees us in Christ Jesus.'[27]

Communion: The Breaking of the Bread and the Sharing of the Cup

At the last supper, while speaking of his impending betrayal and death, Jesus took up the loaf of bread, broke it in his hands, and said: 'This is my body, which will be given for you'. He did the same with the cup of wine after supper, and said: 'Drink all of you from this, for this is my blood, the blood of the covenant which is to be poured out for you'. He invited the disciples to eat and drink this food 'in memory of him' and for centuries the Church has been re-enacting this last supper as the great memorial of his death and resurrection and the profound symbolic action which enables his followers to be taken up into the mystery of his dying and rising.

Catholics have been wary of using the word 'symbol' of the Eucharist (only a symbol?), perhaps unmindful that it is part of the appeal of a symbol that it contains some of the power of the thing that is symbolised. A smile or a warm handshake are not just evidence of welcome; they actually convey the welcome to the guest. A national flag or a national anthem has the power to move soldiers to the same kind of courageous action that the nation itself has. Let us listen again to Frederick Buechner:

As for the symbols of the last Supper, Protestants argue with Roman Catholics, and they both argue among themselves, as to precisely how the power of Christ is present in the symbols of bread and wine. But I think it is not too great a simplification to say that they all agree that one way or another, extraordinary power is there.

Extraordinary because they contain a power which simply does not make the heart beat faster, say, but power that can transform a human life into a new kind of life altogether - a life like his, with some of his power in it.[28]

When the symbols used in the Eucharist are allowed to speak in their fullness, they have an evangelising power. Think of the Book of the Gospels carried in procession and proclaimed in a way that shows reverence for the Word of God; people greeted with a warmth and reverence that recognises the glory of God in them ('christened'); bread broken and shared (bread that is bread to every one of the senses) and wine that is wine for all (in its rich fragrance poured out in fitting vessels) evoking a sense of celebration and festive joy.

This is 'Eucharist', continuing to do what Jesus did, giving thanks over bread and cup in the great *sacrament of unity* of all God's people. This is why we have come; this is what we want to do until we are grasped by it.[29] Not unlike those Christians of north Africa in the early third century who were arrested for gathering together to celebrate the Eucharist on Sunday, and whose reply to the Roman proconsul went thus: 'Quoniam sine dominico non possumus' ('Without the day of the Lord, we cannot possibly live').

Liturgy Speaks the Language of Symbol

The late Gerald Vann OP used to say that the Church speaks and communicates in two ways: in the language of symbol and in the language of dogma. Liturgy speaks the language of symbol, a distinctive language those engaged in liturgy need to understand. Listen again to one of the great seminal statements of *Sacrosanctum Concilium, The Constitution on the Liturgy*: 'In the liturgy, by means of signs perceptible to the senses, human sanctification is signified and brought about in ways proper to each of these signs.' (n.7). In the excellent booklet *A Guide to the Mass* the National Centre for Liturgy in Ireland has a helpful comment on these words:

> The entire ritual complex of actions, objects, words, and persons which constitute the symbolism of the Eucharist is integral to its effectiveness. The more clearly and powerfully each of them signifies, the more directly their effect will be perceived and experienced. Imbued by faith, words clearly proclaimed, actions deliberately and carefully performed, elements and objects authentically made and reverently handled contribute to the integrity of the liturgy and allow its symbolism to work to greater effect ... It is in sharing and experiencing the actions (of the liturgy) in their natural integrity and consistency that their spiritual significance and effect are appropriated.[30]

We live in a culture which has a certain insensitivity to the symbolic and the non-verbal. Perhaps it is worth recalling briefly what the authors were saying about *symbol* in a liturgy textbook we used in the seminary twenty years ago.[31]

1 A sign gives information. A symbol affects the 'heart' of the human being rather than the 'head'. It awakens an experience. It does not just tell us something; it stirs feelings in us. Signs needs to be understood. A symbol cannot be fully grasped or understood; there is always 'more to see'. It is possible that a person may not know what a sign means, for example a jagged yellow line on the road, or a yellow traffic light. But the meaning can be stated in words. Once this is done, the sign says exactly what the words say. Not so with symbols. Their meaning can never be stated in words. There is always more to see, more to be grasped. A symbol has not the clarity of a sign; there is always something hidden, more to be revealed.

All this has evident implications for our response to the profound symbolic activity of our liturgy. A famous ballerina, when asked the 'meaning' of one of her more complicated dance routines, replied: 'If I were able tell you that in words, why should I go to the great trouble of dancing it?' Clearly dance has a power to sound a depth in us, and evoke emotions beyond the power of words. When the bride and groom take to the floor at the wedding reception, the dance and their whole demeanour speak more eloquently of the quality of their relationship and the delightful mystery of human love than any words ever could.

2 A sign can be chosen and altered at will; a symbol is born out of life and has evocative power. Our liturgical symbols were not arbitrarily chosen. They were created in the historical process of our Jewish Christian faith. They have expressed the faith-experience of a people over thousands of years and have an unparalleled power to evoke that same experience for us.

In the Christian Eucharist bread and wine are complimentary. They correspond to two essential urges of all human beings: bread to our hunger, and wine to our thirst. Bread is the fruit of the earth, while wine appears more as the fruit of the sun. Though the Last Supper has a very evident link with the Passover meal, it also reaches beyond it since we know that the Passover meal itself had more distant origins in the ancient spring and harvest festivals of primitive cultures, re-enacting the mysterious events of the past which gave life and fertility to the earth, and not least bread from the ears of corn and wine from the grape.

The Last Supper

In instituting the Eucharist Jesus took over not only the symbols of bread and wine, but also the symbol of the meal. This happened because the Eucharist was instituted during the course of a meal, in the context of the passover feast, the memorial of the liberation of the Hebrew people from Egypt.[32]

We have learned from the Scripture scholars to think of the gathering in the upper room as the '*Last* Supper' with a different emphasis; it was the *last* in a long line of suppers where Jesus was invited to share the meal of friends or officials or of the poor. I read in this morning's Gospel at Mass (Saturday of the first week of ordinary time) not only of the call of Matthew, but also that Jesus accepts an invitation to dine in Matthew's home with all his friends who like him are tax-collectors and people of doubtful reputation. All of these people who find themselves excommunicated from religious society are welcomed by Jesus and share the meal with his disciples.

These community meals, the 'table fellowship' of Jesus, as they have come to be called, were high points of the disciples' time with him in their years together. This was especially true of the meals they shared with Jesus in the evening after the labours of the day, as they became more conscious of their union with him and with one another. Such Jewish meals, however plain and simple they may have been, had a certain ritual about them; a thankfulness for the food and for the blesssings Yahweh had bestowed on his people. After the resurrection Jesus is encountered by the disciples on similar occasions of table fellowship, for example the meeting on the shore of the Sea of Galilee (Jn 21) and on the Emmaus journey (Lk 24). The Easter experience brought home to them who Jesus was and how God had given himself to them especially in the friendship and intimacy of those evening meals.

And they began to see more clearly what Jesus had meant when at the 'last' of those suppers he washed their feet and took ordinary bread and said 'this is my body for you': his body, given literally in their service at the washing of their feet, and his whole self given no less in the great symbolic action of the breaking of bread and the sharing of the cup. And they realised what Jesus had meant when he instructed them to continue 'to do this in memory of him': their common meals became a central feature of those early Christian communities; they gave thanks to the loving gracious God revealed in the life, death and resurrection of Jesus; celebrated their communion with him, and with each other, in the breaking of bread and the sharing of the cup of wine, and then went forth to preach the Good News in difficult and dangerous times.[33]

The Language of Vulnerable Loving

This is the table-fellowship that the disciples of Jesus still continue to practise today. Membership of the body of Christ requires that we be in communion with other disciples. An isolated celebration of the Eucharist cannot achieve very much in the work of evangelisation. It is the exposure to the Eucharist Sunday after Sunday that invites us to a life of ongoing conversion. Ann Thurston puts it well:

> We gather here because we want to practise the rhythms of Eucharistic living ... We learn the art of accepting the stranger not as threat but as gift. We practise the art of hospitality rather than hostility ... This is new to us and we are awkward and sometimes ugly in our response to those who have come to share our new prosperity. We learn about dying and rising, about violence that is not reciprocated but transfigured at the cross. 'This is my body, I give it for you'; 'This is my blood poured out for you'. We continually fail and yet we go on trying, practising the language of vulnerable loving, losing and finding ourselves in the process. Slowly, slowly we take these things into our bloodstream, through words, through music, through ritual until we know them by heart, until they shape us and we become what we say, the body of Christ, *Corpus Christi*.[34]

*Membership of the body of Christ requires that we
be in communion with other disciples.*

The Body of Christ ... Amen!

She refers of course to the moment of communion at Mass
when the minister holds up the host and says: 'The Body of
Christ' and the communicant says a fervent 'Amen' ('Yes, that is
what I believe'). Many times in the year, and especially around
the feast of *Corpus Christi*, I do my best to alert the assembly to
the richness of that response. When the minister says 'The Body
of Christ', their 'Amen' is not just 'Yes' to Jesus in the Eucharist,
but also to his presence in the assembly: all of us here who share
in this Eucharist are the body of Christ.

We have all grown accustomed to speaking of the Church as
the 'mystical body' and of the sacramental presence of Jesus in
the Eucharist as the 'real presence' or 'real body' (cf. the old
Latin hymn 'Ave verum corpus natum'). One of the things that
stands out in my memory from a semester's course on the
Eucharist during my student days in Munster in Germany forty
years ago was the learned professor telling us that for twelve
hundred years of the Church's history the very opposite was
true: the 'real' body of Christ meant the Church and the
'mystical' body of Christ was the Eucharist. The learned
professor was none other than Joseph Ratzinger, and truly
learned and impressive he was despite his youthful appearance
at thirty-six years. An example of the above linguistic usage is a
passage from John Chrysostom, which John Paul quotes in his
Encyclical on the Eucharist:

Do you wish to honour the body of Christ? Do not ignore
him when he is naked. Do not pay him homage in the
temple clad in silk, only then to neglect him outside where

he is cold and ill-clad. He who said: 'This is my body' is the same who said: 'You saw me hungry and you gave me no food' ... What good is it if the Eucharistic table is overloaded with golden chalices when your brother is dying of hunger? Start by satisfying his hunger and then with what is left you may adorn the altar as well.[35]

The words of John Chrysostom remind us that we cannot worthily receive Christ's body and blood unless we have come to recognise Christ in the poorest among us. 'The joys and the hopes, the griefs and the anxieties of the men of this age, especially those who are poor or in any way afflicted, these too are the joys and hopes, the griefs and anxieties of the followers of Christ.'[36] We make our own these memorable opening words of *Gaudium et Spes,* especially when we come to church bringing all the joys and agonies of the world into that special relationship with God and with others which is the Eucharist. Emerging through the church doors we could do worse than have the words of the prophet Micah on the minds and lips and hearts that we signed with the cross as we prepared to listen to the Gospel: 'This is what Yahweh asks of you: this and this only, to act justly, to love tenderly, and to walk humbly with your God.'(6:8) It is when the service in the church is over that the *real service* begins.

Notes

1   *Pre- Pastoral Renewal Exchange,* n.102.
2   Timothy Radcliffe, OP, *What is the point in being a Christian?* (London: Continuum, 2005), p. 55.
3   John Paul II, *Redemptoris Missio: On the Permanent Validity of the Church's Missionary Mandate,*1991, n. 33.
4   Cited by Desmond O'Donnell, 'Down from Tabor', *The Furrow,* Sept. 2005, p. 485.
5   *Redemptoris Missio,* n.33.
6   *L'Osservatore Romano,* English ed., Dec.5, 1988, p. 49.
7   Thomas Rausch, SJ, *Liturgy and Evangelisation in the North American Context,* p. 2; accessed through the Internet.

8 *Evangelii Nuntiandi: On Evangelisation in the Modern World*, 1976, n.21.

9 *Sacrosanctum Concilium, The Constitution on the Sacred Liturgy*, n.2.

10 Donal Harrington, *The Welcoming Parish* (Dublin: Columba Press, 2005), pp. 191-2.

11 Gabe Huck, 'Eucharist of the Assembly', *Church*, Spring 1993, p. 5.

12 R. Hovda, 'The Amen Corner', *Liturgy's Many Roles*, 1994, pp.152-7.

13 *A Guide to the Mass*, published by the National Centre for Liturgy in Ireland, 2005, p. 43.

14 R. Duggan, 'Good Liturgy: The Assembly', *America*, Vol. 190, No. 7 (2004), March.

15 Huck, op. cit., p. 6.

16 Kathy A. Lindell, 'The Ministry of the Parish Liturgy Committee', *America*, Vol. 190, No.12 (2004), April 5.

17 Harrington, op. cit., p. 197.

18 Duggan, op. cit., n.7.

19 General Introduction to the Roman Missal, GIRM, n.34.

20 John Baldovin, 'Presiding at the Liturgy of the Word', *America*, Vol. 190, No. 8 (2004), March 8.

21 Ibid.

22 Timothy Radcliffe, 'The Sacramentality of the Word', in Keith Pecklers, SJ, *Liturgy in a Postmodern World* (London: Continuum, 2003), pp.133-47.

23 Frederick Buechner, *The Magnificent Defeat* (New York, Seabury, 1966), p. 23.

24 Radcliffe, op. cit., pp. 145-6.

25 Cesare Giraudo, SJ, 'The Eucharist as Diakonia', in Keith Pecklers, SJ, *Liturgy in a Postmodern World* (London: Continuum, 2003), p. 130.

26 GIRM., n.73.

27 *Sloyan,Virginia*, cit., Hovda, Robert, *Worship*, January 1988, p. 24.

28 op. cit., p. 107.

29 Huck, op. cit., p. 6.

30 *Celebrating the Mystery of Faith, A Guide to the Mass*, National Centre for Liturgy, Ireland, 2005, p. 27.

31 Gregory Manly and Annaliese Reinhard, *The Art of Praying Liturgy*, Melbourne, 1984, pp. 208-12.

32 Philippe Rouillard, 'From Human Meal to Christian Eucharist', in Kevin Seasoltz (ed.) *Living Bread, Saving Cup* (Minnesota: Liturgical Press, l982).

33 For a scholarly yet very readable account of this background to the Eucharist in the early Church, see A. Greeley, *The Great Mysteries*, 2003, pp. 77-83.

34 Anne Thurston, 'Corpus Christi', *The Furrow*, 2005, p. 396.

35 John Paul II, *Ecclesia de Eucharistia*, n.20.

36 *Gaudium et Spes*, n.1.

Bringing it all Back Home:

The Retrieval of Gregorian/Plainchant and the Forgotten Sense

Nóirín Ní Riain

Overture

Every sound ever to have existed in human history is the sound of God, from the sound of the silent stone to the shrill screech of the blackbird, to the secret sound of one's own voice, to the silent sound of the praying space. This is inclusive of everybody and no different from any aural or oral religious experience imaginable. The human ear is the most sensitive and theologically attuned sense.

Yet hearing, listening, sounding/singing and silence are undervalued, unexplored and unappreciated in our liturgies. The neglect of Plainchant in liturgical practice is but one symptom of this lacuna. This article, firstly, makes a plea for the retrieval of Plainchant (the oldest music in Western history) in liturgical practice. Plainchant is the most highly perceptive aural experience of God's self-disclosure and it has been unfairly dismissed.

Secondly, this paper points out how the entire human sense of hearing has been neglected and ignored in Western theology. Plainchant is a specific, focused, aural prayer which God provides as prevenient grace; the faculty of hearing and the content of what is heard is also prevenient grace. Both are privileged auditory inlets to God, creating an aural ontology, which in the course of this article will be defined by a new word: theosony.

Theme A: Gregorian/Plainchant

'... a music you would never have known To listen for ...
Listen now again'

Seamus Heaney, *The Spirit Level*

Plainchant is the sound of God and of the soul; a music 'to be listened for' to be known. Furthermore, the oldest music in Western history is the sound of God and the sound of the human soul. Our deepest human longings, where the divine/human encounter resides, are balanced and healed in the ear that sings and listens to this Plainsong aptly called 'the speech of angels'. Plainchant is much more than a performance; it is all about prayer. God forms the matter of thought; God is the theme song of Plainsong. God is the ultimate listener or audience. As musicologist, David Hiley, puts it in the opening paragraph of his seminal work on Western Plainchant, '[t]he performance of the music is not ... an end in itself but part of a religious ritual ... Liturgical texts which are sung ... are more solemn, inspiring and impressive, and a more worthy vehicle for human prayer and praise of God'.[1]

Personalising his religious experience, St Augustine attributes it all to the sung sound of Plainchant: 'These holy words fill my soul with greater devotion when they are sung than when they are not.'[2] Once sung and heard, the mystery of Plainchant never leaves the human soul. It is a song that sings about the past, the present and the future. It is about a vertical relationship between us and God; mundane, earth-bound words, song and sound are hurtled upwards to God, the ultimate numinous mystery. Yet in liturgy, religious education and church hymnals, it is not even credited with lip service; since Vatican II, Plainchant has received an insincere profession of good will.

Almost forty years ago, the Second Vatican Council document on *The Constitution on the Liturgy* (116) stated that

Gregorian chant is, 'especially suited to the Roman liturgy. Therefore ... it should be given pride of place in liturgical services'. Over eight years ago, Austin Flannery called for an introduction – or reintroduction rather – of Plainchant into the liturgy: 'The addition of an appropriate amount of sung Latin chant would do much to improve the celebration of our liturgy and indeed to increase its appeal.'[3]

Nothing happened. Worse still, our liturgies replaced this God-directed vertical song by human-directed horizontal song. Human-directed song lacks the mysterious, God-sounding insights of this age-old tradition of liturgical music. Therein, the plane never leaves the runway to make its way to God. My argument here is that Gregorian/Plainchant is especially suited to the *Irish* Roman Catholic liturgy and should be given pride of place in Irish liturgical service. Our ears are attuned to the timbre of Plainsong because it is of the same family as our own *sean-nós* tradition; both are ancient, unmeasured, *a capella* (unaccompanied) vocal and, above all, deeply spiritual. Plainchant must be retrieved and reinstated into its own native dwelling place which is the liturgy in Ireland. This moment is crucial for its timely restoration at a time of dramatic change and possible connection with the Holy Spirit.

The decline of the Plainchant since Vatican II is a great impoverishment of the liturgical wealth of the Church.

Any discussion on the sad plight of Plainchant invariably turns to the Silos phenomenon of the 1990s. Our eyes, or more correctly speaking our ears, were opened to a huge influx of chant in the media in 1993 when a Spanish recording company launched its double CD of plain chant sung by the Benedictine monks of the abbey of St Dominic of Silos in North Spain. This 'clerical chartbuster' as it was called became immensely popular worldwide, selling millions and meriting the title 'Original

International Bestseller'. However, what is significant here is that young people were responding purely to the transcendental, extraordinary *sound* of Plainchant. The integral liturgical context, the actual meaning of the Latin texts, was totally irrelevant. The flower was plucked from its stem and would soon wither and die: the decay continues.

At the end of the day, Plainchant surpasses all sounds only when it is directly connected with the Word of God. It is not necessary to be able to sing Plainchant to experience its deeply transformative power. What is important is the spiritual experience which is *aural*, whether it is received into the soul through the listening, praying ear, or *sonic*, that is, through the vocal cords sounding the chant. It is through the effect of the sound that God communicates to the human ear in all infinite reality. Being becomes fully alive in the singing and the listening. It is precisely because God is beyond Plainchant that God is also behind and within every neume. There is an ancient Greek philosophical adage quoted by such Christian Fathers of the Church as Augustine and Ambrose: *Bis orat qui cantat* [the one who sings prays twice]; *Bis orat qui audit* [the one who listens prays twice] is also true and right.

Austin Flannery draws attention to that which pertains to the senses here: 'If the liturgy of the Western Church were a sensate, intelligent being, it would express a marked preference for Gregorian Chant.'[4] Indeed, such inclusion and retrieval would be a blessed act of kindness to all and sundry, it would appear. 'Not only would the inclusion of Gregorian/Plainchant benefit the liturgy, however, the chants themselves would also surely benefit from being *heard* in their proper liturgical setting'.[5]

The hopeful factor is that we are not springing into life from a new, unfamiliar source. More than a glimmer of this tradition, like *sean-nós,* still resides in our collective memory; everyone, laity and religious, born before 1965 recognises, recalls, retains and responds to the sound of Plainchant. It is part of us.

Many of our church leaders – bishops, priests, administrators, seminary professors, staff and associates – are products of the 1950s for whom Gregorian chant was the first and last breath of their formation.

Yet we all now realise that for many, the times, thus the plainsongs, were thin more than thick. The heavy handed, heady, rational, unemotional introduction to plainsong was, more often than not, for worse rather than for better. The fifties/sixties/seventies chant-learning times were very thin, fear-filled and frightening, when these marvellous chants were largely taught in seminaries and in schools in the strictest, most un-prayerful, unmusical manner, drummed into the soul by rote rather than 'off by heart'. No enthusiasm, no mystery, no vision; no real 'experience' of the powerful, prayerful medium that Western Plainchant was, is and will be in the future. Subsequently, the marriage with this traditional melody of the Western Christian Church and the lived liturgy was on the rocks! This is why Plainchant was ignored; a kind of amnesia by default, a blind failure or lack of energy to act and retrieve this Christian song tradition in lived liturgy because it contains painful memories. Failure to experience the sheer beauty of this practice of praying to God deadens enthusiasm (*en theos*, i.e. 'inspired by or derived from the gods') and no amount of vision will compensate for a lack of energy.

To summarise, our responsibility as a praying people is to bring Plainchant back home; to regain and recover its prayer context. In so doing, we will be the winners because this song is the very door which opens onto the presence of the triune God. In short, Plainchant is listening to the powerful note of wisdom which is God's abundant grace of the Holy Spirit.

The second theme here is 'towards a theology of listening'. There are four strands to this theme: firstly, the fact that the human aural sense (the uppermost human sense in listening to and singing Plainchant) is neglected in all Western society. Secondly, I will present some biological facts about the magnificent, miraculous organ of hearing and listening. Third, the term 'theosony,' which simply means 'the sound of God', will be introduced and, finally, a Coda or postlude will tell a personal theme song.

Theme B: A Theology of Listening

The foundation stone of a listening theology is that the encounter with the incarnate Word of God through the Holy Spirit takes place primarily, although not excepting other media, through the human sense of hearing, listening and its associate silence. God wants us to be 'all ears'; we are 'ear-marked' by God, set aside for the specific use of the Kingdom of God. But first, let us look at this miraculous sense of hearing, which we tend to ignore.

The Ear: The Cinderella of the Senses

Throughout the entire Western culture it is an all-pervasive trait to bypass the ear in favour of the eye. In every discipline throughout Western history the ear has taken second place. 'Ever since the age of Newton and Descartes we have existed in a culture that put excessive emphasis on the eye.'[6] We live primarily in a visual world. Even when we understand something we say, 'I see'. When we try to explain ourselves we say, 'Do you see what I mean?' There is no 'earobics' in e-mailing, net surfing or texting. Medicine is far more sophisticated when it comes to eye surgery; attention to noise pollution is almost non-existent.

Western culture, in general, has tended to over-emphasise the visual and downplay the aural sense. This imbalance has affected the spiritual health of society profoundly.

Yet our undervalued ears are far more accurate than our eyes; the ear is, scientifically, the most sophisticated and sensitive sense in interpreting and understanding the outer physical world. It is the first sense to develop in the womb, some 135 days after impregnation; the last to atrophy, to leave the body. The frequency range of the ear is ten times greater than that of the eye. Furthermore, there are three times as many nerve connections from the ear to the brain as from the eye to the brain. We can hear our own sound because there is a direct channel from the throat to the inner ear so sound does not have to leave the body. The eye sounds 'I', although it can never actually see me. We can also feel, smell and touch ourselves but to see we have to look in a mirror.

The ear generates and provides sensory energy essential to the brain. The brain is dependent upon three main sources of energy: food, air and 'sensory energy'. The aural sense provides most of this third source of energy to the brain. The ear never sleeps; it is constantly providing and supplying energy. According to the French Canadian physician, Alfred Tomatis, 'the ear provides the nervous system with almost 90 per cent of its overall sensory energy'. [7]

The listening process itself, according to audiologists and scientists alike, defies full, verbal understanding. The ear resides in the realm of the mysterious. Audiologist and scientist, J.R. Pierce, concedes: 'A great deal is known about the structure of the ear and about the neural pathways from the ear to the brain, but our sense of hearing is understood only in part.'[8] This resonates theologically: like human understanding of the mystery of God, the aural process defies human knowledge.

Neglect of the aural also affects the spiritual climate of society and I argue that from attention to the miraculous biological detail of the human ear, we can attend to the religious dimension present in all human hearing. Furthermore, in the physical ear resides the seat of emotion; religion is an emotional relationship with God. According to Søren Kierkegaard, the ear 'is the most spiritually determined of the senses.'[9] Favouring the visual and the visible in all areas of life, has, in the words of Joachim Ernest Berendt, generally 'despiritualised our existence'.[10] Hearing 'is THE most spiritual of all our senses'.[11] In short, then, through learning and practising hearing, not only is one's quality of life enhanced but God's self-revelation is more readily and obediently received.

Biological hearing in such a context raises the question of biological deafness and dumbness: Is the person deprived of hearing also deprived of religious experience? Of course not. No human being is deaf to the sound of God. Many people with perfect hearing and perfect pitch choose not to listen. St Augustine describes the moment in his own conversion when such spiritual deafness was dispelled. '*[A]d haec tu dicis mihi, quoniam tu es deus meus et dicis voce forti in aure interiore servo tuo perrumpens meam surditatem* [You answered me, for you are my God and your voice can speak aloud in the voice of my spirit, piercing your servant's deafness]'.[12] Restored sacred hearing is to live in a different reality, to understand the new language of sound. God remains the same; sounds remain the same. What is different is the calling – the 'vocation', the evocation, the perception of the sound.

To summarise this second theme: contemporary theology has also seriously ignored the Ear; it has investigated the nature of God primarily from a visual perspective, largely ignoring the transcendent possibilities of the sense of hearing. For its future survival Christianity *must* address the function of the auditory sense, indeed all sensory functions, in revelation and religious experience. Western Christian theology can do this by showing both how the aural conveys the revelation of God to the human subject, and how the aural holds open the space wherein the world can awaken to the graced presence of God. The proper insertion of Gregorian/Plainchant is one radical way of awakening this presence of God the Creator, God the Redeemer and God the Holy Spirit.

Theosony requires a new kind of listening to the word of Scripture. The original meaning of the Hebrew 'däbär' and the Greek 'logos' embodied an understanding and a reciprocated effectiveness (the effect of the sounding of a word on both the speaker and the listener). The divine Logos, in its sounding and in its hearing, *releases* an understanding of oneself, of the universe and of God. Theosony refers to a revolution in experiencing God's self-communication and love. Christianity shares this aural uniqueness with other great world religions: Hinduism knows that the world resounds to the ultimate, spiritual cosmic sound of 'Om/Aum'; the sound of the Vedas is as important as its lexical sense. The Qur'an is the sacred scripture of Islam and is the most recited book in the world, memorised off by heart. It is the sound of infinite reality, the effect of the sounding of the word on both speaker and listener. Arabic is the sound of divine/human encounter, all about rhythm and cadence, having the aural effect of Western Christian Plainchant. In Christian liturgy, the divine Logos in its sounding and hearing also releases an understanding of oneself, of the universe and of God.

Brief Introduction to the Term 'Theosony'
'Theosony' is a new word for the occurrence or the circumstances where God is heard. Just as any collective term, such as 'fruit', 'family', 'weather', indeed 'theology', is a folder for many different words, 'theosony' contains all the files which refer to the experience of God that is aural. The word itself is a cut-and-paste neologism (Gr. neo-logos, 'new word') from two very old words: Theos (Gr. God) and 'sonans' (L. 'sounding'). Thus, the 'Sound', the 'Word', the 'Silence', the 'Voice' of God and listening/hearing God all live in the realm of 'Theosony'.

Theosony is one word which sums up hearing that Isaiah refers to: 'Morning by morning God awakens my ear to hear.' Theosony is surely the same obedient listening that Christ calls us to through that enigmatic, tautological saying – 'anyone who has ears to hear ...'. God created the human ear and its ingenious ear-work so that the voice of God could be heard and responded to.

The term 'theosony' contains all the files which refer to the experience of God, which is aural.

The auditory religious experience, for whatever and regardless of reason, is a cardinal one in the Christian experience and liturgical practice; it has been neglected and has not matured in scholarship or practice. The Church's failure to understand the 'most spiritual' of all senses is a major lacuna, leading to its failure to understand the power and the virtuosity of the aural.

For instance, during the course of my doctoral research, I consulted some twenty-three reference sources for references to the aural sense. Of these twenty-three, only three, one of which is out of date, find the auditory sense worth mentioning regarding God's self-revelation.

I will cite just two examples here. Firstly, *The Encyclopedia of Religion*, for example, has no entry under 'hearing', 'listening' or 'the ear', yet it includes articles on the human body, the head, the heart, the eyes, the hair, the hands, the knees, the feet and the phallus. Secondly, the recently published second edition of the Roman Catholic equivalent, the *New Catholic Encyclopedia*, has entries on 'sensation', 'sense knowledge', 'senses' and 'sensibles'. These are exact reprints of the 1967 edition of the Encyclopedia. All four bibliographies to these articles remain unchanged in the 2003 editing except for one new text, which is added to the 'sense knowledge' bibliography.

There are three further points here. Firstly, the 1967 edition's entry on 'sensation' incorporates an article on 'physico-chemical factors in sensation' by R.A. Wunderlich. The auditory is considered only on the physical characteristics of the ear and its functions and, as is also the case with the other sensations biologically described here, makes no reference whatsoever to the theological implications of hearing. This article is omitted from the 2003 publication. Secondly, there is an entry for 'sound' in the 1967 encyclopedia which is again scantily scientific, ignoring the theological context. Its bibliographies recommend only scientific, acoustic titles. There is no entry under 'sound' in the most recent edition. Finally, there is an entry under 'deaf' in the first edition that deals only with the education and social rehabilitation of deaf people; there is no biblical or theological discussion. The 2003 edition has eliminated this article altogether.

Although it is a contestable claim, the aural dimension of religious experience to date has been more concerned with mapping a route to God than with actually *experiencing* the contours of that road. Maps are important and helpful in charting directions through the territory. Yet they hardly communicate the lived experience of the terrain; the sensual knowledge which accrues from touching, smelling, tasting, seeing and hearing the reality. This is the reverse of the poetics of experience suggested in *The Dry Salvages* by T.S. Eliot as having the experience but falling short of the meaning: 'We had the experience but missed the meaning'.[13] We have not internalised the Voice, the Sound of God. In short, a diagram of features, although an important initial guide, is experientially unrepresentative of the reality. Reading is in the realm of the cartographer; hearing is the soft, sound-soil of feeling and sensitivity.

Religious experience, both oral and aural, has for the most part given way to the visual. Like Thomas, we believe because we have seen. It asks questions such as what each person's particular experience of hearing the divinity says to that individual; what kind of God is heard in prayer; and how, precisely, can the ear of the hearer be nurtured and supported during these stages of prayer?

I believe that for its future survival, the Church must address the function of the auditory sense, indeed all sensory functions, in revelation and religious experience. Western Christian theology can do this by showing both how the aural conveys the revelation of God to the human subject, and how the aural holds open the space wherein the world can awaken to the graced presence of God. It is our openness to let go, through a certain kind of listening. Connecting the Good News with contemporary living is all about a certain listening wherein God resides and moves.

Coda: Mo Scéal Féin – Scéal Gach Duine (My Story – Everyone's Story)

A Coda is a musical term for a more or less independent passage at the end of a musical composition to bring it to a satisfactory close. To bring closure to this paper, I want to present some personal perspectives on my own observations and limited knowledge of encounters with the sound of God.

Sometimes I feel inadequate because so much of my relationship with God comes from the aural/sound. I spend my time in the ear; listening is a spiritual experience. Any knowledge or practical wisdom gained from a life of prayer has been through the human ear.

This confident conviction in the prayerful power, the accessibility, the universality of 'listening out for and obediently' responding to the divine 'sound of the gentle breeze' of Elijah reflects my own life's pilgrimage; en route, sounding and praying have been inextricably bound together.

For me, to pray is to structure sounds in the silence of my own mind: sometimes in liturgy or performance, to be physically birthed, sometimes not to be, as in solitary prayer. This is a *hesychia* as the Eastern Church would call it, which is in no way the absence of sounds as we have seen earlier but almost a pause between mundane sounds. *Hesychia* is a positive sense of listening resonating fullness not emptiness, divine presence not meaningless void.

Theosony for me is an alertness of the inner ear which listens in the inner room of the praying soul. Of its very essence it carefully, selectively drowns out certain incessant, unnecessary noises. Singing, praying, hearing and sometimes sounding all come from the same source for me; they are one and the same. When I am in deepest song, my ordinary consciousness transforms into one harmonious sound in which I live and move and am. I am transported into a world of sound which is real and not contrived.

The body is an aural sound-board of God, a 'Temple of the Holy Spirit' in direct response to the voice of God – a human resonating chamber for the Divine.

Being in the world is a cosmic sound studio where you can sound and listen – a process of theosonic trial and error – always in flux, always in motion. God is the sound engineer who fine-tunes the organic spiritual melody of each one of us, modifying it to create the most perfect sound of love. So too I feel when I am singing. I can hear myself in the raw naïve subjective listening. Then the God of the silent gaps or within the silent gaps fills in; moulding, editing the sound, splicing the tape to doctor the sound which God wants to hear from me and through which God wants me to hear him.

So much of the human relationship with God is rooted in the aural/sound.

My life is a crusade of the sound and the sacred – 'a mission of pray-sing towards praising'. And this is through singing and listening to Plainchant: Chants to sing – chance to pray!

Sound attentiveness and alertness to the sound of God can nudge the same universal human aural experience above and beyond the mundane into the realms of deepest prayer and transcendence both in personal prayer and in the shared liturgy. Like good liturgy in the widest, most general sense, theosony can be a personal response to the felt presence of God intensifying and heightening that response to become a significant force in the human journey.

Here is a realm of spiritual consciousness and fulfilment, where one encounters divinity either in prayerful listening or prayerful silence in liturgy. The aim of this paper has been to flesh out, through one human sense, the wider, more personal picture of prayer, which Mark Patrick Hederman sees as 'being attuned to the tempo, the texture and the idiom of God's way of relating to us.'[14] The listening adventure with God is characterised by a close and warm relationship, which is deeply personal and even secret.

It is a two-sided listening. Just as we know that message through sound sent from God, so too can we through sound allow that same message to return to sender. It is God singing us all back home if only we could listen, learn and join in that anthem.

Finally, theosony can be that simple human obedient listening to the God who listens as intently to us as He did to that one incarnate logos of the Easter Christ-story. This is the ultimate theosony – penetratingly embodied by the Welsh parson poet R.S. Thomas in the final stanza of the poem 'The Musician':

So it must have been on Calvary
In the fiercer light of the thorns' halo:
The men standing by and that one figure,
The hands bleeding, the mind bruised but calm,
Making such music as lives still.
And no one daring to interrupt
Because it was himself that he played
And closer than all of them the God listened.[15]

Notes

1 Hiley, 1993, p. 1.
2 Gibb and Montgomery (eds) 1908, Bk. X.
3 Ní Riain, 1997, p. 13.
4 Ibid.
5 Ibid.
6 Berendt, 1988, p. 32.
7 Tomatis, 1991, p.186.
8 Pierce,1983, p.96.
9 Kierkegaard, 1944, p.66.
10 Berendt, 1988, p.23.
11 Ibid., p.24.
12 Gibb and Montgomery (eds) 1908, Bk. XIII.
13 Eliot, Faber and Faber, 1969, p. 184.
14 Hederman, 2001, p.131.
15 Thomas, 1972, p. 337.

Bibliography

Berendt, Joachim E., *The Third Edr: On Listening to the World* (Dorset: Element Books Ltd., 1988).

The Complete Poems and Plays of T.S. Eliot (London: Faber and Faber Limited, 1969).

Eliade, Mircea (ed.) *The Encyclopedia of Religion* (New York/London: Collier Macmillan Publishers, 1987).

Gibb, John and Montgomery, William (eds) *The Confessions of Augustine* (Cambridge: University Press, 1908).

Heaney, Seamus, The *Spirit Level* (London: Faber & Faber, 1996).

Hederman, Mark Patrick, 'Personal Prayer', *The Furrow*, Vol. 52, No.3 (2001), March.

Hiley, David, *Western Plainchant: A Handbook* (New York: Oxford University Press, 1993).

Kierkegaard, Søren. *Either/Or*, Two Vols, translated by David F. Swenson and Lilian Marvin Swenson (Princeton, New Jersey: Princeton University Press, 1944 (1959)).

New Catholic Encyclopedia (Washington, D.C.: The Catholic University of America, first edn 1967; second edn 2003).

Ní Riain, Nóirín, *Gregorian Chant Experience* (Dublin: The O'Brien Press, 1997).

Ní Riain, Nóirín, *The Specificity of Christian Theosony: Towards a Theology of Listening*, Ph.D. dissertation, Mary Immaculate College, University of Limerick, 2003.

Pierce, John R., *The Science of Musical Sound* (New York: Scientific American Books Inc., 1983).

Thomas, R.S., 'The Musician', excerpt in *The Faber Book of Religious Verse*, edited by Helen Gardner (London: Faber and Faber Limited, 1972).

Tomatis, Alfred, *The Conscious Ear* (Barrytown/NY: Station Hill Press, 1991).

New Paradigms for Proclaiming the Gospel:

Religious Orders in Search of Identity Today

Anne Codd PBVM

Introduction

The future direction of Religious Life has been of great interest to me for a long time. However, at this point in my life, the search with which I am concerned is not primarily an existential one, that is, it does not concern primarily with meaning and fulfilment in my life as a member of a Religious Congregation. It can be better described as a theological search, i.e. it is concerned with how I understand and interpret my religious vocation as a calling within the Church. In this context, I think of Church as the community of Christian believers on mission in the world, here and now.

In deciding on the theme of this workshop the organising committee of the Summer School has reflected closely the concerns expressed at the international event on Religious Life that took place in Rome in November of 2004. There, the European participants named loss of identity as a major concern of their Religious Orders at this time.[1] Interestingly, they related this loss of identity closely with the fact that, in Europe, many of the roles and ministries formerly associated with Religious have now been taken over by the state. This raises the practical question: has the identity of the Religious been too closely linked to what they do, and has not enough attention been given to Religious Life as a lifeform[2] within the Church in its mission in the world?

Loss of identity is a major concern of religious orders today.

Assumptions

In preparing this paper I have assumed that we are working within the Christian and Catholic tradition.[3] I have taken for granted that when we say Religious Orders, we think of both 'contemplative' and 'active apostolic' forms of monastic life.[4] In this, I have made no distinction between members who are ordained and those who are not. Neither have I gone into detail on the distinction between 'Order' and 'Congregation', between solemn and simple vows, etc. I also want to say that what I am talking about here is Religious Life lived with integrity, but within the limitations of fallen, saved but not yet perfect, human beings. Finally, it is important to state that Religious Life may take very different forms in different cultures. What is happening in Western societies may be quite different from the practice in Asia, Africa or South America.

Perspectives

Given my own background and present ministry, I have taken a very practical approach to the topic. I have also looked at Religious Orders from the point of view of the growth of the whole Church, i.e. pastoral development. Of course, I recognise that there are other important perspectives: spirituality, Canon Law, history, etc. All of these are necessary for a full dialogue on the subject.

Quick Think

It is interesting to invite people to do a quick think on what they consider to be at the heart of Religious Life and then to test what they say in the light of two foundational theological principles, both greatly espoused by Vatican II: the universal call to holiness and the mission of all the baptised.

Any revisioning of Religious Life must take into serious consideration the following two foundational theological principles: the universal call to holiness and the mission of all the baptised.

It is easy for Religious to appropriate exclusively to themselves the Christian calling that belongs to all the baptised. It is arguable that this may have contributed in the past to the way many lay people thought that somehow their place in the Church was simply to be ministered to and directed by 'professed' religious and/or the ordained ministers.

But what, then, is the core identity of Religious Orders? I return, in search of a guide, to the title of this workshop: new paradigms for proclaiming the Gospel: religious orders in search of identity today.

Changes in our Way of Thinking

I now wish to name, first in 'secular' terms, three major shifts in how we see our world, which are taking place in Western societies:

- The shift from compartmentalised ways of thinking to more holistic approaches, which recognise the interconnectedness of all things;
- The shift from understanding human beings as dominating the universe to recognising that human action is a partnership with the universe as it unfolds;
- The shift from a view of leadership as being in charge, independently, to a vision of leadership as enabling all to

discover together and agree, as far as possible, the best and wisest ways forward.

I would like now to consider each of these very radical changes, or 'paradigm shifts' in turn. It is only gradually and with reflection that we see the implications of a holistic way of thinking. For example, when we respond to the awful atrocities which happen so often in our world, we may like to place those who do these things 'out there', as totally different from the rest of humanity. But if we really agree that all things are interconnected, then we must acknowledge that there is a part-terrorist in each of us, and there is part of our peace-loving, life-seeking selves in each terrorist. We are facing a real challenge to grow in reconciliation, in community, in openness to difference. Only when we learn to live well with difference will the threat of the suicide bomber fade in our world.

We can test how far we have grown in a holistic view and way of living by asking: how hurt are we by the reality of poverty, deprivation and exclusion of every kind in our world? In a similar way we ask: can we claim to have moved away from the culture of dominance, of considering that creation is to be subdued and used by us humans, when efforts to reduce pollution in the planet still meet with serious resistance? Has the concept of leadership been thoroughly transformed, when meetings of the G8, for example, must still be made secure behind massive displays of armed force? Just think that in their safe haven, they are supposed to be coming to agreement about what is for the greatest good of the world!

Christian Mission in our World Today

To examine the Christian mission in the light of the paradigm shifts that are in progress and in the light of the current real situation of our world is an ongoing task of practical theology. Does the Good News truly address what is happening in our world, at global and local levels?[5] Let us consider again the three paradigm shifts which I have explored, however briefly, above.

- Does the Gospel offer some insights and resources which can move us as Church, in our mission in the world, towards recognising and honouring our basic interconnectedness with one another and with our cosmos?[6]
- Are we drawn, by reflection on the Gospels, to a vision of all creation as gift of God and God-filled, as entitled to cultivation rather than destruction through our actions?
- And do we find in our Christian message a call to leadership which is ultimately a way of service, empowering people to live in love, to bring about what we call the Kingdom of God?

I believe the answer on all counts is yes.

Throughout the history of Christendom, in our lives and in the Church, we have not lived up to the grandeur of the Christian vision. As Church, with a mission in the world here and now, the challenge we face is to find practical ways of expressing who we are, as ambassadors of God, in Christ, in every aspect of our daily personal, family, community, political and social lives.

As the focus of this workshop is Religious Orders in search of identity, I will move on now to consider again the question: what is the role of Religious Orders, in the service of this Christian mission of proclaiming the Gospel today?

Identity of Religious Life within the Church and its Mission
Religious Life is a lifeform through which is expressed, in a very direct way, that search for the fullness of life through relationship with the Divine (in this case the God revealed by Jesus), which lies at the heart of all religions.

Religious belong to their Orders through the total personal investment of themselves. They do this in the conviction that the Order is gifted by God to be, for them, the community in which they will live fully their Christian calling. This relation to the Order is generated through the vows of chastity, poverty and obedience.

Interpretations of vowed celibacy lived in community as in some way a rejection of the gift of sexuality or as a way of life which is superior to others are seriously flawed. Equally, referring to the fact that Jesus remained unmarried is, I believe, dangerously exclusive. Finally, claiming that availability for ministry warrants a life of vowed celibacy does not, I would argue, stand up to examination today.

There is a real complementarity between self-giving through vowed celibacy lived in community, with its emphasis on openness and inclusion, and the call to Christian marriage, with its emphasis on total commitment to another human being. Together with other vocations within the faith community, these in some measure manifest the infinitely faceted love of God.

The relation of members of Religious Orders to their community can be seen as a symbol of the interconnectedness that I discussed above. Practically, then, Religious communities, including contemplatives and groups of retired people, must see themselves as communities related deeply with the whole Church and the whole human family. When active apostolic religious participate in ministries and in pastoral development the potential of their vocation comes to life in a visible and effective way.

Religious Life is organised so that private ownership of property is not necessary. The way in which Religious order their relation with material goods, through their vow of poverty, symbolises powerfully the partnership with creation that I have named as a major challenge facing humanity. Once again, in the pastoral ministry of the Religious, in their pioneering work at the margins of Church and society, in cooperating with others in the work of Christian justice, this aspect of their lives is manifest and gives witness to the Christian vision of the world.

Religious Life is a lifeform through which is expressed, in a very direct way, that search for the fullness of life through relationship with the Divine.

As Christians, we believe that the ultimate purpose of all living is to become people of the Kingdom – people in whom God's dream for the world is realised. The manner in which Religious relate to their Order, as established through the vow of obedience, is based on the conviction that the Order is gifted by God to be for them the place where they can continually discern what God is asking of them. For our world and for the Church there is much to be learned from the struggle which Religious have had in recent decades to find new 'ways of proceeding' (a term greatly favoured by those who follow the Ignatian tradition). Moving away from the old authoritarian methods has not always been easy, and the search goes on in religious communities for structures and processes which will release the wisdom and power of the Spirit, which is present in all, members and leaders alike.

The radical difference between the way of faith and the way of the 'world' is made vivid and real in current efforts in the Church to encourage participation and communion. The experience of the Religious can be extremely helpful when parishes and dioceses are struggling to develop new structures for collaboration in mission and ministry.

Conclusion

I have argued that, through their lifeform, Religious are integrally related to the tasks of our Church in its mission in the world today. Whether contemplative or active apostolic, engaged in ministerial work or retired, many or few, ordained or not, the basic relationships to which Religious are committed through membership of their Orders are potentially life-springs within the Church and the world. The ministerial activities of religious are closely related to their identity and bring the particular experiences of their lifeform as a resource, in collaboration with others in the Church, to the tasks of Christian mission. Experience also shows that Religious are often the ones to go beyond present patterns in life and ministry, to test new ground, to draw the Church forward through attentiveness at the margins.

Space does not permit further exploration of the practical implications of this reading of the identity of Religious Orders, as they support new paradigms for proclaiming the gospel, and the task of connecting the Good News with contemporary living. For this, the conversation must go on.

I return to the personal note which I sounded at the beginning. For me, life in the Presentation Congregation is the means whereby I live my Christian calling, as a member of the Church, on mission in the world. Anything less would not warrant my total identification with this, or indeed any other, Religious Congregation.

Notes

1 Bernadette Flanagan, *Religious Life Review*, Jan/Feb 2005.
2 cf Sandra Schneiders, *Finding the Treasure, Locating Catholic Religious Life in a New Ecclesial and Cultural Context* (Mahwah, New Jersey: Paulist Press, 2000).
3 We know there are forms of 'monasticism' in many religious traditions.
4 Schneiders, *Finding the Treasure*, p. 9. Here, it is important to distinguish between monastic *life* and monastic *lifestyle*. Active apostolic Religious were invited by Vatican II to go back to the inspiration of their founders, their 'charisms'. This involved a serious examination of their lifestyle and a move away from 'monastic' practices such as strict *horaria* (timetables) and communal exercises, insofar as they work against the active ministry. By monastic life is meant a lifeform which orders itself around the quest for fullness of life, on the understanding that it is to be found in relation with the transcendent.
5 For an exploration of the Church's mission to be a community at service of Kingdom of God, see, for example, John Fuellenbach, SVD, *Church, Community for the Kingdom* (Maryknoll, NY: Orbis Books, 2002).
6 For an exploration of ecclesiology revisited in light of the new cosmology, see, for example, Cletus, Wessels, OP, *The Holy Web, Church and the New Universe Story* (Maryknoll, New York: Orbis Books, 2000).

News and Good News: Christ in the Marketplace

Salvador Ryan

Introduction

Many years ago, I remember a priest, renowned for both his holiness and learning (but not necessarily for his preaching style), who visited our parish to speak. Many parishioners awaited this event with anticipation; even some visitors from outside decided to come to hear him. When the ceremony was over, I recall asking one of these visitors, a wise and astute grandmother, what she thought of the sermon. I expected a positive response, as I was aware that both she and the guest preacher held similar viewpoints on most matters concerning the Church. Her reply, however, took me by surprise: 'Yes,' she replied, 'he had a lot of valuable things to say, but I must admit that his delivery let him down. You see, it's not enough to have valuable things to say: we are also called to be good salespeople for Christ.' This curious expression caught my imagination at the time and has stayed with me ever since.

What exactly does it mean to be a good salesperson for Christ? This is the question that I wish to pose as I begin a discussion on the relationship between the Church and the media today. This relationship is often strained and distrustful and, at best, one of mutual misunderstanding. And yet, both the media and the Church can learn from each other. After all, the Church has a long history of success in the transmission of its message (something that must necessarily be of interest to those who work in all kinds of media) and yet contemporary society at least appears to be listening more attentively to what is presented in the most popular talk shows, newspapers, magazines and internet sites than to the message proclaimed in their local church on a Sunday morning. This anomaly presents the Church with a problem: how can it effectively communicate the Christian message in the twenty-first century and what can be learned from the modern media, particularly the advertising world, in this regard? Does becoming a 'salesperson for Christ' mean buying into all the methods of modern advertising and will such a move eventually discredit Christ rather than promote him? These are valid questions and they warrant serious examination.

The Divergent Approaches of the Church and the Media to News

The relationship between the Church and the media, at first sight, appears to be doomed before it begins. Firstly, their approaches to the transmission of news (whether daily news or the 'Good News' of the Gospel) are fundamentally different. Modern media corporations are interested in getting news out fast. They realise that individual news items are ephemeral things and the timing of their release is paramount. The news must, preferably, be 'breaking news': once it has 'broken' it has already begun to become stale. Its shelf life is limited and it must be given blanket coverage when it is still 'fresh' or 'hot' or whatever other expression you might like to use. Reactions come, inevitably, in sound bites and even when more in-depth analysis is afforded, there are always, understandably, time limits. Most of what is today or tomorrow's news will become a crumpled copy in a bin by the end of the week. News desks in the world of modern media are places of constant and rapid change, driven by the insatiable hunger of the public for the latest story. Their world is a world of flux.

In contrast, of course, the wheels of the Church grind slowly. The Church, as the well-known adage goes, thinks in terms of centuries rather than days at a time. Tradition rather than the latest fad is what is important to her. A second-century Christian text entitled the *Shepherd of Hermas* depicts the Church as an old woman, presenting her as almost timeless. It is quite an appropriate image. Like older people who remember living in a less hectic society, the Church is not interested in 'getting there quickly' when relating a story to her grandchildren. She becomes irritable and frustrated when modern media interviews demand that she does. How, she wonders, can you transmit the complexities of the Christian message in a sound bite? The Church certainly wants to be heard by the media but she gets irked when the media only wish to listen to and report certain aspects of her life. Like a grandchild who only wishes to hear the words 'and now let's see what sweets nanny has bought for you' and who becomes restless when having to listen to the prelude to such a declaration, which might consist of the protracted story of nanny's schooldays, many modern media commentators appear to be interested in only certain keywords when reporting Church affairs. They also become impatient when they encounter what they perceive to be hesitation and caution on the Church's behalf in answering the issues that they want addressed. After the Synod of Oceania in 1990, one of the bishops attending was quoted as saying that if the theme of the Synod was on agricultural science, there would still be elements in the press talking of ordaining married men. Similar thoughts were expressed more recently concerning the Synod held in Rome to mark the close of the Year of the Eucharist in October 2005.

The Church must engage with the media. There is no question about that. However, the challenge is to present the message meaningfully without compromising its content.

There appears to be a clear divergence between what the Church wishes to say in the modern media and what the modern media wishes to hear. While 'Good News' may be important to the Church, 'Good Copy' is what is ultimately important to the media. Both Church and media have different priorities and thus do not always speak the same language. If the Church is to be a major player in the world of communications, what can it do to make its voice heard? How can it become, in the words of my friend, 'a good salesperson for Christ' without compromising its position? First of all, it must be admitted that the language of the 'salesperson' is problematic to begin with. The term conjures up images of a person who is willing to cajole, bargain with and even compromise in order to 'cut a deal' or 'market a product'. The salesperson, moreover, does not necessarily have to believe in the product that he or she sells. More importantly still, surely Christ should not be reduced to 'a product' to be sold to people in the first place? This kind of language smacks of the sort of promotion that televangelists like to make on obscure television channels. And yet, despite these misgivings, it must be admitted that the twenty-first century has become a marketplace for, if not religion, then certainly spirituality, and the Church will ignore such a development at its peril. Jeremy Carrette and Richard King, in a recent study of this phenomenon, argue that 'in a context where brands and images are becoming more important than the products themselves, 'spirituality' has become the new currency in the task of winning human minds and hearts'.[1] The challenge for the Church is a tricky one. Does it engage the minds and hearts of people by entering the marketplace and setting up its stall, for example, beside those representing the burgeoning industry that is *New Age*? Should it offer Christ as an alternative to reiki, crystals, astrology, psychic healing, etc., or should it abstain from the marketplace altogether, claim to retain some respectability and thus avoid the risk of being seen as just another 'product' in the race for twenty-first century souls? The *New Age* phenomenon seems to have little problem using the media to market its product. The adverts for psychic tarot lines seen frequently on our television screens are proof of that. What should the Christian response be?

Paul the Master Communicator

It appears to me that one of the best exponents of the success of the Church in the marketplace is St Paul. Here was a 'salesperson for Christ' who undoubtedly believed in what he preached but who was also savvy in his presentation of this message. Paul was aware that there were many other voices in the marketplace and that these would continue to manifest themselves after his death: 'The time is sure to come when people will not accept sound teaching but their ears will be itching for anything new and they will collect themselves a whole series of teachers according to their own tastes' (2 Timothy 4:3). However, he urged his followers to 'put up with suffering; do the work of preaching the Gospel; fulfil the service asked of you' (2 Timothy 4:5). The most interesting account of Paul entering the marketplace of religions with his eyes wide open is surely found in the story of his speech at the Areopagus in Athens. Here, he preached a resurrected Christ to pagans but couched this teaching in categories that they might understand by singling out their statue to an Unknown God as evidence that they had already been on the right track. This Unknown God that they revered, Paul claimed, was the one that he proclaimed to them as Christ. A point of entry for the Christian message had been established and the consummate Christian salesperson had won the right to be heard.

Dropping out of the marketplace is, therefore, not an option for the Church. One response over the past number of years to the booming spiritual economy by many groups within the Church has been to acquire some of these new 'products' for their own stand. Thus we find many Christian centres offering courses in popular elements loosely associated with the New Age phenomenon such as reflexology, enneagram, eastern styles of meditation, etc. While many of these practices, which have sometimes been given a 'Christian spin', have been helpful to people, this response of supplying only what is in popular demand contains the danger of creating an impression that Christianity has nothing of its own to offer a 'spiritual age'. The renewed interest in spirituality in contemporary society might perhaps be a good incentive for the Church at both a universal and local level to revisit the sources of its own faith and draw from a rich spiritual heritage that includes a tradition of meditation and mysticism. A recent document from the Pontifical Council for Culture and the Pontifical Council for Interreligious Dialogue states that *New Age* offers Christians a positive challenge to take the message of the cathedrals to the people in the fair and that Christians must not merely wait for an invitation to do so.[2]

What Does Engaging with the Media mean?

This engagement with 'people in the fair' entails an engagement with the world of modern media. The Church, therefore, must learn what it means to be a good communicator. The market is already there and this, of course, is half the battle. There have been many recent success stories proving that slick (but not tacky) marketing can be used effectively by representatives of the Church. A notable example has been the marketing of the Lough Derg pilgrimage site as a place of refuge and cleansing from the stress of modern day life. One particular advert, which was designed to appeal particularly to people engaged in the frantic pace of the business world, proved immensely popular. The Diocese of Westminster's recent public advertising for the priesthood seems also to have been effective. Interestingly, the business world itself sometimes borrows the sort of language that one might expect to hear in church on a Sunday to invite customers to stroll around its shopping centres. One recent advertisement that I spotted encouraged shoppers to 'come away and rest awhile'. Christ, it seems, has been contracted to compose slogans for marketing moguls. Clearly, both the religious and business worlds can learn from each other. In his message for World Communications Day in 2000, Pope John Paul II stressed the importance of proclaiming Christ in and through the media. While he adverted to the importance of the Church making skilful use of its own means of communication (books, newspapers and periodicals, radio, television and other means), he also emphasised the need for the Church to make use of the opportunities that it receives to present its message in the secular media. This Pope was under no illusions about the importance of not confining the Church's message to religious publications which have, relatively speaking, a limited readership.

Time is of the essence in the media's approach to news. However, the Church's approach tends to be slow and cautious.

In attempting to dialogue with the secular world, religious publications are faced with the challenge of presenting the message of Christ in an intelligible and accessible style, but also in a form that will attract attention. This is not always easy. Publications often err on the side of appearing stuffy and dogmatic or lightweight and cheap. It is sometimes difficult to avoid including the sensational headline that will attract the attention of potential readers. And yet headlines such as *Religion Is Good For You: Fact* with the subheading *Belief in faith and family is good for your heart, soul and wallet says new research*, which appeared on the front page of one Irish religious newspaper recently, seem to advocate a utilitarian approach to faith. The reader gets the impression that he or she should believe because of the various benefits that are to be acquired by doing so rather than because of the inherent truth of what the system teaches. The trap that some publications can fall into is essentially that of making themselves into religious versions of the sensationalist secular tabloid press. The tension is, of course, between dialoguing with the world in its own language while at the same time preserving the depth of the Christian message. Often it is easier to argue one's point at a superficial level than to engage with the real issues. One prominent example of this kind of approach can be found in many headlines in religious publications (sometimes quoting prominent Church figures) concerning the issue of contraception. Many pages of Catholic publications over the years have been given over to debating the effectiveness or otherwise of the condom as a means of 'safe sex', for instance. Invariably, religious and secular commentators quibble over the percentage rates of success. However, what is often overlooked by those who think they are arguing the Church's case by pointing out these practical flaws is the following: if a scientifically certifiable condom that had a one hundred percent success rate were to be produced in the morning, would that change the Church's position on contraception one jot? The success rate or otherwise of contraception is not the issue at all. Failure to engage with the real reasons behind the Church's opposition to artificial contraception only opens the Church to ridicule as a curious body quibbling over statistics. A religious media that allows itself to become embroiled in irrelevant nit-picking does no service to the Church at all.

In joining the marketplace, it is important that the Church realises the uniqueness of what it can offer and, therefore, that it does not choose to play to other spiritualities' strengths rather than its own. And these are many. The Church offers, above all, a community of believers. Or at least it should. There is a fundamental difference between many of the *New Age* spiritualities, which focus on the massaging of the self, and the Church, which is centred firmly on the community. In a society that feels itself increasingly alienated, due, among other things, to urban living, hectic lifestyles, long commutes to and from work and the disintegration of community life, the Church should ideally offer fellowship and a sense of belonging. This can be found to a greater or lesser extent in well-organised parishes. The Sunday gathering of the parish for Eucharist should ideally be an occasion for more than the gathering of bodies in a liturgical space but should also be a gathering of minds and hearts. It makes no sense for people to both enter and leave the church as strangers on a Sunday morning. That would be, in effect, the antithesis of what happens at Eucharist. Simple measures such as a priest's greeting after Mass at the door, social gatherings centred on the parish, wide participation in the liturgy, etc. build community and sustain it. Community living simply cannot be found in engagement with the media; nor can it be bought from a *New Age* website.

The Message and the Messenger

Unarguably, the most effective acts of communicating the Christian message are achieved at a local level. More importantly, they are achieved not by words but by example. An old parishioner once said to a priest 'When you speak, your words are whispers but when you act they become shouts'. The personal acts of witness by individuals to Christ are, indeed, the Church's best advertisement. Ronald Rolheiser draws attention to the passage in Ezekiel when the prophet was asked by God to eat the scroll of the law (Ezekiel 3:1-3), remarking that we are invited to digest the Word of God and turn it into our own bodies so that people may be able to see the Word of God in a living body rather than on a page.[3] The message of Christ then becomes incarnate. Words become much more than words.

They become the expression of a life lived. Mother Teresa was a good example of an individual Christian who spoke with authority because of the way she lived. She could stand before thousands of people, utter the words 'God loves you' and whole congregations would be in tears. The message worked because it was seen to be authentic and to have been internalised. Here was a salesperson who believed in what she said. For many people still, the Church is present both at some of the most wonderful and fragile times of their lives. To a heartbroken family that has suffered bereavement, it speaks at a different level than a newspaper article on grieving ever will. These are the encounters in which Christ's message (which is not an easy one and which invites people not to instant gratification but to take up their cross everyday) can sometimes find an attentive ear. Personal encounter with Christians who have internalised Christ's message will always remain the most effective means of advertising Christianity.

> *The personal witness of believers is the greatest advertisement for the Church.*

These individual Christians will also be the greatest ambassadors for Christ in the secular media. Prominent Christian figures such as Mother Teresa, Brother Roger of Taizé, Pope John Paul II and many others transcend the perceived barriers between the Church and the media and are celebrated by a world that can recognise and admire both their holiness and their authenticity, even if it does not always agree with their views. These are the sort of people who carry 'Good News' with them by the very way they live and, thereby, create a place in the secular arena where 'Good News' and 'News' can truly meet. By no means, of course, is this transmission of 'Good News' in the secular media confined to the more famous representatives of Christianity. The secular media also provides regular glimpses of the extraordinary lives of ordinary individuals who, inspired by the Christian message, make this world a brighter place by individual acts of charity, mercy or heroism. They shine through the darker storylines like stars that give us hope. It is people like these that truly bring Christ into the marketplace; perhaps not explicitly, often very quietly; but it is these stories that endure in our hearts.

Notes

1   Carrette, Jeremy and King, Richard, *Selling Spirituality: The Silent Takeover of Religion* (Abingdon: Routledge, 2005), p. 25.
2   *Jesus Christ: The Bearer of the Water of Life: A Christian Reflection on the 'New Age'* (Vatican, 2003), p. 67.
3   Rolheiser, Ronald, *Seeking Spirituality* (London: Hodder and Stoughton, 1998), p. 97.

Nourishing the Faith through the Lens of Patrick Kavanagh's Poetry

Una Agnew SSL

Introduction

To some it may seem strange that I have chosen to reflect on spirituality for everyday life through the lens of Patrick Kavanagh's poetry. However, I can cite at least two reasons in support of my choice. Firstly, it may be said that Kavanagh was an unlikely religious model. However, unlikely instruments are often chosen to communicate God's Mystery. In a strange way, Kavanagh knew that his poetry had a mission, which he states as that of delivering 'God's commands/into the caressing hands of/a holy hearing audience.'[1] He spoke these words to an audience in UCD in 1956. No priest could have said it better. The second reason for choosing him is, in a strange way, his relevance for the contemporary world. Some might question his relevance for a twenty-first century audience. However, I beg to differ. If he is not relevant, why then do we return to him today? Have we not left Kavanagh behind? It often takes time for a writer's thought to filter down into the currency of everyday thinking. This is what I see happening today. People are looking for something of this poet's spiritual vision, his unorthodox approach, his focus on essentials, his unwillingness to be seduced by superficial values, etc. They are looking for glimpses of God in everyday life and struggling, as he did, to find images of God consonant with the realities of their lives and in tune with the deepest longings of their hearts. Moreover, Kavanagh brought to his writing a wonderful sense of fun and perspective. He could be reverent and irreverent, earthy and spiritual. He could, as his sister once said of him, 'curse and pray in the one breath'. Irish people, for some reason, like a spirituality that is neither too pious nor too harsh. Our God, we feel, is also partial to a bit of 'craic'! Kavanagh's spirituality reassures people who are afraid that they will lose all the fun of life if they embrace God.

> *Kavanagh's genius consists in helping people find images of God consonant with the realities of their lives and in tune with the deepest longings of their hearts.*

Let me highlight three elements in Kavanagh's search for everyday spirituality and integrity:

1 His capacity for transcendence in cramped oppressive situations;
2 His continuous confrontation and interaction with his own experience in the light of Mystery;
3 His fascination with images and metaphors for God that turn their backs on a harsh Jansenistic religion and reflect, rather, the contours of the Irish landscape and a face of God that answers the soul's deepest longings.

Kavanagh's Theological Background

Let us begin with a brief examination of the religious background out of which this poet emerged. Born in Mucker, Inniskeen in 1904, Kavanagh grew up in a Church emerging from the Famine. The Irish Church of that time was strongly Jansenistic, and had become so in the wake of the famous

Synod of Thurles (1850) when Archbishop Cullen summoned together the bishops of all dioceses and drew up guidelines that virtually ensured that this country's faith became thoroughly Romanised and steered safely away from its native religious practices: its patterns, pilgrimages and devotions around holy wells. As a result the Irish Church became laden with continental devotions with a distinctly anti-modernist mentality.[2] Despite the oppressive Catholicism of his time, Kavanagh was a man of faith who probed incessantly for the deepest springs of Christianity, determined to distil, as it were, an essence for himself. He was proud of his religious inheritance and celebrated its mysteries in original ways.

The theological method (if we could call it that) that he adopted was to continually set himself up as what many might consider 'bad Catholic'. In this way he did not seem to be a threat to anyone and in adopting the guise of a 'fool' he gave himself the freedom to be outrageous without censure. In an autobiographical note, he called himself: 'A Catholic, though not of the Lourdes and Fatima variety.' He did not want to appear pious, a 'craw thumper' or a 'voteen'! He was keen to establish himself more as who he was *not* than who he was. He was also pointing to a possibility that there was an essential brand of Catholicism to which he could subscribe, under the autobiographical guise of the day-dreamer, poet-farmer Tarry Flynn. Tarry is chastised by the parish priest for 'talking religion to fools' at the crossroads. The parish priest pompously explains to the unlettered Mrs Flynn: 'that is what we spend years in colleges for'.[3] Kavanagh's humour is deliciously barbed and conveys the sense of superiority with which many clergy of his time treated lay people.

Kavanagh continued to challenge many of the 'sacred cows' of Irish society, outrageously highlighting the accepted 'superior role' of the priest and the alleged ignorance of ordinary people. He poked fun at the Church's negative teaching on sexual mores, its widespread condemnation of 'company-keeping' and its exaggerated reliance on external devotions such as confraternities, missions and novenas. He condemned current Jansenistic attitudes, which, he says, 'cut all the green branches'.[4] This, he showed to be a sin against life, and therefore not of God. In fact, his major work *The Great Hunger* is not solely about poverty and sexual frustration, but about a famine of the heart in which the Church seemed to collude by 'pressing its low ceiling' over its people. Imprisonment by the penury of small subsistent farms and entrapment in a negative theology of sexuality and marriage left many bachelors and spinsters tied to the land and to the many frustrations that ensued:

> Life dried in the veins of these women and men
> The grey the grief the unlove
> The bones in the backs of their hands
> And the chapel pressing its low ceiling over them
>
> 'The Great Hunger'

Kavanagh retains his sense of perspective amid all that is going on around him. He searches for meaning, integrity and self-transcendence, since he knows that, however 'small' a person appears in the eyes of others, he is 'great as God has made him'. In his recent book entitled *Vulnerable to the Holy*,[5] Enda McDonagh suggests that some of Kavanagh's poetry 'expresses something of the modesty and penitential discipline to which [both] artist and Christian are called'. From my own study of his work, I would be willing to venture further by suggesting that Kavanagh was an exponent of some exceptional theological reflection and wise spiritual guidance. Let us look at his contribution to Irish spirituality.

Glimpses of Transcendence

Despite the cramped and oppressive circumstances of his life and life around him, Kavanagh nevertheless discovered the capacity and key to transcendence. By transcendence I mean some glimpses of ultimate significance and even a hint of God's presence in his constricting circumstances. He became a cherisher of the gaps, chinks and shards of light, hidden from most, but celebrated by the poet.

When Kavanagh described his '10x12' attic room where he read and worked as a writer and poet, he realised that his room, like his life and even the society of his time, was cramped and in some ways claustrophobic:

> 10x12 and a low roof
> If I stand by the side-wall
> My head feels the reproof

Not only was he spatially constricted, he was also held in the claustrophobic ambience of highly devotionalised religion, almost entirely imported from Rome and the continent of Europe. The five holy pictures that hung on the wall were undoubtedly his mother's prized possessions, bought at the local Mission or in some Catholic Truth Society shop:

> Five holy pictures
> Hang on the walls
> The Virgin and Child
> St Anthony of Padua
> Leo XIII
> St Patrick and
> The Little Flower

'My Room'

As rural electrification was not yet in place, he was constrained to write by candlelight or by the light of 'an old-fashioned kitchen lamp',[6] with a Howe sewing machine table for a writing desk, a steel pen and a half used accounts register for writing-paper. There were practically no books in the room, except for a few old school books, cuttings from the papers, Moore's *Almanac* and *Ireland's Own*. His room was his den, a cramped claustrophobic place, but its little window let in the stars. Thus the poet was able to engage with his experience, interpret it and reach some tiny aperture of transcendence. A window that lets in the stars is a metaphor for transcendence.

As readers of Kavanagh, when we engage with this window-of-light metaphor and allow it to work on our right-brain image and symbol-making mechanism, it weaves its way into the soul. Left-brain theological concepts often stack themselves up in linear succession, argue for position and fail to influence faith. Cardinal Newman has said it very well when he asserts that the heart is commonly reached, not through the reason, but through the imagination.

The poet was further able to glimpse a soul-warming moment in a shaft of light when he saw 'between the ricks of hay and straw ... a hole in heaven's gable'. He remembers, with vivid recall, how on Christmas morning as a six year old, though his Christmas was simple in material comforts, it was rich in wonder at the magic of ordinary things like 'the music of milking' and 'wafer-ice on the potholes'. He was rich most of all in owning his 'prayer like a white rose pinned on the Virgin Mary's blouse' (*A Christmas Childhood*).

Later, as a ploughman, he found, in the dark up-turned sod at his feet, the raw material for his writing and his soul-work: 'I find a star-lovely art in a dark sod, O joy that is timeless O heart that knows God' (*Ploughman*). By imaginatively using the mysteries of his inherited faith he found, with a new rush of inspiration in spring, that 'in the green meadows/the maiden of Spring/[was] with child by the Holy Ghost' (*April*). His landscape became impregnated with God and thus began his gospel of the sacramentality of the earth, so central to his thinking.

As a ploughman, he found, in the dark up-turned sod at his feet, the raw material for his writing and his soul-work.

Parish life offered one small consolation to this cobbler-farmer in that the parish priest with his silver-voiced sermons could charm the attention of his congregation so much that 'even a man hurrying to the fair with the thickest fasting spit wouldn't find his sermons long'. Yet the priest he knew had too much power; he was 'the centre of gravity' in the parish and had a say in everything – even in how to treat a sick animal, not to mention taking over their recreation initiative by running the dances of the Parish Hall. He was no encourager of writing either and simply dismissed the apprentice poet's efforts by saying: 'Cobbler! Stick to your last.'[7]

In Drumcatton chapel, Kavanagh listened to the priest say the prayers before Mass: 'O God who did so love the world.' He felt he alone took these words seriously. He alone was *The Green Fool* who loved to the heart of any ordinary created thing, who found Christ transfigured without fear at the heart of a primrose and was the lone bystander: the 'king of banks and stones and every blooming thing'.

When, as a dreamer of the fields, he felt the criticism and non-acceptance in his begrudging neighbours, he was able to see that, despite narrow-minded attitudes and inculpable ignorance, they too were capable of transcendence:

> From every second hill a neighbour watches
> With all the sharpened interest of rivalry
> Yet sometimes when the sun comes through a gap
> These men see God the Father in a tree
> The Holy Spirit is the rising sap
> And Christ will be the green leaves that come at Easter
> From the sealed and guarded tomb
>
> 'The Great Hunger'

His was a vindication of the gift for transcendence that could be learned in the school of life:

And I have a feeling
That through a hole in reason's ceiling
We can fly to knowledge
Without ever going to college
                    'To Hell with Commonsense'

This was not said by way of an anti-intellectual attitude, but in
the firm conviction that 'the heart has its reason that reason
does not know'. He believed in intuition as a gateway to
knowledge.

The bedlam of the little drumlin fields of his Monaghan
landscape became for him the playground of the Holy Spirit.[8] Yet
his mother kept urging him to attend the Redemptorist Parish
Mission, which, to her mind, was a far more orthodox form of
current religious practice. Kavanagh, who could find God in the
fields and backward places of his life, believed that people in their
quest for happiness often 'pushed closed the doors that God held
open' (*Lough Derg*). They were standing before the miracles of
God and couldn't see them. Organised religion, he felt, was
possibly directing people away from their native, instinctive
orientation towards the transcendent and was urging them to
deal instead with a God whose hand could be forced by the right
novena or number of Hail Marys. In his own simple family
environment, where the everyday care of hens and pigs was the
order of the day, Kavanagh knew somehow the dignity of life
around him where he sensed the presence of God at work:

In the sow's rooting
Where the hen scratches
We dipped our fingers
In the pockets of God

                    'The Long Garden'

And so, in this small subsistence farming community where
people even enviously compared lots and said uncomplimentary

things about one another, there were chance windows of poetry and prayer, narrow slices of divine instruction and even moments of graced transcendence, moments of Trinitarian epiphany.

Conclusion to Part One

Having looked at Kavanagh's ability to find transcendence in the poor, cramped, oppressive atmosphere of the Irish society of fifty or sixty years ago, the very last thing I wish to do is to glorify that kind of oppression or poverty and make it the necessary seed-bed of authentic spirituality. Less still is it my intention to canonise the poet Patrick Kavanagh. My intention is to ask what sensibility have we lost that we can no longer feel or experience moments of transcendence in our busy lives or recognise the fact that the life we experience has its intrinsic potential for transformative moments. And does the Church direct us toward finding transcendent meaning in our life-experience?

What remains universal and still contemporary in Kavanagh's work is the fact that cramped circumstances and dysfunctional systems still leave the possibility of 'pockets of God'. The sun can still shine through the gaps of oppressive systems. Narrow, repressive ambiences can still have windows that let in the stars. But have we lost our capacity for wonder and for gratitude, for perspective? Why, despite better living conditions and a more vibrant economy are we, as Emily O'Reilly says, still whingeing?[9]

God in the Bits and Pieces of Everyday

The second way in which Kavanagh pointed towards a spirituality of everyday was the manner in which he dealt with the events of his life; in a word, his experience. It was by dealing with his experience of personal failure and the collapse of his dreams that Kavanagh's poetry convincingly shows the struggle to find meaning and Christian significance. As poet he becomes powerful in his spiritual lessons; his life-experience became food for his poetry and spirituality. Despair dogged his path until he had to counsel himself into holding on when all seemed lost. Straining to hold on to his gospel of faith and love he counsels himself to hold on to essentials:

> And do not lose love's resolution
> Though face to face with destitution
>
> 'Prelude'

He asks the crucial question many people at sometime want to ask: Can you grow meaning out of failure? Does despair hide in its dark recesses any consoling flower or worthwhile fruit? By asking these hard questions Kavanagh also leaves us his guidance for dealing with despair, a salutary guidance for today:

> Can a man grow from the dead clod of failure
> Some consoling flower
> Something humble as a dandelion or a daisy,
> Something to wear as a buttonhole in Heaven?
> Under the flat, flat grief of defeat maybe
> Hope is a seed.
> Maybe this is what he was born for, this hour
> Of hopelessness.
> Maybe it is here he must search
> In this hell of unfaith
> Where no one had a purpose
> Where the web of meaning is broken threads
> And one man looks at another in fear
> O God can a man find You when he lies with his face downwards
> And his nose in the rubble that was his achievement?
> Is the music playing behind the door of despair?
> O God give us purpose.
>
> 'From Failure Up'

Here Kavanagh deals with an experience at the very depths of human existence. Here is a man on the margins of life, desperately looking for a reason to live, to repair, even to pull together, the 'broken threads' of his life. Nothing remains but the dead clod of hopelessness. He asks the hardest questions of all. Can anything, even the humblest, least-wanted flower, grow out of failure? Without diminishing the pain of loss or hopelessness, he asks the penetrating question of God! Can one find God when one's nose is to the ground and dangerously close to being devastated by failure? Kavanagh shows courageous insight into the generally un-talked about experience of failure and loss of purpose. There is no adequate theology of failure. This is why I feel it worthwhile examining his spirituality. He ends, not with a prayer for *comfort*, as perhaps Gerard Manley Hopkins did in a similar situation of despair (*Send my roots rain*); he asks for *purpose* instead! O God give us purpose!

Kavanagh's poetry represents his struggle to find meaning and Christian significance in the midst of personal failure and the collapse of his dreams. Can you grow meaning out of failure? Does despair hide in its darkest recesses any consoling flower or worthwhile fruit?

He had a similar moment in 1954 when he remonstrates with a year that has given him nothing but pain: a lost law-suit, the failure of his newspaper project, a public humiliating cross-examination by a powerful barrister, the dreaded diagnosis that he had lung cancer and, worst of all perhaps, the loss of a long-term relationship which had given him companionship and support, that with Deirdre Courtney. He curses a year that sought to shatter 'his lamp of contemplation', that left him once again under the low sky of disintegration: 'Everywhere I look a part of me is exiled from the I'.

Eventually he realises that naming his condition, confronting his problem is all he can do just now. Meaning will follow, if he is honest and takes personal responsibility for his life:

> Making the statement is enough. There are no answers
> To any real question
>
> 'Nineteen Fifty-four'

He must summon up his resources, re-find his purpose in life and steer his life onwards into the unknown. Kavanagh by this stage has acquired the art of ritually taking stock or auditing his life. He had done this in a major way in 1951 in the poem 'Auditors In' when he assessed the assets and debits of his life. In Ignatian terms, it was a major *révison de vie*! And so Kavanagh's pilgrim journey continues, struggling with illness and lack of recognition, until he eventually finds healing for body and soul. In a mid-July moment of healing, he finds himself, redeemed and exuding gratitude on the banks of the Grand Canal in 1955.

What is the secret of Kavanagh's ongoing spirituality, his search for meaning, integrity and self-integration even when dealing with the most painful vicissitudes of life? He knows himself, knows his own weaknesses thoroughly and openly confesses them. Once he asks God to give him perfection. He did not much like the awkward contours of his personality. He pleads with God to make him 'calmly wise, all the world's virtuous prize'. Having made his request he listens in his heart to God's reply:

> And God spoke
> The only gift in my giving
> Is yours – Life. Seek in hell
> Death, perfect, wise, comfortable
>
> 'The Gift'

He discovers that no yardstick of perfection, from whatever source, can legislate for the unique original life of each human person. The great compliment we can return to God is to celebrate the life given us. In another place Kavanagh says: 'God only makes geniuses'; yet often people don't like God's work of art. Life itself is the real gift to be chosen, to be embraced and to be celebrated.

So what can be learned today from a struggling poet learning to come to terms with his life? He took one of the symbols most meaningful for his life, 'the land', and extended it to his soul. He knew he had inner work to do and that this was essentially his own responsibility. He self-counsels himself wisely:

And you must take yourself in hand
And dig and ditch your authentic land

Kavanagh knew well the universal significance of what he was saying. He had already sold his Shancoduff fields, so he knew that the land of which he now spoke was a metaphor for an inner territory of the soul which cried out for cultivation. The crops to be planted now were compassion, healing, equanimity, contemplation and gratitude. Experts today say that spirituality is a self-implicating discipline; it begins with the self but does not end there; it rather reaches out to find the incipient traces of Christ in ourselves in the other. Personal experience, lived in the light of Mystery, becomes the raw material of a robust spirituality.

Kavanagh's gift was to see beyond appearances to mystery present in the other. He saw the face of Christ lurking beyond the tattered outward garb of a beggar:

I saw Christ today
At a street corner stand
In the rags of a beggar he stood
He held ballads in his hand ...

He finishes by saying:

> And I whom men called fool
> His ballads bought
> Found him whom the pieties have vainly sought
> 'Street-Corner Christ'

Similarly he traces the imprint of the Incarnate God over the fields of Inniskeen, marked out by the Magi symbol of three within bushes that rode across the horizon. Closer to home, he sees the Nativity, the Birth of Christ, occur in his own backyard, where the music of milking is its accompaniment and the twinkling of a stable lamp makes way for the Light of the World!

Conclusion to Part 2

Taking failure, desolation, weakness and limitation on board he confronts the experiences life throws at him. He strives to find significance and meaning by digging deeply into his own spiritual reserves, facing the harsh realities of life and somehow finding traces of God present in the vicissitudes of his life. Kavanagh compels himself to find significance even in the meanest experience.

Kavanagh's Original Metaphors for God[10]

The third and final area I wish to examine is, perhaps, the poet's greatest contribution to Irish theological reflection. He is not normally numbered among Irish theologians, yet he is the poet most often quoted from the pulpit. This is where he grappled with a variety of images of God. No Irish poet writing in English has, more repeatedly than he, attempted to figure God out. It would seem to me that he tested every smallest detail of Christian belief handed on to him. He did not merely appropriate religion and teach it unthinkingly, but gave all a thorough going over until he ultimately grew into the essential tenets of his faith, adapting them to the contours of his own awkward, but original personality. He reflected himself uncompromisingly into Christianity.

No Irish poet writing in English has, more repeatedly than Kavanagh, attempted to figure God out.

He puzzled long over the Overarching Mystery that surrounded his life. He felt that God was so often misrepresented. By dint of constant searching, he states that what he had learned about God, is that God is not the Abstract God (of Scholastic theology), nor the God of middle-class respectability. God is not one made important in terms of worldly status, 'One who might be appointed to a Board or gathering of art lovers'. Gradually he succeeded in penetrating beyond conventional labels. His interpretation sought to break out of the moulds of stagnant religious practice. God for him is One who is neither solemn nor boring, neither self-important nor pompous or serious about unserious things, and yet not insignificant! His God was One who must be allowed 'to surprise us'. At special moments too, God could be resplendently garbed in the colours of the rainbow: proclaiming His Presence, down in the bogs and marshes, or at other a God barely visible, hidden in the dead clod of failure. But above all he believed with some considerable vigour, as if countering false theologies:

> God was not all in one place complete
> and labelled like a case in a railway station
> Till Hope comes in a takes it on his shoulder.
>
> 'The Great Hunger'

Kavanagh's multifaceted God could be sacramentally present in 'a kiss,' 'a laugh' and 'sometimes tears'. These were revolutionary statements for an Irish society imprisoned, at this time, in Jansenistic attitudes towards the flesh and in the grip of a pessimistic notion of sanctity. Kavanagh felt that Ireland was in the grip of the anti-life spirituality and wryly proclaimed in his *Kavanagh's Weekly* (10 May 1952) that the entire nation was being presided over by an undertaker 'in his long black coat'!

All of these statements were considered to be outrageous. Insinuations such as these were certain to give Kavanagh a reputation of irreverence and even heresy. But still he persists in his search for God and ultimately learns that God, the One who surprises, who 'caresses the daily and nightly earth', is revealed in unexpected joy, leniency, gentleness and understanding, especially towards those who are down in their luck. And yet this is the Transcendent God, the Mind that has baulked the profoundest of mortals. It is by countering false images of God and claiming a God in love with human life that Kavanagh chips away at all that is not God until a firm intuition of God remains.

His Christmas poems keep us attuned to a God who keeps the personal *dream* of existence safe for each one, despite interference. It is easy to be so deafened by the idiosyncrasies of Kavanagh's personality that we fail to hear the dominant notes of his spirituality. A poem such as 'Having Confessed' shows him unusually perceptive and contemplative in his understanding of the human condition:

Time has its own work to do ...
God cannot catch us
Unless we stay in the unconscious room
Of our hearts. We must be nothing,
Nothing that God may make us something

Kavanagh was subversive in his ideas of God; he was, indeed, the first Irish theologian who lays claim to the possibility of a feminine God, generous in praise, understanding of the poet and affirming of creativity. Although he may not have been a true feminist in the fullest sense, his declaration that 'surely my God is feminine' is well ahead of his time and might have carried more theological clout had he achieved the literary status that was his due. Only now, one hundred years after his birth, do people see in Kavanagh's ideas, a glimmer of the more all-embracing God than was preached in his time.

Conclusion

And so when we ask for a secular spirituality for today, one in tune with everyday life, we come to realise that spiritual life is rooted firmly in our daily life experience and is available to all. Spirituality requires that we refocus our image of ourselves, as human persons, that we acknowledge our openness to Mystery and trust the glimpses of transcendence and meaning that we receive in the daily events of life. We nurture those fleeting brushes with the Transcendent, with a God who is very far and very near us. With a great deal of humour and honesty, Kavanagh asks the meaning questions, struggles to reach integrity, integrates his life and finds his God. He is eager to give back his spiritual inheritance to 'a holy hearing audience'. He may often portray himself as a 'bad Catholic', but today, we can assert with some confidence that he steadily tapped into those clean springs of *essential* Christianity to which this country aspires today.

Notes

1 'Thank you, Thank you', Peter Kavanagh, 1984, p. 349.
2 Corish, 1985, pp. 197-201.
3 Patrick Kavanagh, 1947, *Tarry Flynn*, Chapter 7, p. 142.
4 See, Agnew, 1998, pp.109-118, where I have given this topic more complete treatment.
5 'Temptation in Harvest', *Complete Poems*, pp. 156-7.
6 *Tarry Flynn*, pp. 14-16.
7 *Tarry Flynn*, pp. 29-30.
8 O'Reilly speaking at the Céifin Conference, Ireland, 2004.
9 Agnew, *Studies* Vol. 93, 2004. pp. 437-47
10 'The Great Hunger', VI, p. 88.

Bibliography

Agnew, Una, *The Mystical Imagination of Patrick Kavanagh: A Buttonhole in Heaven* (Dublin: The Columba Press, 1998).

——— 'The God of Patrick Kavanagh', *Studies*, Vol. 93, No. 372 (2004), pp. 437-47

Corish, Patrick, *The Irish Catholic Experience* (Dublin: Gill and Macmillan, 1985).

Kavanagh, Patrick, *Tarry Flynn* (Middlesex, England: Penguin Pbk), Chapter 7, p. 142.

Kavanagh, Peter (ed.) *Patrick Kavanagh: The Complete Poems* (Newbridge: The Goldsmith Press, 1984).

Quinn, Antoinette (ed.) *Collected Poems of Patrick Kavanagh*, (London: Alllen Lane, 2004).

——— *Selected Poems* (Middlesex, England: Penguin Books, 1996).

Connecting the Good News with Contemporary Living:

European and Global Perspectives

Cardinal Keith O'Brien

What is Contemporary Living?

Before we can consider contemporary living, I think that, first of all, we must look to the past and consider what our 'previous living' was like. I do not intend looking back too far. Perhaps considering the stability that existed more or less in the world and certainly in our Church up to the time of the Second Vatican Council, we should look back some fifty years to consider what our previous living was like.

Previous Living

One might say that at that time some fifty years ago we were at the height of the missionary movement in our world, conducted with very great optimism following the Second World War. Answers were seen as being clear and inevitable. Christianity was winning and there was the possibility that soon we would be conquering the whole world for Christ. One might also say that the fact that God was there before our arrival was not even acknowledged!

Being a Christian and being a missioner meant having power – we were the soldiers for Christ out to conquer the world. The sending of money to conquer the world was seen as being important – what one of us does not have hundreds if not thousands of 'black babies' to our name. I still remember those wonderful missionary magazines, some of which are still in existence and flourishing. They were magazines like *Africa, The Maynooth Mission to China*; the magazines of the various missionary orders then thriving with increasing numbers of members and more and more magazines being sold each year. All these magazines and the reports from missionaries themselves gave great accounts of success stories, of countries being converted to Christianity, and of a great increase in missionary vocations, as well as increases in vocations in the missionary lands themselves.

At that time we must say that the Church was on a 'high'. And perhaps it was something of the vision of the great Pope John XXIII that helped to bring us face to face with reality.

Developments without and particularly within the Church, including the child sexual abuse scandals, have helped us to come to the realisation that we are not a Church of saints but very much a Church of sinners.

Contemporary Living
With regard to our contemporary living, we might say that now we have been brought down to earth with a very great bump. We realise the actuality of our present situation: we are not a Church of saints – we are very much a Church of sinners. So much has helped to open our eyes to the reality of our present situation, not least the horrible situation of child sexual abuse, which has affected so many of our countries in the Western World and especially priests and religious.

Now we realise that we ourselves are in poverty – not particularly material poverty but spiritual poverty – and we must bear witness to exactly who we are before trying to hand on Christ ourselves. We must see the spreading of the Good

News as a sacred responsibility given to us because of our very nature as Christians and especially because of the nature of God himself who wants his love to be shared, not just within the Trinity but with a magnificent outreach to all creation.

Our *connecting the Good News with contemporary living* must ensure that we are in dialogue with those we are meeting – and it must be a prophetic dialogue. We are called upon, as Jesus himself said in that magnificent statement when he stood up to preach in the synagogue in Nazara, 'to preach the Good News to the poor' – and we ourselves must realise our own poverty as we preach to the poor in our midst at this present time.

Our approach to social problems must not be simplistic but realistic.

At this present time *action regarding justice must be at the centre of the Gospel.* While in the past charity was, in some sense, understood in a simplistic way, now we must realise that it is a lot more complex and we must get to the roots of the real problems that exist in the world. Following on from this we must take a stand against war and strive to safeguard creation, the creation of God. We must have a particular concern for the homeless, the migrants, the refugees, etc. They are some of the poorest of the poor. We must become aware of the reality of the situation in the world of today and be clear where we stand in it with our own particular responsibilities.

Differences between Previous Living and Contemporary Living

What emerges from what I have said so far is that there are *clear differences between living fifty years ago and living at this present time,* between our previous living and contemporary living, between our membership of the Church prior to the Second Vatican Council and our membership of the Catholic Church at this time.

CONNECTING THE GOOD NEWS
WITH CONTEMPORARY LIVING

Our Christianity prior to the Second Vatican Council was seen *as a wonderful gift from God* given to us to be lived by us and handed on to others as a sign of our thanks for what we have received. Now we see our Christianity as something to be lived, as a gift not just static, but a gift to be communicated by our living. By living the Christian message in our own world, we communicate that gift to others.

Perhaps we could sum up what I have been trying to say already thus: it is necessary for us to realise that the Church is missionary by its very nature; that the Church is called to be a witness to Christ and that this witness must be deeply Trinitarian, with ourselves realising that we have come from the Father and we must hand on the Christ of history endowed with the power of the Holy Spirit. The Church is not out to destroy the cultures of different societies with Christianity being Western and having to be preserved as such. In recent years rather we have taken other cultures seriously and we must continue to do that. But Christ is the 'Lord of history' and we must hand on that message, in season and out of season, welcome or unwelcome!

Perhaps it might be of interest if I mention something of *the example of my own life and that of my contemporaries* - given that we have experienced something of both previous living and contemporary living.

I was ordained a Priest in 1965, ordained a Bishop in 1985 and created Cardinal in 2003. In my life as a Bishop I have experienced tremendous changes in the past twenty years - with the fall in vocations to the priesthood and religious life being the most obvious. In those past twenty years one junior seminary and two senior seminaries have been closed in Scotland. I am aware that similar drastic closures have taken place here in Ireland both with regard to seminaries and religious houses.

However, on the positive side, what has been most heartening for me and my colleagues has been the tremendous awareness of the importance of the lay vocation. This was stressed at the Second Vatican Council and also at the Synod of Bishops on the laity that followed. I remember those words of your outstanding leader of the time, Cardinal O'Fiach, who described the laity as 'a sleeping tiger'. And then of course at the end of that Synod, Pope John Paul II spoke of the 'exalted vocation and the many and varied forms of mission' of the lay faithful!

Since then priests, religious and laity have worked together increasingly well. In my own Archdiocese we have parish pastoral councils, deanery pastoral councils and an archdiocesan pastoral council.

One of the positive developments in the contemporary Church is the central importance being given to the role of the laity in the mission of the Church.

However, it is necessary for each one of us to grasp the reality of the present situation without closing our eyes to it. I would stress that it is relatively easy to convert buildings whether they are cathedrals or churches, convents or seminaries, but it is much more difficult to convert people.

Perhaps that is the reason for our being here this evening – to convert ourselves in an evermore vital and vivid way to the reality of our vocations while reaching out to convert others.

Of course one of the greatest difficulties at this time as we live through the present changes is quite simply *resistance to change*! Perhaps people of my age and older just cannot change; those who are younger perhaps will not change; and it is the responsibility of those in positions of responsibility, including, of course, bishops, to say you must change!

When travelling yesterday to my father's hometown of Wexford I purchased the local paper *Wexford People*. The front page indicated precisely something of the change about which I am talking, the headline being 'Church Shake Up – Number of parishes to lose priests as twenty clerical changes are announced'. The Apostolic Administrator Bishop Eamonn Walsh stated: 'We don't have enough priests to go around. There are not enough to meet the needs of all the communities that have their own churches. We will not be closing down any churches. There may not be a resident priest in the parish but there will be a priest to say Sunday Mass'. The Bishop also said that in the future the laity will have to take on a greater role in their own parishes to assist their priests.

Perhaps each one of us could think for a few moments as to what is the greatest change in the lifetime of each of us in the Church as we know it.

European Perspective

Before considering the wider European perspective, I think it might be appropriate for me to consider the Scottish perspective – the one with which I am most familiar.

The last *Ad Limina* visit of the Scottish bishops to the late Pope John Paul II was in March 2003. In my statement to Pope John Paul II on behalf of the Bishops Conference of Scotland I said: 'Despite the fact that we live in an often secular and a materialistic world, it is heartening to realise that 74 per cent of Scots still describe themselves as Christians. In Scotland we value the national and cultural diversity of our country and the varied origins of its people. We remain committed to providing a place of safety and tolerance for those who have suffered persecution and violence elsewhere in the world and strive to welcome the strangers in our midst, namely, 'refugees and asylum seekers''. I also went on to indicate something of the involvement of Catholics in ecumenical and interfaith activities, which continue to grow at both local and national level.

In his message, the late Pope John Paul II said to the bishops of Scotland:

The reports you have brought from your various dioceses attest to the new and demanding situations which represent pastoral challenges for the Church today. In fact we may observe that in Scotland, as in many lands evangelized centuries ago and steeped in Christianity, there *no longer exists the reality of a Christian society*, that is, a society which, despite human weaknesses and failings, *takes the Gospel as the explicit measure of its life and values*. Rather, modern civilization, although highly developed from the standpoint of technology, is often stunted in its inner depths by a tendency to exclude God or keep him at a distance. This is what I refer to in my Apostolic Letter 'Tertio Millennio Adveniente' as *'the crisis of civilization'*, a crisis which must be countered by 'the civilization of love, founded on the universal values of peace, solidarity, justice and liberty, which find their full attainment in Christ'. The new evangelization to which I have summoned the whole Church can prove a particularly effective instrument for helping to usher in this civilization of love. [My emphasis]

What I have stated with regard to Scotland can, I am sure, be applied to Europe as a whole. One might say that most, if not all, countries of Europe can indeed be called secular societies at this present time.

Europe is no longer seen as a Christian society - it no longer is a Christian society.

One might think of the words of Archbishop Diarmuid Martin of Dublin, who told a conference recently in Donegal, that he was confident that Ireland in twenty-five years will not be a godless society, but 'one where the love of God lived out by men and women will continue to surprise and open new ways for all'. The Archbishop added that whether or not Ireland would be Christian in 2030 depends on how well the Church carries out its mission, adding that whether the Gospel is going to be important in people's lives in the future will be determined by the style and the pastoral structures of the Church today.

Shortly after having been created Cardinal, I made as my principal goals the 're-Christianization of Scotland' and 'improving the standards of marriage and family life'. I have proclaimed those goals in my preaching, when on pastoral visits to my parish in Rome, on a pastoral visit to Malta for the two-hundredth anniversary of a parish and recently to the Ukraine commemorating the fourth anniversary of the visit of Pope John Paul II.

Shortly before my departure for this Conference I received a letter from the secretary of the Consular Corps in Edinburgh, who is from the Czech Republic. He lamented the fact that the media had declared the Czech Republic to be the most atheistic country in the European Union, even though at the Velehrad Shrine in Moravia to commemorate the arrival of Christianity to the Kingdom of Moravia through the ministry of St Cyril and St Methodius, Cardinal Vlk celebrated Mass attended by over 30,000 pilgrims.

I believe that this is the Europe in which we now live. Europe is no longer seen as a Christian society – it no longer is a Christian society. As you know, any mention of God was excluded from the recently produced European Constitution; Sunday is not observed as the 'Day of the Lord' by the majority of our citizens; a Christian lifestyle is not seen as the norm. One has only to consider the fact that the greater majority of Christian Catholics do not enter into the Sacrament of Matrimony, but rather live together; we have only to consider the moral aberrations permitted by our laws at this present time; we have only to look at the Europe around us to realise that we can no longer say that the Gospel is the explicit measure of our lives and values.

Global Perspective

Having considered something of what is happening in Europe, we now look at the global perspective. Perhaps the most startling thing we notice when we look at our world in this time is the stark contrast that exists between those who have and those who have not; those in the northern part of the world compared to those in the southern part of the world; those in USA, Canada and most of Europe compared with those in Africa, Central and South America and India. Obviously one cannot generalise, but what happened in Scotland prior to the recent G8 Summit perhaps brings the reality of the present world situation more close to us. We do realise and want to do something about the stark contrasts in our world, about that great divide between the haves and the have nots. The Make Poverty History Campaign brought together almost 250,000 people to the city of Edinburgh, all trying to protest and heighten the awareness of the G8 leaders and, indeed, the whole world, about the present situation with regard to poverty.

After 2,000 years of Christianity the world is far from being Christian; following on the wonderful teaching of Jesus Christ, there are so few who heed that teaching and even fewer who hand it on.

Initially I was talking about the differences between living some fifty years ago prior to the Second Vatican Council and our living at this present time. It was shortly after the Vatican Council that my predecessor Cardinal Gray adopted the territory of Bauchi in Northern Nigeria as our particular archdiocesan mission receiving the support of priests, religious and lay people. It was our responsibility to staff it with religious and priests, and to help finance the Church's missionary endeavour in that part of the world, an area where Islam is the dominant religion and poverty is rife.

CONNECTING THE GOOD NEWS
WITH CONTEMPORARY LIVING

This region was also crippled by lack of education, appropriate health care and often the basic necessities of everyday living. Most of the bishops of the world and the great bands of missionaries, including missionaries form Ireland who have accomplished such amazing work down through the centuries, are familiar with the above conditions and encounter them in their travels. I know that Archbishop Clifford has just returned from a pastoral visit to Malawi. It is hard to conceive of any bishop remaining unchanged by what he witnesses in mission territories. All bishops, I am sure, are only too happy to communicate something of their knowledge and experience to their own people back home.

Since my appointment as Archbishop I have been privileged to visit the area of Bauchi. It is now the State Capital and I will be returning there in October of this year to open a new church. I have also been happy to visit my priests, while on loan to El Salvador, Chiapas in Mexico and Guatemala. Under the auspices of our Scottish Catholic International Aid Fund, I have been able to visit Rwanda and the Democratic Republic of the Congo last year. This year I visited Ethiopia and at the beginning of next year I will be visiting India. Even though I cannot speak from a huge experience, whatever I say is from lived experience.

The most startling feature of the contemporary global scene is the stark contrast between the lifestyles of the rich and the poor.

The poverty of the Third World is a tragic shame – it is something barbaric, especially when it exists and co-exists with the wealth and the riches of our own first world. It is something which we must do something about; it is something which more and more people realise they must do something about. In these countries which I have visited, as well as in other parts of the Third World,

I see a shortage of vocations to the priesthood and religious life. I encounter priests and religious who have to care pastorally for many thousands of people, and yet we ask them to help us in our own vocations crisis. I see and realise that countless thousands are dying everyday from diseases that have long ceased to be a problem in the Western World and there are many thousands dying of HIV/AIDS. We have for a long time tried to share our religion – are we equally enthusiastic about sharing our wealth?

Can we say that a Christian society exists in other parts of the world outside Europe? I think rather the opposite is the case. We know of the great spread of Islam throughout the world; we are aware of the increasing presence and growth of sects in Africa and in South and Central America. We realise that often Christianity is indeed in decline – particularly because of a lack of personnel and a lack of willingness from the first world to help.

The tendency to allow the poverty in our world to continue at present levels without doing anything much about it is a clear symptom of our disregard for life in all its aspects. We know of the disregard for life in the womb; we are aware of the disregard for those suffering in abject and dire poverty throughout the world; and we are also aware of the increasing moves to legislate with regard to euthanasia throughout the world. All these are manifestations of the one problem – a disregard for life given by Almighty God himself, a life that stretches from the first moments of natural conception to natural death. Ultimately the above manifestations are a disregard for the rights of the individual – whether unborn, living in abject poverty or near the end of life on earth.

Perhaps the disregard for life in all its aspects is one of the reasons why there has been such a growth in terrorism throughout the world at this present time. We read of terrorist activity in many places in which there has been war and unrest – whether in Ireland or Iraq, whether near at home or far away.

And we must also consider those major cities in which terrorist activity took place in the recent past including New York, Madrid and, just a few weeks ago, London itself. People have no regard for their own lives and the lives of others if they commit such acts of terrorism. From a global perspective, our world seems to have been reduced almost to a terrorist state with the lives of so many innocent people constantly at the mercy of others.

What are we Going to Do About it?

I do not think there is much use for us as Christians just to look back to the past and say how wonderful it all was and then look to our present and the future to say just how sad it all now seems. Rather we must indeed be missionary in our outlook and missionary in our lifestyle. We must do something.

What then must we do? With regard to both the European and the global situation, I would suggest three things. You might think they are rather simplistic. Nevertheless I will state what they are first and then explain them: Talk, Speak Out, Do Something.

A blueprint for action: Talk, Speak Out, Do Something!

Talk

I think we must indeed talk about the situations such as we know them and learn more about just where we are and where we are going. In talking about our situation, I believe that we must never forget the great wealth of experience we already have, in and through our former missionaries. They were, indeed, stalwarts of the faith, who acknowledged the world as it was in their youth and left their homelands, families and friends, not unlike those who had heard the first call of the

Gospel from Jesus Christ himself. Now many of them are in their retirement in their native lands and we must indeed benefit from their experience. We have wonderful opportunities for talking together in our own countries. However, I think not only of the opportunities of talking together as Catholics, but also, in Scotland and in so many other parts of Europe, of talking together with members of other Christian religions and other faiths.

In this regard, from my own experience, I recognise the work done by ACTS (Action of Churches Together in Scotland), bringing together all the main Christian denominations, with a certain oversight being provided at national level with associated bodies throughout our country. Obviously I am also aware of similar groupings existing in Britain and Ireland, a link being provided through CTBI (Churches Together in Britain and in Ireland).

At European and indeed at world level there are also ways of talking together within our Church and with others of goodwill. Within our Church there is COMECE (linking together the Bishops of the European Community) and CCEE (the Episcopal Presidents of the Conferences of Europe). I have no doubt there are similar bodies existing in other parts of the world bringing together Conferences of Bishops. These groupings, of course, can liaise with similar bodies in other Churches and in other faiths, so that the European and, indeed, world experiences can be shared.

I think if members of our Church speak together, then members of different churches will also speak together with their leaders and share their views. This process then percolates down to those who are not leaders, but who would regard themselves as ordinary members of the community. Indeed, this process might enhance faith in their ability to speak out. The speaking out might help them to look at what others have been able to achieve and realise the benefits that can accrue from speaking out.

Speak Out

I think it is vital at this time that we do speak out concerning the Good News of Jesus Christ and connect that Good News with our contemporary living. This can be done at a variety of levels. I can think of the various levels of speaking out, some very recent, at the European level. I can also think of my own role in Scotland with regard to the re-Christianisation of Scotland. We now enact a Nativity Scene annually in Princes Street, the main shopping thoroughfare in Edinburgh. Last year, for the first time, an Easter Play was performed in Princes Street Gardens on the afternoon of Holy Saturday and similar plays have been performed in other parts of our country. There has been an increased demand for Christmas cards and Advent calendars, cards and calendars that will recall the Nativity Scenes rather than simply portray a variety of Santa Clauses and robins.

If Church leaders can speak out, I think it is also vitally important that the lay members of our Churches speak out – on the shop floor, in their offices and in their places of recreation. It is good to remind ourselves of the often forgotten words of our late Holy Father following on the Synod of Bishops on the laity: 'You have an exalted vocation and there are many varied forms of mission open to you!'

A crucial part of our speaking out is quite simply portraying our Christian views and our Christian living to those who perhaps are not aware of the standards we have, the standards of Jesus Christ. When we think of our own lifestyles as Christians, we must ask whether these lifestyles are any different to those of others.

And of course this must not only be done in our own countries. When we think of handing on the Christian message, the Good News of Jesus Christ, we must think of those who have been suffering under Soviet oppression, overburdened with national debt, exploited by multinational debt or crushed by dehumanising poverty – and think how they will receive the Christian message. We must think of a possible outreach to peoples of other faiths who may now be living in our countries and of our need to dialogue with the interfaith movement.

When I say 'Speak Out', I also mean that our Church must use the most effective means of communication at this time. We are more than aware of complaints about the standards of television and radio programmes coming into our homes. How can we respond to them effectively? Invariably on my travels – whether in a country like Rwanda or in Gozo, the small island of Malta – I am aware of Catholic broadcasting stations keeping the Catholic community up to date with news while also evangelising those who may be listening to the particular programmes. I would also ask whether or not programmes which are broadcast worldwide are of the highest possible standard or are rather providing a view of Catholicism from some fifty years ago. Perhaps the EWTN (Eternal World Television Network) falls into this particular category.

I am very happy when I think of the ways in which modern means of communication are often used in our Catholic secondary schools. Just recently I took part in a television link-up in which a secondary school liaised, not only with its associated primary schools, but also with a secondary school in Bangalore in India with which it was having increasing links. Such links were becoming evermore commonplace.

Do Something

With regard to doing something, we must think of ways of doing something both at home and abroad. One most recent example remains in my memory – the recent Make Poverty History Campaign in Edinburgh, bringing together peoples of goodwill from all over the world prior to the G8 Summit. Unfortunately much of the publicity concerning the Make Poverty History Campaign was overtaken by the G8 Summit itself and the various protests in parts of Scotland prior to and at the time of this campaign.

However, no one can deny that the Good News of Jesus Christ on behalf of the poor was lived by and handed on by almost one quarter of a million people gathered in Edinburgh on the Saturday before the G8 Summit opened. No one could have denied that a tremendous example of Christianity was being handed on by all of those taking part in the campaign proclaiming that poverty must end and that the teaching of Jesus Christ must be handed on with regard to our love and care for the poor and powerless.

Perhaps a personal example of evangelisation at this time is given to us by Bob Geldof and his direct way of acting. I myself was at the meeting of bishops from the first and third worlds prior to a meeting with the Chancellor of the Exchequer Gordon Brown when Bob Geldof was given ten minutes input into our preparatory meeting. He simply said with regard to world poverty: 'Now you must do something about it! The situation in the world at present is horrible; it is obscene!' And you know what response he got throughout the world – countless millions listening to his words and many millions taking positive action.

Conclusion

We might ask just where we go from here. Let me conclude with one practical story from my visit to El Salvador some ten years ago. On a previous visit I had been asked by a small community in El Higueral to visit their community and pray with them as they had been evicted from their homeland. They were now prepared to return there after the civil war. I got up early and prayed for them, comparing them to the people of the Old Testament as they travelled through the desert en route to their homeland led by God in the form of a pillar of cloud by day and a pillar of fire by night. I continued my pastoral visit to their country and met up with them immediately prior to our entry into their homeland of El Higueral on the top of a rather steep hill. We eventually reached our destination by jeep, mule and on foot. On reaching the clearing at the top of the hill, it all seemed desolate to me: the shattered remains of some homes, cooking utensils scattered on the ground and, in general, an air of degradation and loss. However, the Chief of the community said to me: 'Father, is this not beautiful? It is our home!' And then he said to me: 'Can we not celebrate Mass here?' I was taken aback with his invitation. Initially I thought he was going to ask me if I would like some coffee and something to eat. We were certainly tired. We celebrated the Eucharist in as simple a setting as possible. For an altar, we used a sack of corn. The priest who was with me had the necessities for the celebration of Mass and the Mass was celebrated in the open air by the light of the moon. And then we relaxed, ate and went to bed.

The lesson I was taught by those Salvadorians was quite simply the need to have priorities right in our lives – the priority of spiritual food before material food, the priority of putting spiritual things before material things. That small group of people wanted to have their spiritual food before they shared in material food.

I think this is a good lesson for us as we struggle to spread the Good News in the Church and in the world today, whether our perspective is European or global. We must focus on the spiritual. We must indeed spread the Gospel of Jesus Christ. We should share his love for others and show his love by our own lifestyles. We must share our love by handing on the Gospel and providing the means by which Christianity will continue to be handed on to future generations.

However, we must also go beyond. Following on the basic evangelisation, we must also stress the need for increased healthcare, education and improvement of the basic needs of the people we are ministering to. However, the spiritual must come before the material and perhaps a reminder of this is contained in that old phrase: 'The right relationship between prayer and action is this: it is not that action is all important and prayer helps, but rather that prayer is all important and good actions flow from our lives of prayer'. Perhaps we need to bear these words in mind particularly today as we strive to connect the Good News with contemporary living.

Jesus came on earth, first of all, to bring the Good News to the poor – but he himself was living the life of God as the Son of God and Son of Man. It was because of that relationship to his Father and inspired by the Holy Spirit that he managed to accomplish so much good, in a material sense, in the world.

It remains so with us too. Just recently Father Raniero Cantalamessa spoke in London on 'Faith which overcomes the world'. He stressed there that 'it is possible to have an impersonal knowledge of the Person of Christ' and went on to state that 'to be a true relationship, that relationship with Jesus has to lead to recognition and acceptance of Jesus for what He is, that is to say, Lord'. The personal knowledge of Jesus consists in this: 'That I acknowledge Him as my Lord and Saviour, which is like saying: 'He is my centre, my meaning, my reason for living, my purpose in life, my glory, someone to whom joyfully I surrender all!'

We must acknowledge our need for Jesus Christ and then pray that God may indeed continue to help us and inspire us both to live that Good News of the love of Jesus and hand it on in our own countries, in Europe and throughout the World.

Witnessing to Solidarity and Justice in the World:

Trócaire's Contribution to the Church's Mission Today

Lorna Gold

Introduction

Trócaire was founded by the Irish Bishops' Conference in 1973 as an expression of the solidarity of the Irish people with the developing world.[1] The Bishops gave the organisation a dual mandate, with responsibilities both abroad and at home: 'Abroad, it will give whatever help lies within its resources to the areas of greatest need amongst the developing countries. At home, it will try to make us all aware of the needs of these countries and of our duties towards them. These duties are no longer a matter of charity but of simple justice.'[2] Since then, Trócaire has grown and developed into an entity which is highly regarded both within the Irish development community and internationally. It has recently received a number of external accolades for its work in the field of development cooperation[3] and continues to play an important role in the education of the public in Ireland. The question this paper would like to consider is: how does this work relate to the mission of the Church in the twenty-first century? Is there something specific about Trócaire's work that sets it apart as a faith-based agency with 'simple justice' at its core? And what specific challenges does this pose in the context of its work today both at home and abroad?

*Trócaire's aim is to help those in greatest need
abroad and educate those at home about their
plight.*

Mission and Catholic Development Agencies

Before coming on to discuss Trócaire's role in particular, it is
important first to clarify some aspects of mission, particularly
those that relate to Catholic development agencies in general.[4]
Mission can be regarded as the core of the Church's action in
the world. In Matthew's Gospel, Jesus is reported to have told
the disciples to: 'Go, therefore, make disciples of all the nations;
baptise them in the name of the Father and of the Son and of
the Holy Spirit, and teach them to observe all the
commandments I gave you.'[5] This command to bring the Good
News to all peoples can be defined as the original missionary
impulse which continues to the present day. Over the course of
the Church's history, the understanding of mission has changed
and developed, shaping the Church, peoples and contexts in
which it is being accomplished. An important recurring feature
of mission within the Catholic tradition, however, has been the
call to transform society and human relationships as a
constitutive part of the Christian vocation.

Throughout the twentieth century, and into the twenty-first
century, there has been a growing understanding of the inter-
linkages between the mission of the Church and the
transformation of social relationships and structures. The
development of mission theology itself has had an important
influence in this evolving understanding of mission for the
Church. According to Miriam McHardy, a number of these
theologies have had an important influence on the
establishment and development of Catholic development
agencies such as Trócaire.[6] The theology of Missio Dei, in the
early part of the twentieth century, for example, underlined the
idea that mission is an act of 'Godself' and that the Church is

God's instrument for proclaiming that mission.[7] The conclusion that Coleman draws from Missio Dei is that if the Church is an 'agent of God's purpose', then its actions must reflect God's call: 'the Church as the new Israel is called to work for justice in human relationships and structures'.[8] This understanding of mission goes back to the first half of the century and gave rise to a range of social movements and organisations aimed at lay apostolate.[9] The creation of the various lay associations, including Caritas organisations, has its origins, at least in part, in this theological tradition.

Transforming human and social relationships is a constitutive dimension of the Christian vocation.

Another influential mission theology that has shaped the Catholic development agencies, again according to Miriam McHardy, is liberation theology. Liberation theology grew out of the understanding within Vatican II that the Church should 'be the Church of the poor', as reflected in the core documents of Vatican II. *Gaudium et Spes* sets out a radical vision of Christianity centred around the quest for social justice.[10] According to Berryman, liberation theology is an interpretation of Christian faith in the light of the suffering of the poor, as well as a critique of society and the Catholic faith through the eyes of the poor.[11] Liberation theology focuses on Jesus as a liberator, emphasising those parts of Scripture which describe Jesus' mission in terms of liberation and justice. Liberation theology is very much rooted in the praxis of everyday life and is oriented towards the transformation of this life. One can 'know God' in the *'doing* of justice'.[12] It requires active engagement in the transformation of lives and the changing of structures of injustice.

Catholic Social Teaching

A closely related element in the changing understanding of the Church's mission in the world that has had a deep and continuing influence on the Catholic development agencies is the growth of Catholic Social Teaching (CST). Over the past 100 years, this body of social teaching has grown in importance and has served as the sure guide for discerning the practical implications that the Christian message has for society. This body of teaching, compiled most recently in the *Compendium of the Social Thought of the Church*,[13] represents the vision of a new humanism aimed at transforming social and economic structures – not only within the Church, but also in society at large. This body of teaching represents key elements of a Christian anthropology that often stand at odds with prevailing social and economic norms. Central tenets of CST, such as human dignity, rights and responsibilities, value of community, stewardship, subsidiarity, participation, solidarity and the common good, etc., are key social values which offer a perspective through which to critique current economic and social order. They also offer a value base by which to propose alternatives which reflect more fully God's unfolding will for humanity.

Development of every person and of the whole person is at the very heart of evangelisation.

This body of teaching has provided particular insights into the complex relationship that exists between the Church's mission and the humanitarian work of development agencies such as Trócaire. The publication of *Populorum Progressio* was a key moment in the process of questioning the dominant vision of economic and social development that was prevalent at the time. The encyclical argued that progress is multifaceted and has ethical and spiritual dimensions. Human development knows no geographic boundaries. All people are called to integral development, particularly those with financial resources and power. It questioned whether those in rich countries can call themselves 'developed', for example, if the model of development they espouse systematically deepens divisions between people and destroys the natural environment. This dimension of development is a constant theme within the Church's teaching. Pope Paul VI questioned the 'moral underdevelopment' of a society that can sit back in comfort and watch others suffer. Pope John Paul II cites the co-existence of poverty and inadmissible 'super-development' side by side as the greatest challenge to authentic human development today.[14]

This new vision acknowledges that there are profound links between integral development and evangelisation, and that these links go back to the very heart of the entire anthropological vision underpinning the Catholic Tradition: 'Integral human development, the development of every person and of the whole person, especially of the poorest and most neglected in the community, is at the very heart of evangelisation. Between evangelisation and human development and liberation there are, in fact, profound links. These include links of an anthropological order, because man who is to be evangelised is not an abstract being but is subject to social and economic questions.'[15] This underlying notion of transformation, centred in an anthropology based on 'evangelical' values, is an essential element in understanding the contribution of Catholic development agencies to the Church's mission.

The late Pope John Paul II's extensive contribution to CST elaborated this relationship between mission, evangelisation and social transformation. The acceleration of the processes of globalisation in the 1980s and 1990s prompted him to question the underlying 'structures of sin' which perpetuate injustices in the world. In particular, he interpreted the mission of the

Church as one of restoring authentic human relationships in a world order driven predominantly by profit and self-interest. The Church's mission, shared by all Christians and people of good will, is that of tempering self-interest in the interest of the common good, particularly the good of the poor. In one of the most concise passages from *Sollicitudo Rei Socialis*, he wrote:

> [Solidarity], then, is not a feeling of vague compassion or shallow distress at the misfortunes of so many people, both near and far. On the contrary, it is a firm and persevering determination to commit oneself to the common good; that is to say, to the good of all and of each individual, because we are all really responsible for all. This determination is based on the solid conviction that what is hindering full development is that desire for profit and that thirst for power already mentioned. These attitudes and 'structures of sin' are only conquered presupposing the help of divine grace by a diametrically opposed attitude: a commitment to the good of one's neighbour with the readiness, in the gospel sense, to 'lose oneself' for the sake of the other instead of exploiting him, and to 'serve him' instead of oppressing him for one's own advantage (cf. Mt 10:40-42; 20:25; Mk 10:42-45; Lk 22:25-27).[16]

Towards a New Paradigm
The letter *Novo Millennio Inuente*, written at the beginning of the twenty-first century, in many respects marks out a development in this vision of the Church as called to build a 'civilisation of love'. In this letter, Pope John Paul II highlighted the Church's mission today, above all, as one characterised by witnessing to God's Love through its presence in the world, building up the unity of the one human family.[17] Jesus called on his disciples to become one in him, through mutual and continual love, in the knowledge that it is through such love that

he is present: 'Where two or three are gathered in my name, I am there'.[18] It is this love that brings many into one and reveals the very essence of the mystery of the Church, which is to make us of 'one heart and one soul'.[19] It is in building this communion of love, through the Eucharist, that the Church appears as the 'sign and instrument of intimate union with God and of the unity of the human race'.[20]

> *The Church's entire mission can be described as witnessing to God's presence in and love for the world by building genuine communities at local and global levels.*

First and foremost, according to John Paul II, mission means becoming witnesses of love through contemplating the mystery of the Trinity dwelling within us and seeing that light reflected in our brothers and sisters. It means reflecting on the profound unity of the Mystical Body, which links each of us together as one human family under God, and which makes us able to share joys and sufferings, sense desires and attend to needs, and offer deep and genuine friendship. It implies the ability to see what is positive in others and welcome it as a gift from God. It means knowing how to make space for others and learning how to 'share each other's burdens'.[21]

This kind of love, by its very nature, opens out to a service that is universal and to a commitment to practical and concrete love for every human being. It opens our eyes to see the face of Christ in the faces of those with whom he identifies himself most: 'I was hungry and you gave me food, I was thirsty and you gave me drink, I was a stranger and you welcomed me, I was naked and you clothed me, I was sick and you visited me, I was in prison and you came to me' (Mt 25:35-37). This Gospel text is not merely an invitation to love, but also a passage which sheds light on where we can encounter Christ: 'Whatever you did to the least of these brothers of mine, you did it to me.'[22] It is a call to radical simplicity of life, so as to encounter God's love.

This love is universal in nature and cannot exclude anyone. Yet, at the same time, it must recognise the special presence of Christ in the poor, and it must make a preferential option for them – both near and far. It must open the eyes of Christians to the many contradictions of economic, cultural and technological progress, which offer immense possibilities to the few who can avail of them, while leaving millions of others on the margins and below the minimum demanded by human dignity. Shortly before his death, Pope John Paul II called for an 'urgent ... economic and moral mobilisation'[23] to address the problems of hunger and injustice in the world.

Trócaire and the Church's Mission

How does the work of Trócaire relate to this shifting paradigm of mission within the Church? As discussed at the outset, Trócaire was established by the Irish Bishops' Conference with a dual mandate. This mandate has enabled Trócaire to evolve as an organisation that is still closely linked to the mission of the Church. As with the other Catholic agencies, it has drawn on Church teaching and mission theology to frame its work in the developing world. In particular, it incorporates a vision of mission centred around justice and social transformation. I would like to discuss here four aspects of Trócaire's relationship with the Church's mission: sharing of resources, building global solidarity, being a prophetic voice and educating for peace and justice.

Vision, Mission and Values
Before elaborating on the specific aspects of the above-mentioned relationship, I would first of all like to reflect, in

general, on how this mission of the Church is integrated into the core vision, philosophy and values of Trócaire. Trócaire's vision, philosophy and values have strong links with both the liberation theology tradition and Catholic Social Teaching. If one examines Trócaire's mission statement, it states that 'Trócaire envisages a just world where people's dignity is ensured, rights are respected and basic needs are met; where there is equity in the sharing of resources and people are free to be the authors of their own development'.[24] This mission statement, in many respects, clearly reflects the core elements of Catholic Social Teaching. It embraces both the 'rights-based' approach to development, which has become mainstream throughout the development field, and also provides a specifically Catholic perspective on the whole debate on human rights.

Ultimately Catholic social teaching can be defined as proclaiming and defending fundamental human rights as sacred and inviolable because every human being is created in the image of God.

Trócaire has placed particular emphasis on the link between human rights and Catholic Social Teaching, seeing the human rights discourse as a bridge between Church teaching and the dominant development discourse. Human rights have a profound meaning within the Christian tradition as they flow from the nature of the human person made in God's image and likeness.[25] Within such a vision, every human being, regardless of his or her wealth or poverty, race or religion, is looked upon as a brother or sister within the one human family. As such, all share the same fundamental rights and unique gifts. This vision is reflected in a special way through the manner in which the relationship between rights and responsibilities is articulated and the manner in which rights are achieved through human actions.[26] Human rights can only be fully realised through recognising mutual responsibilities towards each other, in particular through community. Underpinning these rights and sustaining them must be a shared value system that reflects certain basic principles such as equality, justice, truth, honesty, fairness, non-violence, tolerance, participation and solidarity. Without these values, which affirm the centrality of the human person, the idea of human rights becomes meaningless. This is at the very heart of the vision and mission Trócaire espouses.

Sharing resources
Perhaps the most obvious contribution of Trócaire to the Church's mission is through its role as the vehicle through which the assistance of the Irish people is channelled to the poor. *Sharing* is a value that is deeply rooted in a Christian understanding of economic life, and one that could offer a new perspective on building a more equal and just world. The Church upholds the right of individuals to own private property, but underlines the universal destination of goods: that God created goods for all to share in. According to the teaching of the Church, material wealth gives its owners a greater chance to show their inner wealth and reveal who they really are. It is not so much that a large personal fortune, of itself, either brings happiness or causes misery in the biblical sense, but that the person who uses it in one way - metaphorically speaking, to build 'bridges' with others - is blessed or happy, while the person who uses it differently - to build 'walls' against others - is not. With wealth, therefore, comes a grave responsibility. This responsibility is both towards those in need and towards ourselves. For the Gospel tells us that it is only through opening our hearts to others and giving freely that we will find true happiness. In the recent Pastoral Letter on International Development, *Towards the Global Common Good*, the Irish Bishops' Conference underscores the Gospel imperative to

share our wealth with those less fortunate than ourselves. 'What is clear from the Scriptures', the bishops state, 'is that our salvation is intimately connected to our attitude to the poor.'[27]

Over the 33 years of its history, Trócaire has encouraged the Catholic community within Ireland to respond to this commandment of putting Christian love into practice through financial giving and through donating time, energy and prayers. The Lenten campaign and Trócaire box have become institutions within Irish society. Through the Lenten Campaign, individuals are reminded of the Gospel imperative to put the needs of the poor before their own and to give generously. This emphasis on voluntary giving has an indispensable role in building the Kingdom of God in the world. Through financially giving to charity, one is demonstrating one's solidarity with those in need. On a deeper level, each contribution helps to build up a vibrant civil society imbued with the values of solidarity, commitment, self-sacrifice and generosity. Every act of true giving is valuable in God's eyes, no matter how small, as the Gospel teaches us in the parable of the 'widow's mite'. Such contributions enable partnerships between the North and the South to grow, thus building up a global culture of solidarity and sharing. These values can act as a powerful antidote to the values of consumerism and self-interest that underpin much of globalisation.

Building Global Solidarity
Another dimension of Trócaire's work that reflects the Church's mission is its emphasis on building solidarity *with* the poor. Within Trócaire's vision, the poor are not simply regarded as passive recipients from rich donors. Instead all are regarded as brothers and sisters – equal partners who share a common heritage as members of the same human family. This deep underlying vision of 'partnership' translates into concrete practices within Ireland and on the ground. Within Ireland, for example, it is reflected in the kind of imagery selected for

campaigns such as the Lenten Campaign. The images always seek to respect the dignity of the individual involved. The images seek to reflect not only the hardship and difficulties of people living in poverty, but, above all, their immense dignity, resilience and hope for a better world. Takes the images of the past two Lenten campaigns, for example: in both cases, the images have reflected the humanity of the families involved. Choosing such images is not easy, as statistically it has been proven that distressing images tend to raise more cash.

Trócaire's international work also seeks to bear witness to the values of solidarity and human dignity. This explains, for example, why Trócaire does not, by and large, run programmes in the developing world. Instead, it seeks out those people who are promoting those values through doing good work on the ground and supports their actions. In many instances, those people are themselves members of other Catholic organisations such as Caritas, Justice and Peace commissions or members of missionary congregations. In such circumstances, the shared values and mission can strengthen the direct link with the Church's mission on the ground.

Many of the programmes supported by Trócaire in the developing world point to those living on the margins and hence, the preferential option for the poor. The focus areas of the programmes – working with those affected by HIV/AIDs, conflict prevention and peace building, and support for those challenging human rights abuses – all reflect this ethos.

Being a Prophetic Voice
A second way in which Trócaire witnesses to faith and justice is through its role as a public advocate for the values of the Gospel. This role as 'prophet' goes to the heart of the vision of mission within the tradition of liberation theology, but also reflects the vision of CST underpinning John Paul II's teaching. According to this theology, as outlined above, Christians have a responsibility to stand up to injustice through resisting those

structures, attitudes and behaviours that perpetuate inequalities. At the same time, Christians are called to witness to the existence of an alternative to the dominant structures of inequality. When the Irish Bishops founded Trócaire in 1973 they recognised the importance of this aspect of the organisation's work. The founding document explicitly states that 20 per cent of the budget should be used for projects to support the education of the Irish public on the causes of poverty.

Being a voice for the voiceless goes back to the very roots of the Judeo-Christian tradition.

Throughout its history, Trócaire has played an important role in deepening understanding of development issues within the Irish public. It has placed a particular emphasis on research and analysis of the causes of underdevelopment and Ireland's role therein. In the 1980s, for example, there was no dedicated academic department doing systematic analysis of development co-operation. Trócaire responded to this through stimulating research in the Trócaire Development Review, as well as through the commissioning of major pieces of research on issues such as the reform of the Common Agricultural Policy.

In 1998, Trócaire launched a series of books examining the 'Christian Perspectives on Development Issues', which sought to combine theological analysis with development studies. The Christian Perspectives on Development Issues series emerged in the late 1990s, as part of Trócaire's desire to rediscover its roots in the Christian faith. The idea behind the series was the production of a number of short booklets on development issues, which would relate the teachings of the Church to contemporary debates. The research for the books was commissioned out to leading researchers in the various fields in

Ireland and was seen as a contribution to Catholic thinking around some critical development issues.[28]

This emphasis on understanding the root causes of poverty has been further strengthened through the creation of a Policy and Advocacy Unit within Trócaire in 2002. The objective of this unit is to provide a critique of the current policies of international institutions in which the Irish government has a role – the EU, the UN, World Bank, IMF and WTO – and to propose alternative policies from the perspective of Catholic Social Teaching values.[29] This work is increasingly carried out in conjunction with other Catholic agencies across the world[30] and through working with parallel networks in other Christian traditions, as well as secular organisations.[31] The partner organisations with which Trócaire works also play an increasingly important role in setting the agenda of advocacy priorities.

This policy and advocacy work has been accompanied by a growing emphasis on campaigning for changes in society which reflect the values of CST. A major part of this has been the mobilising of those who share these values to speak out against injustice. In some cases, this means linking with the hierarchy of the Church, as was done in May 2005 through a Bishops' lobby of the G8 leaders. This joint lobby action involved eight Catholic bishops from the North and the South visiting the G8 leaders to call for changes to aid, trade and debt policies. In this instance, Trócaire, together with the other Catholic Agencies, was able to provide the bishops with detailed technical expertise on policy proposals. Another key element of recent campaigns has been the ecumenical dimension. This has involved joining forces with other Christian denominations to build joint actions in favour of policy changes. One example of this in Ireland was the joint statement of the leaders of the ten Christian churches in support of the aims of the Make Poverty History campaign. Such a joint action around shared values is a small, yet valuable contribution towards building unity between divided Church denominations.

Educating for Peace and Justice
Finally, the work of Trócaire in witnessing to solidarity and justice can be seen in the work of the organisation in educating for justice and peace. This work centres on bringing the Gospel values into schools all over Ireland and integrating them into the whole curriculum. Trócaire has worked in the area of development education since 1973 and has seen this work grow, develop and reach out to all the sectors of Irish society, from the very youngest in the pre-school sector, through to primary and post-primary sectors and the adult audience through its adult literacy work. The work varies according to this wide audience. The basic objective, however, is the same: to challenge people's perceptions of and relationship with the poor and vulnerable in our world and to provoke them into taking meaningful action. Trócaire's education work, therefore, is always linked to campaigning work, giving people a chance to act once they have internalised and absorbed information on the issues of human rights, justice and peace.

It is important to ask for people's material help to fight poverty and injustice. It is equally important to raise their consciousness about poverty and injustice.

Some of Trócaire's education work, such as the Trócaire Lenten resources, link closely with the Religious Education curriculum and have a strong religious content. Through this work, Trócaire is playing a catechetical role in schools, by drawing attention to the justice dimension of the Church's mission. Another aspect of this work is responding to the changing demands of teachers through linking the Lenten resources with the other aspects of the curriculum. Trócaire education officers are kept involved and informed on curriculum development so that they can ensure that issues of peace, justice and human rights continue to gain more prominence within the relevant subject areas, and not only religious education. This transition beyond religious education in many ways reflects the Catholic Social Teaching perspective of transforming all areas of social activity.

Two examples of resources where this transition is obvious are *Watoto* and *Pamoja*. *Watoto*, meaning 'child' in Kiswahili (a language widely used in East Africa), is one resource and, developed by Trócaire, it aims at introducing development issues to pre-school educators. The idea is to provide three- to five-year-olds with ways of exploring different cultures, poverty and wealth issues, etc., in ways that are appropriate to their age. During its research into developing this pack, Trócaire came to the conclusion that:

> There is clear evidence that children notice human differences at a very early age and that these distinctions become part of the earliest construction of their social world. Not only do they see differences, but their ideas about them begin to reflect the prevailing adult attitudes at an early age ... Furthermore, as they engage in their early peer interactions, they begin to form their general social orientations and beliefs about what people are like. Early childhood educators have the opportunity to expand, challenge and influence children's social perceptions.[32]

The central aim of this resource is to teach children to see the unity of the human family enriched by diversity. In a very simple way, this message introduces children to the themes of universal love and respect for others, which are at the heart of *Novo Millennio Inuente*. Its popularity led to the production of a new *Watoto* supplement last year and the introduction of a pre-school Lenten resource annually.

Pamoja, another Kiswahili word meaning 'together', is part of the wider Lenten education programme. Developed three years ago, the *Pamoja Kwa Haki*, 'Together for Rights', project is an invitation to senior cycle students in post-primary schools to simply do a project on the Lenten theme. This project work begins in the first school term and is supported by an education officer so that by Lent the participating students have gained a deep insight into the issues affecting the chosen Lenten country and the Lenten theme. The aim of this project – and there is a corresponding project in Kenya – is to offer interested students the opportunity to explore human rights issues in a way that meets their level of interest and capacity, and to facilitate the growth of skills and attitudes that remain with them for life. In the last three years participating students have accomplished an incredible amount of work and furthered the common good by involving themselves in projects such as peer education, community talks, church talks, street campaigning, radio interviews, newspaper articles, primary school talks and joint campaigning initiatives with Kenyan students.

All education work undertaken by Trócaire is a learning experience in itself, but *Pamoja* stands out in that it displays clearly the inner wealth of our youth – a wealth that is not necessarily based on material wealth, but built on unconditional beliefs in the form of commitment to basic human rights and unconditional love in the form of sharing and solidarity.[33]

Some Challenges for the Future

As the Church and society change, witnessing to solidarity and justice is a constant challenge. Here, I will touch on three challenges and opportunities that Trócaire as a Catholic development agency faces in its efforts to embody the mission of solidarity and justice in the world.

The first set of challenges emerge from the international work which Trócaire undertakes. As it seeks to build solidarity through partnership, it has to adapt to the changing external environment. Over the past decade, the context in which this work is taking place has become more complex and insecure. Whilst the number of conflicts may have decreased, levels of social violence within communities has increased. This means that in many parts of the world, there is a heightened security risk in carrying out development work. This makes the challenge of building partnership both more urgent and difficult at the same time. In particular, it heightens the need for solid trust between the various partners. Moreover, the Catholic identity of agencies like Trócaire can present particular risks in regions of the world where there are Christian minorities. This challenge, however, is also an opportunity to contribute to the Church's mission through building, where possible, stronger inter-faith cooperation and promoting dialogue and understanding.

A second challenge which Trócaire faces relates to the changing context of Irish society. Economic prosperity has brought many positive benefits, but there is a risk that this same prosperity will result in weakening the traditional social values that underpin CST. Vested economic interests may make it more difficult to speak out on policy issues that have a negative impact on the developing world. This economic prosperity, however, is a real opportunity for the Irish people to transform the structures of globalisation which Pope John Paul II called 'structures of sin'.

As Ireland becomes more prosperous, it is to be hoped that it will not become immune to the cry of the poor.

Moreover, it is an opportunity to move beyond a model of giving based solely on charitable donations. Building a just world requires a transformation of the market structures so that they embody the values of human dignity. Such a transformation requires a shift in thinking towards 'ethical globalisation' in which people are mindful of the human relationships underpinning economic transactions.[34] As people who regularly make choices about what to consume and how to invest one's savings, we need to recognise the importance of being informed about what we are purchasing. Behind each product or service, in fact, is a long chain of decisions and actions all of which involve relationships between people.

Finally, the phenomenon of declining Church attendance in Ireland presents Trócaire with a challenge and also a key opportunity. As Church attendance is falling, the role of the laity in the mission of the Church will come to the fore. One area of Trócaire's relationship to the mission of the Church, which is perhaps underdeveloped at present, is the whole area of the future role of the laity. The changing paradigm of mission outlined above highlights a shift away from a highly clericalised and hierarchical vision of mission, to one in which each lay person has a mission by virtue of his or her baptism. Groome emphasises four ministries for lay people in the mission of the Church: worship, community witness, word and service.[35] According to Miriam McHardy, in each of these areas, Catholic agencies such as Trócaire could play a key role in the future.[36] Trócaire, through its Lenten campaign, has had a limited role in each of these areas, but there are opportunities for growth in the future.

Conclusion

In this paper, I have sought to provide an analysis of Trócaire's contribution to 'mission', as understood within the Church today. Mission is a multifaceted concept which, whilst applicable to the universal church, has different meanings in different contexts. Trócaire's contribution to mission, I argued, is to be seen in the context of its role as a promoter of the 'values of the kingdom', of solidarity and justice in the wider world. The internalisation of the principles of CST within the organisation means that it offers a concrete expression of solidarity and justice in action within the contemporary context. This is seen both in the mission and values the organisation espouses, as well as in the practical nature of the work it undertakes. In particular, the 'partnership model' developed by Trócaire and its sister Catholic agencies, is a concrete example of Catholic principles transforming structures. However, as outlined above, being a Catholic agency in the contemporary context also presents a number of challenges.

Notes

1 The views expressed here are those of the author.
2 *Bishops of Ireland on Development*, Pastoral Letter of the Bishops of Ireland on the establishment of Trócaire, the Irish Catholic Agency for World Development, 2 February 1973.
3 For example, the 'People in Aid', the 'Best Companies to Work for in Ireland 2004' and 'Excellence through People' awards.
4 Trócaire is one of many such 'Lenten agencies' set up by European and American Bishops' Conferences in the post-Vatican II era. Others include Catholic Aid for Overseas Development (CAFOD), Scottish Catholic International Aid Fund (SCIAF), Cordaid, CCFD, Development and Peace. Sixteen such Catholic agencies are members of the CIDSE network.
5 Matthew 28:19-20.
6 M. McHardy, Workers for the Kingdom: The Catholic Development Agency and its contribution to the wider mission of the Church, Masters Dissertation, Unpublished, University of Edinburgh, 2004.
7 Karl Barth, speaking at the Brandenburg Conference 1923. Bosch, *Transforming Mission*, p. 391.
8 J. Coleman in J. Provost (ed.) p. 123.
9 For example, the creation of Catholic Action.
10 'The greater part of the world is still suffering from so much poverty that it is as if Christ Himself were crying out in these poor to beg the charity of the disciples. Do not let men, then, be scandalised because some countries with a majority of citizens who are counted as Christians have an abundance of wealth, whereas others are deprived of the necessities of life

and are tormented with hunger, disease, and every kind of misery. The spirit of poverty and charity are the glory and witness of the Church of Christ.' *Gaudium et Spes*, 1965. See Gutiérrez, G., *A Theology of Liberation: History, Politics and Salvation* (New York: Orbis Books, 1988).

11 P. Berryman, *Liberation Theology* (New York: Pantheon Books, 1987).
12 D. Carroll, *What is Liberation Theology?* (Herefordshire: Gracewing Publishing, 1987), p. 7.
13 *Compendium of the Social Doctrine of the Church* (Vatican Press, 2004).
14 *Sollicitudo Rei Socialis*, n.28.
15 *Ecclesia in Africa*, n.68.
16 *Sollicitudo Rei Socialis*, n.38.
17 *Novo Millennio Inuente*.
18 Matthew 12:24.
19 Acts 4:32.
20 *Novo Millennio Inuente*.
21 Galatians 6:2.
22 Matthew 25:40.
23 Pope John Paul II, Message for World Peace, January 2005.
24 Trócaire Mission Statement, Annual Report, 2005.
25 See *Populorum Progressio* for an overview of the Catholic vision of human rights and authentic human development.
26 E. Deberri et al., *Catholic Social Teaching: Our Best Kept Secret* (New York: Orbis Books, 2003).
27 Irish Bishops' Conference, 2005, *Towards the Global Common Good*, p. 3.
28 The CPS series are *Human Rights, Land* and *Famine* and they came out in 1998. These were followed by *Food* in 1999, *Refugees and Displaced Peoples* in 2000 and *The Reality of HIV/AIDS* in 2003. The final book in the series on *Ethical Globalisation* was published in Autumn 2005.
29 See: www.Trócaire.org/policyandadvocacy
30 For example, through the CIDSE and Caritas Internationalis networks.
31 For example, through working with Eurostep, Action Aid, Oxfam, etc.
32 Ramsey, P., *Teaching and Learning in a Diverse World: Multi-cultural Education for Young Children* (New York: Teachers College Press, 1987).
33 The education projects mentioned here do not fully represent the work of the Trócaire Education unit. For more details, please visit our website on www.Trócaire.org/education where you can also share comments and questions.
34 See Gold, L. and Leen, M., *Ethical Globalisation*, Christian Perspectives Series (Dublin: Veritas, 2005).
35 Groome, T., *Sharing Faith: A Comprehensive Approach to Religious Education and Pastoral Ministry* (San Fransisco: Harper San Fransisco), p. 302.
36 McHardy, 2004, p. 19.